D1154174

Angels and Principalities

The background, meaning and development of the
Pauline phrase *hai archai kai hai exousiai*

WESLEY CARR
Canon Residentiary, Chelmsford Cathedral
Deputy Director, Chelmsford Cathedral Centre for Research and Training

CAMBRIDGE UNIVERSITY PRESS

CAMBRIDGE
LONDON · NEW YORK · NEW ROCHELLE
MELBOURNE · SYDNEY

Published by the Press Syndicate of the University of Cambridge
The Pitt Building, Trumpington Street, Cambridge CB2 1RP
32 East 57th Street, New York, NY 10022, USA
296 Beaconsfield Parade, Middle Park, Melbourne 3206, Australia

BS
2655
.P66
C37
1981

First published 1981

Printed in Great Britain by
Redwood Burn Ltd
Trowbridge Wiltshire.

British Library Cataloguing in Publication Data
Carr, A. Wesley
Angels and principalities. – (Society for New Testament Studies.
Monograph series; 42).
1. Paul, *Saint* 2. Angels – History of doctrines 3. Demonology
I. Title   II. Series
235'.3   BS 2506   80-41242

ISBN 0 521 23429 8

CONTENTS

PREFACE

The substance of this book was originally presented for the degree of Doctor of Philosophy in the University of Sheffield in 1974. That study was made possible by the Trustees of the Sir Henry Stephenson Fellowship who, in electing me to that Fellowship, provided for two years' research. My thanks are due to them. In addition I also make grateful acknowledgement of the welcome I received during that time from Professor James Atkinson and the staff of the Department of Biblical Studies. All were generous with their time and in giving advice and criticism when it was sought. I must, however, particularly mention Dr David Hill, Reader in the Department, who has continued to make his help, encouragement and advice freely available since my leaving the University.

This monograph is a considerable abbreviation of the original thesis. I am very grateful to Professor R. McL. Wilson, Editor of this series, and his associate, Dr M. E. Thrall, for useful criticisms and suggestions, which saved me from several errors. For those that remain I take full responsibility. The production of the original thesis owed much to Mrs Pat Clarke, who has also typed the manuscript of this book.

Chelmsford Cathedral   Wesley Carr

March 1978

ABBREVIATIONS

APOT	*The Apocrypha and Pseudepigrapha of the Old Testament,* ed. R. H. Charles (Oxford, 1913)
ARW	*Archiv für Religionswissenschaft*
ATR	*The Anglican Theological Review*
AV	The Authorised Version of the Bible
BA	*The Biblical Archaeologist*
BAG	*A Greek-English Lexicon of the New Testament and Other Early Christian Literature,* by W. F. Arndt and F. W. Gingrich. A translation and adaptation of W. Bauer's *Griechisch-Deutsches Wörterbuch zu den Schriften des Neuen Testaments und der übrigen urchristlichen Literatur* (Chicago and Cambridge, 1957)
BASOR	*The Bulletin of the American Schools of Oriental Research*
BCH	*Bulletin de correspondance hellénique*
BCLARB	*Bulletin de la classe des lettres de l'Académie Royale de Belgie*
BDF	*A Greek Grammar of the New Testament and Other Early Christian Literature,* by F. Blass and A. Debrunner. A translation and revision of the 9th/10th edition of *Grammatik des neutestamentlichen Griechisch,* incorporating supplementary notes of A. Debrunner, by R. W. Funk (Chicago, 1961)
BT	The Babylonian Talmud
BibSac	*Bibliotheca Sacra*
BJRL	*Bulletin of the John Rylands Library*
BSA	*The Annual of the British School at Athens*
BZ	*Biblische Zeitschrift*
BZNW	Beiheft zur ZNW
CA	*Cahiers archéologiques*
CAH	*The Cambridge Ancient History*

CBQ	*The Catholic Biblical Quarterly*
CCL	*Corpus Christianorum Series Latina*
CIG	*Corpus Inscriptionum Graecarum*
CIL	*Corpus Inscriptionum Latinarum*
CP	*Classical Philology*
CQR	*The Church Quarterly Review*
CR	*The Classical Review*
CRAI	*Comptes rendues à l'Académie des inscriptions et belles-lettres*
CSEL	*Corpus Scriptorum Ecclesiasticorum Latinorum*
DSS	The Dead Sea Scrolls
ERE	*The Encyclopaedia of Religion and Ethics*, ed. J. Hastings (Edinburgh, 1908–26)
ET	English Translation
ÉtBib	*Études bibliques*
EvTh	*Evangelische Theologie*
ExT	*The Expository Times*
GCS	*Die griechischen–christlichen Schriftsteller*
Hennecke–Schneemelcher	*New Testament Apocrypha*, ed. E. Hennecke and W. Schneemelcher. English translation, edited by R. McL. Wilson (London, 1964–5), of *Neutestamentliche Apokryphen* (Tübingen, 1959 and 1964)
HTR	*The Harvard Theological Review*
HUCA	*The Hebrew Union College Annual*
IDB	*The Interpreter's Dictionary of the Bible*
IEJ	*The Israel Exploration Journal*
IG	*Inscriptiones Graecae*
IGRR	*Inscriptiones Graecae ad Res Romanas Pertinentes*
ILS	*Inscriptiones Latinae Selectae*
Insc BM	*Ancient Greek Inscriptions in the British Museum* (Oxford, 1874–1916)
Interp	*Interpretation*
JAC	*Jahrbuch für Antike und Christentum*
JAOS	*The Journal of the American Oriental Society*
JBL	*The Journal of Biblical Literature*
JHS	*The Journal of Hellenic Studies*
JNES	*The Journal of Near Eastern Studies*
JQR	*The Jewish Quarterly Review*
JRS	*The Journal of Roman Studies*
JSS	*The Journal of Semitic Studies*
JT	The Jerusalem Talmud

JTS	*The Journal of Theological Studies*
KuD	*Kerygma und Dogma*
LexTQ	*The Lexington Theological Quarterly*
LSJ	*A Greek–English Lexicon*, H. G. Liddell, R. Scott and H. S. Jones (Oxford, 1940)
M	The Mishnah
MélArch	*Mélanges d'archéologie et d'histoire de l'École française de Rome*
MM	*The Vocabulary of the Greek Testament*, 4th ed., J. H. Moulton and G. Milligan (Edinburgh, 1963)
NEB	The New English Bible
NovT	*Novum Testamentum*
NTA	*New Testament Abstracts*
NTS	*New Testament Studies*
OCD	*The Oxford Classical Dictionary* (Oxford, 1949)
OGIS	*Orientis Graecae Inscriptiones Selectae*
Peake	*Peake's Commentary on the Bible*, ed. M. Black and H. H. Rowley (London, 1962)
PG	*Patrologiae Graecae Cursus Completus*, ed. J. P. Migne (Paris, 1857–94)
PL	*Patrologiae Latinae Cursus Completus*, ed. J. P. Migne (Paris, 1844–80)
RAC	*Reallexicon für Antike und Christentum*, ed. T. Klauser (1950–)
RB	*Revue biblique*
RBN	*Revue belge de numismatique*
RE	*Real-Encyclopaedie der classischen Altertumswissenschaft*, ed. A. Pauly and G. Wissowa
RechSR	*Recherches de science religieuse*
RevArch	*Revue archéologique*
REJ	*Revue des études juives*
RHE	*Revue d'histoire ecclésiastique*
RHR	*Revue de l'histoire des religions*
RhMP	*Rheinisches Museum für Philologie*
RMM	*Revue de metaphysique et morale*
RP	*Revue de philologie*
RQ	*Revue de Qumran*
S–B	*Kommentar zum neuen Testament*, by H. L. Strack and P. Billerbeck (Munich, 1922–61)
SEÅ	*Svensk Exegetisk Årsbok*
SEG	*Supplementum Epigraphicum Graecum*

SIG	*Sylloge Inscriptionum Graecarum*
SJT	*The Scottish Journal of Theology*
SNTSBull	*The Bulletin of the Studiorum Novi Testamenti Societas*
ST	*Studia Theologica*
TB	*Theologische Blätter*
TDNT	*Theological Dictionary of the New Testament*, ed. G. Kittel and G. Friedrich. English translation and edition by G. W. Bromiley (Michigan, 1964–74)
TLZ	*Theologische Literaturzeitung*
TS	*Theological Studies*
TZ	*Theologische Zeitschrift*
VC	*Vigiliae Christianae*
Vermes	*The Dead Sea Scrolls in English*, edited and translated by G. Vermes (London, 1962)
Vg	The Vulgate
VL	Vetus Latina
VT	*Vetus Testamentum*
ZAW	*Zeitschrift für die alttestamentliche Wissenschaft*
ZNW	*Zeitschrift für die neutestamentliche Wissenschaft*
ZThK	*Zeitschrift für Theologie und Kirche*

GENERAL INTRODUCTION

One of the most influential books for the study of the New Testament in the twentieth century has undoubtedly been *Die Geisterwelt im Glauben des Paulus*, which Martin Dibelius published in 1909. He himself owed much to a slimmer volume from Otto Everling, *Die paulinische Angelologie und Dämonologie* (1888). Both authors attempted to establish that a world dominated by supernatural forces was central to Paul's thought; that these forces were hostile to mankind; and that this was the context within which Paul worked out his thinking on man's existence and the work of Christ. Although not the first to deal with this subject, Everling and Dibelius are mainly responsible for the centrality of these notions in the study of Pauline theology today.[1]

In Britain there was less interest in the subject. J. S. Stewart in 1951 described it as 'a neglected emphasis' and G. H. C. Macgregor developed the idea in his stimulating address to the Studiorum Novi Testamenti Societas in 1954.[2] The books of Everling and Dibelius were never translated into English. Those of Oscar Cullmann, however, were, and they exercised a wide influence in the world of scholarship. Both in *The State in the New Testament* (1957) and *Christ and Time* (ET 1951, revised 1962) these principalities and powers were given a central place in his dogmatic scheme. By the time that G. B. Caird published his small collection of lectures in 1956 – *Principalities and Powers: A Study in Pauline Theology* – it was almost universally accepted that Christ's victory over cosmic forces was for Paul a fundamental concept. In particular it was suggested that this vision constituted a major and direct link between the world of the first century and that of the twentieth, especially in Europe and the United States. The problem of the state, which had been experienced acutely by the Germans under Hitler, coupled with the powerfully Christocentric theology that prevailed at the time, sought resolution in the concept of *Christus Victor*, especially as described in Col. 2: 15f. Indeed after the Second World War it appeared for a time that celebration of Christ's triumph enabled Christians respectably on the one hand to urge triumphalist courses of action, whilst publicly on the other hand to reject the apparent triumphalism of the western Church.

Whatever the detail, however, the concept of the victory of Christ over evil powers has been regarded as central to Pauline thought. Certainly there remained the problem of the continued activity of these powers, which Christ was supposed to have conquered once and for all on the cross, but this was only the old problem of theodicy in a distinctively Christian guise. Generally, Cullmann's analogy of the pause between D-day and VE-day received assent, thus allowing the Church to affirm the reign of Christ as Lord and to involve itself in programmes of social and political action. It would appear now, however, that there is less confidence in this assumption. This attitude once again allows us to examine those passages in the writing of Paul in the light of contemporary knowledge and evaluate the significance of the powers in Paul's mind.

The aim of this present study is to carry out such a re-examination. It falls into three parts. In the first place, the environment in which Paul worked and wrote is of fundamental importance. In recent study emphasis has been given to the Jewish background of Paul's thought. Important as this is, it is worth recalling that he lived and worked in the main in Asia Minor, where even the Jews had to a large extent forgotten their past. The letters that we possess were written to churches that occupied an environment that repays careful study in its own right. There is also the matter of chronology. It is rarely noticed how isolated and peculiar a period of history was that in which Paul lived. The Augustan peace in Greece and Asia Minor was a distinctive experience, which can only be understood by a carefully examined chronology of the material that relates to that area.

The central section of this work is given to detailed exegesis of the passages in Paul that deal with the powers. This is done at some length, since it has been necessary not only to suggest a new exegesis of some well-known verses, but also to justify it by outlining the consequences for the particular epistle and for Pauline thought in general.

The final section attempts in short compass to trace the major developments of the idea of the powers in Christian thinking during the first two centuries. This enables us more clearly to see Paul within the Christian tradition as a whole. It is interesting to observe how his understanding is also that of his near contemporaries and immediate successors. When, however, Pauline texts begin to be quoted freely, they seem to be used in somewhat different senses from those that Paul intended. This study ends with Origen, since he appears to represent a turning point in the understanding of Paul's thought.

Finally, it should be noted that two major allied topics are on the whole excluded from this study. The demons, which are prominent in the Gospels, hardly feature in Paul. Thus, although there are inevitably references to demons in the course of the work, no detailed attention is paid to demons and exorcism. Secondly, no separate treatment of Satan or the Devil is offered. This figure looms larger and larger in the course of Christian history, but whilst he is mentioned and discussed on many of the following pages, the temptation to deal with him has been resisted, for that would require another complete study.

PART 1

The background to Paul's thought on the powers

INTRODUCTION

A major difficulty in the study of the language of the powers in the NT is that there is no immediately obvious source from which it derives or background into which it fits. Evidence that is adduced in various lexicons and word studies is often taken from the second century A.D. or later. Moulton and Milligan (*The Vocabulary of the Greek Testament* (London, 1929)) offer no examples of ἀρχή, ἄρχων, ἐξουσίαι or δύναμις prior to the second century A.D. in any other meaning than the recognised classical uses, among which a supernatural sense, when the words are used absolutely, is not found. There is a similar lack of evidence in the LXX, where the words all occur, but not necessarily in an explicitly angelic sense. One exception may be noted: in Dan. 10 there are references to οἱ ἄρχοντες, 'the princes of the nations', and in 7: 27 the ἀρχαί are mentioned. But immediately to relate the two words here, as does Delling, does not take account of the different provenance of these two sections of the book.[1] In the absence of further evidence it is doubtful whether such an association may validly be made, as will be demonstrated. ἄρχοντες also appear in Ecclus. 10: 14 and elsewhere in that book. Again, however, there is no obvious reason why in any passage they should necessarily be interpreted in an angelological sense.

When we turn to the evidence of inscriptions from the Greek East in the first century A.D. we find no use of these terms other than in the recognised political senses. In the Jewish communities too there is plentiful use of ἄρχων, but not in connection with angels.[2] In addition the plural terms ἀρχαὶ καὶ ἐξουσίαι, whether singly or as a couplet, appear not to be used in Jewish or pagan sources. The language appears to be peculiar to the NT and is not found in hellenistic religion.[3] Yet, subsequent to the time of the writing of the NT, we find this type of language proliferating. It is therefore the period of the first century A.D. that requires investigation.

The culture into which Christianity spread and in which Judaism itself shared was an amalgam that had developed since the time of Alexander the

Great. Nowhere was this clearer than in the fields of language and of religion.[4] Greek became the language of the known world. This was not solely a matter of convenient communication. It was itself evidence of the dominance of Greek ideas and attitudes throughout the Mediterranean area. For example, the characteristics of Theophrastus' *Deisidaemon* are also typical of the devout Jew.[5] It is also notable that in the Maccabaean wars it was only the extremely pious who reacted strongly against any syncretism. When emissaries were sent into the countryside to introduce the new cult, they went unarmed. This seems to suggest that they expected no opposition.[6] The ordinary people were not noted for their resistance to foreign ideas. Even the community at Qumran, which has sometimes been used to support the notion of a Judaism that stood over against the hellenism of the Graeco-Roman world, has clear parallels with the Pythagorean brotherhoods. The similarities may not be too strongly pressed, and it seems likely that there was no direct link between the communities. Nevertheless, the similarity does show that even when some Jews were being self-consciously Jewish they were not at this time behaving in a manner so very different from other peoples in the contemporary world.[7]

There is a more deeply rooted assumption that needs questioning. This is the claim that by the first century A.D. men had lost their ties with the old gods and were looking for a vital personal religion that would rescue them from despair. Yet not only was personal religion an aspect of much ancient Greek belief, but even an apparently political act, such as the Augustan religious settlement, could not have succeeded in its restoration of religion unless it also matched up to some sort of real belief. The recovery and augmentation of the *lares compitales* evidences this.[8]

For the study of the language of the powers in Paul's writing, therefore, an awareness of the complex religious and social background of the time is vital. Certainly there is ample evidence for the significance of Paul's Jewish antecedents in his thinking. However, three questions immediately come to mind. First, his use of language and concepts that are derived from recognisably Jewish sources does not necessarily mean that he took them in the traditional sense. The impact of his conversion can easily be underestimated. Secondly, much recent study has emphasised Paul's use of early Christian material. Clearly, therefore, Paul entered upon a Christian tradition that was already advanced in its process of formulation. And thirdly, it is known that his public ministry took place in the main in Asia and Greece. Thus, whatever his own background, the day to day world against which Paul worked out his faith was the ordinary Graeco-Roman world of the first century. In this connection we must also work on the assumption that what he wrote made sense to his readers, who also lived in Greece, Asia or Rome. The question is not only why Paul spoke of the powers, but also what he succeeded in communicating to the recipients of his epistles in the mid-first century A.D.

1

THE ENVIRONMENT IN WHICH PAUL WORKED

1 Asia Minor in the first century A.D.

The letters of Paul may be placed somewhere between *c*. 50 and *c*. 60 A.D. It is not really possible to be more precise, and therefore we should be wary of drawing direct connections between particular historical events and specific episodes in the epistles. The letters were addressed to people living in the world of Graeco-Roman thought, politics and religion. Even where he addressed himself to Jews, as is reported in the Acts of the Apostles, his audience was by no means isolated from the pagan world. There was a common culture with its own attitudes, fears and hopes. The period may be defined, as Tacitus noted, by reference to two main events: the battle of Actium in 31 B.C. and the year of the four emperors in A.D. 68.[1] Both events were of significance in affecting the world of Asia and Greece. The battle of Actium was the culmination of a series of events, each of which had involved the inhabitants of Asia Minor in an exaction. Caesar, Brutus and Cassius, and Antony all made their demands. As for the year 68, not only was there the well-known devotion of the eastern provinces to Nero, which issued in the persistent myth of Nero Redivivus, but the inhabitants also had to stand the cost of Vespasian's army as it moved through the provinces under C. Licinius Mucianus.[2] Between these two events, however, there was a genuine Augustan peace. It is this period that requires careful examination, since it is the background to Paul's work and thought.

Under Augustus and the Julio-Claudians both Rome and the Eastern provinces recognised there was a mutuality of interest.[3] Asia was important within the imperial strategy. Through the heart of the provinces ran the geographical boundary of the Anatolian highlands. The essentially Greek cities of the coast looked westwards and the cities of the hills faced to the East. Thus the cities of the Aegean tended to relate to Greece, whilst the area of Pisidia, which was significant in the life of Paul, was colonised by Roman veterans. This binding together of Asia and the West had a twofold effect. Certainly there was the ever-increasing influence of Greek and Asiatic culture upon Rome, which was at the end of the first century to call forth Juvenal's condemnation.[4] Yet there was also significant Roman influence upon Asia, which was felt in a way not discernible elsewhere in the empire. At the beginning of the principate there was total economic distress. The earthquake of 12 B.C. added to this, but Augustus stepped in and paid the tribute of Asia from his personal funds. In return he soon received the genuine devotion of the people. From this moment Asia flourished impressively, primarily because of the personal interest of Augustus.[5] As a result the Romans looked to 'mollis Ionia' for relaxation and many made the journey.[6] The presence of these tourists coupled with the permanent settlements of Roman veterans had considerable influence. Whilst there was no systematic colonisation of Asia, some colonies were founded in order to extend Roman influence in the area. In time they were absorbed into their environment, but at the time of their founding they were aggressively Roman, and, with the trading posts, greatly affected the surrounding area.[7]

This influence of Rome upon Asia extended beyond the political and commercial. In matters of religion the marks may also be seen. Augustus took singular pride in his re-establishment of traditional Roman religion in the capital itself. In part it was a means of justifying the new by appeal to the old.[8] Yet, although it is not always noticed, he also did something similar in Asia. Here he inherited the *koina*, which flourished in the cult of the famous dead and, on occasion, of living benefactors. As a result of his success at Actium, Augustus was inevitably caught up in this aspect of indigenous religion.[9] In A.D. 11 he banned the practice of voting cults to Roman governors during their period of office, although the custom had in fact ceased.[10] Taking this tradition, however, he invigorated it and reclaimed it to his own advantage. What is most worthy of note is the way in which Augustus was able to manipulate and monopolise a religious custom, even though it was deeply ingrained in Asian religious life. He here exemplified the general influence of Rome in modifying and directing Asian religion in this period. This would suggest, therefore, that the age was less one of new awareness and religious insight than one in which the old was being revitalised in a quiet hope that it would suffice.

Asia recognised and accepted her dependence upon Rome, and in her social and religious life looked in that direction, not always for ideas, but certainly for inspiration in the application of these ideas.[11] This attitude was not confined to the reign of Augustus. In most matters Tiberius was concerned to implement the Augustan ideal; if Gaius proved erratic, his time was short. Claudius succeeded with his own brand of conscious archaism: roads were built, colonisation recommenced, and towns recognised their devotion to him.[12] Throughout the period of Paul's activity in Asia, then, the area was feeling and adjusting to the renewed impact of Roman life and attitudes. The attraction between Rome and Asia was mutual, but while Rome perhaps failed to perceive the influence that Asian thought, life and culture was having upon its own *gravitas*, it is equally clear that the Asian cities and towns had not fully grasped their own rate of change, as what sometimes seemed to be merely administrative decisions also affected at root their cultural and religious heritage. The recovery of Asia after the depredations of war was accomplished through energies being channelled mainly into administration and economic endeavour. This, in its acknowledged and grateful dependence upon the West, meant that religious and cultural life tended towards a *polis*-oriented conservatism, almost archaism, which mirrored life at Rome itself. The flowering of religious belief and inquiry in Asia occurred in the main from the end of the first century onwards. Paul moved about an Asia that was characterised by religious quiet and acceptance of the past. We may test this general thesis by examining two specific areas, each of which has at times been adduced as part of the background to Paul's work and both of which are of direct relevance to the question of the powers in his thought. These are the question of personal religion in the mysteries and the rise of astrology. Final evidence will be sought in the Acts of the Apostles, itself a valuable source for knowledge of Asia in the mid-first century.

2 Personal religion and the mysteries

Since the work of Reitzenstein the significance of mystery religion for early Christianity has been a matter of intense debate. In a most important article, B. M. Metzger has clarified the conditions within which the discussion must be held. In particular he has emphasised that we must distinguish the faith and practice of the earliest Christians from that of those in subsequent centuries.[13] This position is also fundamental to the present study. It may easily be shown, for example, that the cult of Asclepius or the syncretistic religion of Sabazius or the universal appeal of Isis all greatly influenced the Mediterranean world. The question is, however, to what extent they were active in the mid-first century and, if they were active, to what extent they demonstrably affected Christian faith and practice.[14] Such detailed evidence as we have for the mystery religions is mainly late and dates from the third century or later. This naturally does not imply that they began then. Although for centuries they had been part of Greek life, under the Roman Empire they revived in Asia, and the evidence that we have suggests a particularly strong revival in the second century. In any religion there are changes and variations at different times and places, and the mysteries were no exception. In A.D. 376, for example, we have two inscriptions about the efficacy of the taurobolium that are mutually contradictory.[15] Christianity itself, as Metzger reminds us, originated in Palestinian Judaism. This did not necessarily remain significant, in itself, and E. R. Goodenough has sufficiently demonstrated the wide variety of beliefs that were maintained within Judaism.[16] It is the period within which Christianity began that is of primary significance. Nationalistic fervour among the Jews was strong and this, as may be suspected, appears to have gone hand in hand with a heightened religious consciousness. Into this atmosphere of conservative, almost reactionary, Judaism, Christianity was born. There is, therefore, an inherent improbability that the first Christians would have borrowed concepts from any mystery religions. In addition, there is scarcely any archaeological evidence for mysteries in Palestine itself. There are always likely to be apparent connections between different religions, and this was noted as much in the ancient world as it is today. Mutual borrowing was not unusual. Nevertheless it is the differences between religions rather than their similarities that are usually more important. The absence of the language of the mysteries from the earliest Christian writings is significant, as is the marked contrast between the avowed mythology of the mysteries and the distinctive claims of the early Christians.[17] Various studies have demonstrated that pagan sacramental rites have not significantly affected those of the early Church. Above all, the absence of claims to a resurrection in the mysteries prior to the end of the second century is highly remarkable.[18]

The mysteries, then, made no measurable impact upon the Christian faith in the first half of the first century. The reason for this may well lie partly in the Jewish origins of that faith and in the nature of its message.[19] Yet also it must lie in the state of the mysteries themselves. They appear at the time of the rise of Christianity neither to have regained the significance that had earlier been theirs, nor yet to have had the status that they were to claim from the end of the first century until the end of the third. The evidence for this claim is diffuse, but cumulatively it is convincing.

Unquestionably the supreme mysteries of the ancient world, until their demise in A.D. 396, were those at Eleusis. One of Augustus' first acts after his victory at Actium was to be initiated and his successors usually followed this lead.[20] The act seems to have been another part of Augustus' repristinisation of religious life, and in his attitude he appears to have shared a general Roman view that the mysteries were less an experience than a means by which men were civilised.[21] Thus by example in Greece, and later by precept in Rome, Augustus tried to ensure that for a time religion in all its forms would direct men to the past and thus into safe channels. Socially the mysteries were important, but experientially they were clearly weak. Augustus was able to demand an extra performance at Eleusis for the benefit of an Indian, Zamarus, who seems to have been unimpressed.[22] That Augustus could so impose his will upon the most ancient of mysteries argues a certain weakness of the cult at that period. The economic distress of Greece and Asia could only have contributed to this. If, however, such was the case at Eleusis, it would not be surprising if the many lesser mysteries of Asia Minor were in a worse case.

There is another piece of fragmentary evidence that the mysteries gained prominence only in the period after the original steps by Christianity into the Greek world. Towards the end of the first century there appear hints in Ephesus, Ancyra, Pergamum and Bithynia of a connection between the imperial cult and local mysteries. This cannot be evidence for the accept-ance of the imperial cult at the roots of popular religion, since its place there was already assured. Rather this suggests the revival of local mysteries through their association with the more powerful cult of the emperor. In the main the imperial cult was adopted and encouraged by local nobility. Association therefore with it by small local mysteries may well have been the means by which they survived and from which they recovered their importance, which reasserted itself in the second century.[23]

At the time of Trajan it would appear that oracles too were enjoying a renewed vigour.[24] One of the most famous was that at Claros, the history of which seems to confirm the picture of a quiet period in the religious life of Asia in the mid-first century. The excavations by Louis Robert have brought to light an oracle whose history goes back to the third century B.C. but whose period of glory seems to have begun in the second century A.D. From this time a large number of votive notices have been uncovered. The first mention of this oracle in the first century A.D. recounts a visit by Germanicus in A.D. 18. Tacitus, writing in the early part of the second century from the vantage point of one who had been proconsul in Asia, seems to attribute little significance to this oracle and regards it as almost unknown to the Romans. The inscriptions, therefore, together with this literary mention would suggest that at Claros there occurred what we have noticed elsewhere: a religious revival took place in the second century, rather later than the date of the first Christian writings. Even if we dis-allow the witness of Tacitus, the inscriptions alone point to a lively oracle in the second, but not in the first, century A.D. The oracle is one of a new style, combining with its oracular function some sort of mystery cult. The primitive rite described by Tacitus, whereby a man had to be fetched from Miletus to deliver the message, has given place to a sophisticated ceremonial.[25] And what happened at Claros appears also to have occurred elsewhere in Asia Minor, especially the connecting of oracles with mysteries in this new lease of life.[26]

Finally we may point to the literary history of the period to demonstrate the sudden increase of religious feeling from the second century onwards. Towards the end of the first century examples of the romantic novel reappear. Although this genre has its origin in Parthenius and Ninus, it reached its zenith in the third century A.D. Not only is the second century the significant period of development, but Asia itself is the home of several leading writers: Longus of Lesbos, Chariton of Caria, and Xenophon of Ephesus. The ideas of the Orient here enter the western world and Greeek authors publish literature of what is in fact a most un-Greek style. In these novels are reflected the religious concerns of the age, with the demand of the individual for redemption, mysteries, oracles, and 'the general air of the transcendental'.[27] The basic concept is that of the purification of the soul through tribulation. After a period of economic and social upheaval and restoration, various religious conflicts reassert themselves at the beginning of the second century: the individual against the nation; personal religion and the efficacy of the old gods; East and West; the old and the new in oracles and mysteries; the rise of astrology. This resurgence provides the background for these novels, which are uniquely works of their own day, a day far removed from that of the first Christians.

These pieces of evidence cumulatively suggest a period of religious quiet rather than of turbulence in the middle of the first century A.D. There is a wider gap between that time and the second century than is sometimes realised. The second area of argument on this and its relevance for the understanding of the earliest Christians are seen in the problem of astrology, its power and significance in the mid-first century.

3 The rise of astrology

It is sometimes claimed that some of Paul's language reflects the astrological concerns of his age.[28] There can be no disputing the presence of astrology in the Graeco-Roman world of the first century A.D.[29] The term 'astrology', however, needs to be used with circumspection. Knowledge and awareness of the stars is a significant aspect of any society prior to the invention of street lighting. They are unavoidable and their progress across the heavens has an attractive inevitability when compared with the chances of life. For the farmer astrometeorology is an essential professional skill, but it constitutes no evidence for an interest or belief in astrology. Columella, for example, is quite able to argue the case for astrometeorological skills alongside a denunciation of astrology.[30] We cannot, therefore, assume that any mention of the stars automatically implies a belief in their direct influence upon the lives of men.

Astrology may be divided into two main types: universal astrology, which tends to be fatalistic, and individual astrology, which is catarchic. 'Human nature being what it is', writes F. H. Cramer,

> 'the harsh principle of fatalistic astrology was appealing to the sober, scientific minded minority only. Most of those who believed in astrology at all preferred the catarchic doctrine, permitting man to "outsmart" the heavens. As for the masses, star worship and catarchic astrology with them remained popular at all times from the hellenistic era to the end of paganism in the Roman empire.'[31]

Unless this distinction is observed it is all too easy to overestimate the significance of astrology in Asia Minor and the West in the first century A.D. Horoscopic or catarchic astrology differed very little from the art of *haruspicina*. Juvenal at the end of the century, naturally ridiculing astrology as an eastern import, noticed the connection: 'motus astrorum ignoro . . . ranarum viscera numquam inspexi.' He also noted the connection between astrology and oracles.[32] We have already seen that oracles revived from the beginning of the second century. Similarly the general dominance of astrology also begins then. Although astrological belief does have an influence in the first century, the evidence requires careful sifting. If it dates from the second century it may only be used with extreme caution. And some things, which in the light of a later context appear to be evidence for astrology, when examined in their own context, prove simply to be popular superstitions with no astral connection.[33]

In Rome itself, for which we have most evidence, fatalistic astrology in the first century was primarily a pursuit of the dilettante. Its close connection with Stoicism ensured among some its acceptance.[34] Aratus' work was popular, but less for its content than for its style.[35] The *Astronomica* of Manilius, which dates from the beginning of the century, suggests that the author writes less within an environment that has accepted the ideas of universal astrology than as an evangelist for his cause. The view that Roman society was becoming interested in the subject, but that it was not yet of dominant significance, is confirmed by the *Satyricon* of Petronius. At his feast Trimalchio is shown as excessively superstitious. His wall-chart of the phases of the moon and lucky and unlucky days, his zodiacal dish with appropriate foods, and above all his droll astrological nonsense – at which the guests praise 'urbanitatem mathematici' – combine to create an extravagant picture of astrology among the *nouveaux riches.*[36] But the sheer superstition emphasises that it is still merely the expensive pursuit of the idle rich and not a serious matter. And this was not peculiar to Rome. In the provinces, except in Africa, which had its own sidereal religion, astrology remained to a large degree an interest of the leisured. It was not a popular belief, which the intellectuals refined; it rather attached itself to ancient beliefs as an intellectual refinement of them, which later and gradually permeated the lives of ordinary people.

A further piece of evidence from Rome is suggestive. It appears that during the period between A.D. 16 and 93 there were approximately eleven expulsions of astrologers from Rome. The details of some are doubtful, but these seem to have been the sum of public moves against astrologers.[37] The expulsions were always to do with unrest, usually believed to involve plots against the emperor or his family. Significantly, however, in the first sixty-eight years of the century there were only five such expulsions, and since two of these occurred in the same year (A.D. 16) and since those under Nero are highly problematic, almost certainly fewer. After this, however, the incidence of expulsions in the first century doubled. The influence of fatalistic astrology was always likely to increase in times of unrest, real or imagined. The second half of the century, after the events of A.D. 68, offered a climate in which it could develop, but this was not so in the peace of the first half. This may be confirmed when we note that astrology is frequently mentioned in Juvenal, but only twice in all the work of Horace: the *pax Augusta* ensured that there was little need for interest. The totally different approach to the subject between the mid-first century and the second century is exemplified by one small example. According to Suetonius an astrological prediction of the death of Vitellius was frustrated by him. By the time that Dio Cassius retells the story, however, the astrologers are vindicated. This is not merely a matter of Dio being more credulous than Suetonius, since the latter is usually prepared to allow oracles and prophecies a key role, as, for example, in his account of the demise of Vitellius.[38] It represents a genuine social change in the attitude to astrology.

The question must now be asked of the relevance of this evidence from Rome to the world of Paul, to Greece and Asia Minor. The tendency for astrology to come into prominence in times of political uncertainty is also typical of Asia.[39] Certainly, as we have seen, the period was one of political quiet and therefore not likely to be conducive to widespread astrological belief. In addition it may be that an edict published by Augustus in A.D. 11, which forbade certain astrological practices, applied to the whole empire.[40] It is impossible to be sure, but it does suggest that horoscopic astrology was dominant and not a universal fatalism. Certainly the idea of fate as it affected the individual was prevalent, but it was not yet so oppressive that it created in men a fear of the elements. The cults of Isis and of Mithras contained aspects of astrology, but these notably increased in significance in the second rather than in the mid-first century. Again, there was a close association in the minds of the populace between the stars and success in the races. This is clear in the late republic, but it is observable how this popular belief was strengthened and developed in the second and third centuries by a progressive engagement with fatalistic astrology.[41]

The original religious settlement of Augustus included the revival of the worship of *lares compitales* along with the *genius Augusti*. This was not an imposition by the emperor, but a perception that the Roman people looked for their popular worship not in any new importation but in a revived local cult.[42] On the basis of our study of the attitude of Asia towards Rome in the first half of the first century it would appear that the same principle applied there at the same time. Old cults were encouraged and indigenous religion with a bias towards Rome and the emperor revived. It is here that we should look for evidence of popular belief in the first part of the century and not to any fear of the stars. In general there is evidence for the swift increase in the importance of astrology outside Africa and the Orient from the second century onwards, culminating in its dominance under Antoninus Pius. Christians encountered it in the second century and answered its challenge in the language of the day, but it would be an anachronism to claim that it was an issue of the mid-first century.[43] Astrology was already in the world, but Christians only encountered the small indications of potential. The actual growth was yet to come.[44]

4 The evidence of the Acts of the Apostles

There is available to hand in the Acts of the Apostles a contemporary source of information on some social and religious attitudes in Greece and Asia Minor at the time of Paul. The book has generally been undervalued from this perspective, largely because scholars have been occupied with questions concerning the theological and apologetic aims of the book and with the question of sources. Even this search for sources, however, implies that the book rests on evidence that is derived from the mid-first century. As such, therefore, it should be available as evidence, when used critically, for the religious attitudes to be found in Asia Minor and Greece at this time. One means of testing the overall reliability of the book is to stand its information alongside what is known from other sources. This has been done for the social and political situation by A. N. Sherwin-White.[45] Here we consider alone the encounters with contemporary religion, other than Judaism, which are narrated in six episodes. The passages are assessed solely for their value to us in attempting to understand the religious environment of Asia and Greece in which Paul worked.

The presence of a Jewish magician, Elymas, in the entourage of a Roman governor occasions no surprise (Acts 13: 6ff). Romans, especially when in the East, were inclined to draw upon local wise men and include astrologers and soothsayers in their company. Clearly Elymas is a Jew, but of his duties we can discern nothing. He functions in the story only as an opponent of the gospel. Haenchen introduces the notion that the story is a paradigm of the encounter between the gospel and demonic forces.[46] Yet we should affirm on the contrary that the author consciously does not personalise the evil in Elymas. Thus Paul is described as πλησθεὶς πνεύματος ἁγίου; the sorcerer is merely πλήρης παντὸς δόλου. This is no struggle between opposing forces, for there is no direct comparison between the phrases. The Christian apostle is energised by the power of the Spirit which pervades the Christian, whereas the sorcerer is replete with wickedness, a description of his state.

When Paul and Barnabas reach Lystra (Acts 14: 8ff) they heal a cripple, are taken by the Lycaonians to be Hermes and Zeus, and only just avoid having sacrifice offered to them. The episode is highly problematic. Although the function of the difficulty of the local language is probably to explain how Paul and Barnabas allowed themselves to get into so compromising a situation, the fact of its mention is wholly consonant with what is known of this colony in the first century. In addition to the story of Baucis and Philemon, there is epigraphical evidence from the third century A.D. that links Hermes and Zeus in Lystra.[47] Even if we have here a story devised for edification, it is notable that, if Zeus and Hermes represent a hellenisation of local gods, in the first century the important gods are still the old ones and not any new religion.[48]

Little need be remarked on the encounter with Python in Philippi (Acts 16: 16ff). She appears to have been a medium, and both pagan and Jewish traditions associate mediums with demons.[49] The exorcism is, therefore, the natural response. Far more instructive is the episode in Athens (Acts 17: 16ff) where Paul speaks of the Unknown God. The aspects of the story that alone concern the present study are the two references to religion. The recorded reactions of the Epicureans and Stoics to Paul's message certainly fit what is known of them. Secondly, the altar to the Unknown God remains a mystery. However, even if Luke invented it to give Paul's argument a starting point after the initial *captatio benevolentiae*, it is not unreasonable to suppose that we have here an early reference to one of the known marks of religious devotion in Athens, namely worship at altars to unknown or unnamed gods. Wycherley's attractive suggestion that this reference is to the rebuilding of altars for the dead whose graves had been disturbed during the rebuilding of Athens would certainly fit what we know of the city in the mid-first century. Unlike the rest of the Greek mainland Athens was, as we have noted, enjoying imperial patronage and the corresponding commercial recovery.[50] This is, however, only an hypothesis and we must therefore conclude of this episode that, while there is nothing in Luke's account that hinders our seeing it as an accurate reflection of the first century, there is equally no positive evidence that demands that we do so. This raises the problem of the distinction between possibility and probability in historical studies. If we do take the account at its face value, then it certainly has the marks of historicity and therefore the possibility is that it is an accurate account of life in Athens in the mid-first century.[51] In this case, the absence of further evidence may allow us to regard it as an historical probability. The picture is of a city that in its religious expression is still tied to the old gods. The term 'The Unknown God' is not a pointer to religious uncertainty and the attempt of a people to cover themselves fearfully against all divine possibilities (which may be Luke's interpretation), but to a continued devotion to the old ways and customs.

The two most dramatic encounters in the book between Paul and pagan religion occur at Ephesus. The burning of the magical books (Acts 19: 18ff) forms the conclusion to the most puzzling story of the sons of Scaeva. Luke chiefly has in mind the exorcism, but the portrayal of Ephesus as a centre of magic is accurate for the time of Paul. Of far greater interest is the riot that Paul is recorded as having caused around the worship of Artemis (Acts 19: 23ff). There are again many problems associated with this story, but it is significant that the episode, which involves several nice points of law, has been dated by a historian to a period prior to the middle of the second century. This era, 'the last age of civic autonomy', began in the Augustan period and then declined to an end in the second century.[52] All the key cities of Asia, including Ephesus, had been part of Antony's eastern empire prior to Actium. Among the aims of Augustus was the restoration to them of pride and prosperity after the doldrums at the end of the republic. In this story the concern not only of the religious leaders but also of the civil authorities at Ephesus witnesses to a time of civic awareness, which is wholly in keeping with the restored fortunes of Ephesus in the mid-first century A.D. The charge against Paul and his companions is that they wished to seduce the population away from the old gods. This is described by Haenchen as 'heathen belief in its crassest form'. In this, however, he has supposed too much for this particular period in the history of Asia Minor. Not only was all that was old being revalued during the first part of the century, it was also being given a new religious infusion, possibly by association of the imperial cult with the worship of Artemis.[53] Although the livelihood of Demetrius and his fellow silversmiths was threatened and there was undoubtedly a certain amount of self interest involved in the behaviour of the citizens, the significance of this religious fervour should not be underestimated. Historically much of the authority and autonomy of Ephesus derived from her central position in the cult of Artemis. Several centuries earlier some ambassadors from Ephesus to the dependent shrine at Sardis had been abused, and the Ephesians had sentenced the criminals to death in an episode of which we know little, except through one inscription.[54] At the time of Paul's visit Ephesus was again a key city, which, after its restoration from the preceding decades of trouble, was again exerting her civic autonomy. The way in which she had done this in the past was through her central importance in the cult of Artemis. There is then every probability that this was the way in which she would do it again. The age of scepticism had not yet dawned, and Artemis was the focus both of civic pride and of genuine religious feeling. Luke's account exactly fits this specific period in the history of the city.

In these six episodes, even allowing for Luke's formalisation of the Christian mission and the literary problems in each passage, it is clear that the religious world portrayed by Luke matches what we know from other sources. The world is one of old gods, exorcisms, magicians and philosophers. The ideas that are missing, however, are even more intriguing. There are no hints of mystery religion, nor of astrology, nor of men bound by decrees of Fate. The conclusion must be that these were of little or no significance in Asia and Greece in the mid-first century. The argument is from silence, but the silence is eloquent. Similarly Luke's interpretation of the progress of the mission from Jerusalem to Rome is never characterised in terms of principalities and powers. The few encounters with demons occur in a way reminiscent of those between Jesus and the demons in the Gospels. The Acts of the Apostles, therefore, appears to provide corroborative evidence that the time of Paul's mission was not one of great religious awakening, but one of quiet and determined revival of the old ways as the world finally settled after the traumas of the end of the Roman Republic.

5 Conclusion

No period of history may be treated in isolation from the years that precede and follow it. It would certainly be a mistake to separate the period *c.* 30–60 A.D. out of its wider context. Yet equally it should be remembered that this was the exact period in which the Christian mission took the gospel out of Palestine into the wider world, and, in the case of Paul, specifically into Asia Minor, Greece, and Rome. There is also reason to think that this particular period was in several ways isolated from the years preceding and following. The decline of the Roman Republic did not only affect Rome and Italy, but, as we have seen, it also had an impact upon Asia Minor, which even prior to Actium was an area of major disturbance. The rich economic resources of Asia were drained during the death throes of the republic, so that the dawning of the empire was the final stage in a long drawn out process of political and economic change. At the same time this beginning laid the foundation of the heyday of empire, which unarguably came in the second and third centuries. In this period the true flowering from the roots that were laid in the first century took place. The peace and prosperity, *pax et securitas*, was no longer a slogan in this century; it was an experience from which a cultural reassessment and corresponding religious revival sprang.

The Christianity that Paul brought spread only in the geographically limited area of Greece, Asia Minor and Rome. Here he appears to have been regarded and to have behaved like a cultivated 'Jewish-Greek'. The incident at Lystra is instructive: Luke portrays their instinctive horror that they might be seen as gods as an expected Jewish reaction. It is also, however, that of cultivated Greeks when confronted by barbarians. This Luke stresses by his emphasis upon the problem of language. It is with this type of cultivated Greek that Paul seems to have dealt in much of his mission and to whom he assimilated himself whilst in Asia and Greece.

The world in which these Greeks lived had been considerably affected by the inauguration of the Roman Empire. Romanisation was in progress, partly through the new colonies, but chiefly through economic encouragement and renewed prosperity. This had begun before the time of Paul's activity in the area through the direct involvement of the imperial family, and this fact contributed to a greater acceptance of Rome in Asia than there was, say, fifty years later. The world as a whole was at this time highly dependent on Rome, resulting in a more relaxed period of history; the Greek world was once again self-consciously providing ideas and life for the West. This change is almost typified in the difference in attitude to Greece that may be discerned between Trajan and Hadrian. The former could not understand Dio of Prusa when he heard him speak, whilst the latter was noted as a philhellene.[55] Further examples may be found in the coinage and in the art of the time. In Asia under Augustus there were about 100 centres that were allowed to mint their own coinage. By the end of the century, however, Rome's public hold was being relaxed and the number had risen to nearer 300.[56] At the beginning of the century

Asia, in close dependence on Rome, was undergoing a period of repristini-sation similar to that which was taking place in the capital. Although the early life of the empire seemed to be vigorous, this impression is mislead-ing. For the vigour was being carefully channelled into the old and the safe, not into new or exploratory ideas, least of all in matters of religion and culture. In art also we note that new approaches and developments are discernible in the second century. In the first part of the first century, however, the Graeco-Roman world was too conscious of its immediate past to risk much for the future.[57]

It was due to this conscious conservatism that the revival of the mysteries, of oracles, of local cults, and the inbreaking of popular astro-logy did not occur until the end of the first century onwards. This was the age of the new religions and a revived emphasis upon experience. It was also the time of the rise of individualism, because in Asia and in Rome the consequences of the principate were being reaped in terms of the collapse of the social structures that gave value to the concept of society or the city. The concept of *polis* revived in Greek cities in the early empire, but from the time of Trajan local political significance began to decline rapidly.[58] Compensation for this imposition from above was in part found in the local assertion of independent cults and *collegia*. In such groupings men sought their identity. 'The failure of the cities to continue their Romanisation in the second century is not due to the upwards movement of the lower classes; it reflects the failure of the urban classes themselves to be satisfied with their inherited culture.'[59] As public life declined and men felt free from old obligations, the way became open for a reassess-ment of the meaning of life. The mysteries revived and witnessed to a renewed concern with questions of eternal life and the consequences of this for the significance of life in this world.[60] Astrology, with its claim to explain the movement of history and to give sense to even the most apparently meaningless of lives, spread through all levels of society. Above all, the individual's experience of isolation and his feeling of being in-capable of handling it characterises the men and women of the second century. At the turn of the first century the difference in attitude is marked. Epictetus, for example, speaking of the *pax Augusta* acknow-ledges its existence, but emphasises that this is no peace from the passions of personal experience – love, grief, or envy. This view contrasts starkly with the relief, which finds regular epigraphical expression earlier in the century, when peace as freedom from war and from want is greeted with enthusiasm.[61] This problem at the end of the century was not that of vigorous society, but of a de-politicised, prosperous society, which turned men in on themselves and raised questions that appear not to have been so prominent earlier. Culturally and politically the second century may have been one of decay; religiously it was one of new directions and original ideas. Whereas the promise of peace was acknowledged under the Julio-Claudian emperors, the events of A.D. 68 reminded the world of its fragility.   Although the potential civil strife did not materialise, questions of human existence were posed with renewed force. This time the answers were sought in a different direction, not in terms of peace and prosperity (which were largely realised) but in terms of individual identity and the nature of the soul. And the answers were religious.

The world into which Paul ventured with his gospel, however, was quite different. It was religiously a somewhat sterile world, upon which the Augustan peace still fell. It was not seething with religious quests, but was preoccupied with prosperity and recovery. The hand of Rome, which later had such a paralysing effect on local life and initiative, was at this stage welcome. Only under the Flavians did the relationship between central government and local autonomous bodies become important. There was a pause in the world of the mid-first century, and into that pause Christianity quietly spread. Its period of growth and consolidation coincided with the renewed religious concerns of the second century onwards. But as the challenge came, Christianity, having already found its base in the Graeco-Roman world, did not bother with borrowing from Mithras or from Isis or from the mysteries, but encountered Greek thought face to face and to a large measure adopted Roman patterns of organisation. Such behaviour is that of a movement that is fully at home in the world and that is mature in its outlook. This maturity was itself a product of its gentle introduction into a foreign world during a period that culturally and religiously was, as Tacitus perceptively observed, one of *quies et tranquillitas.* [62]

The background to Paul's language and thought, therefore, is not simply to be sought in Palestine or in Judaism, for his life was lived in the main apart from the developing political and social unrest of that province. He lived and worked where the imperial peace was a matter of daily experience in an industrious and thriving world. Nor, on the other hand, is the source of his language to be sought in the realms of mysteries and astrology. These were at the time of his mission at a low ebb and use of any technical language derived from them, even if it was known to Paul, would have conveyed little to his readers. We cannot take the existence of a serious belief in the oppressively demonic for granted in the world into which Paul went. In our examination, therefore, of his language of αἱ ἀρχαὶ καὶ αἱ ἐξουσίαι we must carefully try to understand it against this background of the mid-first century, and not against that of the end of the century, the beginning of the second, or later.

2

THE POWERS IN JEWISH AND PAGAN THOUGHT

1 Jewish thought

It is not the intention of this section to attempt a full account of Jewish angelogy and demonology. Questions of origins do not arise, for we are concerned with the Jewish background only in so far as it may have affected Paul's concept of the powers.

The concept of angelic or demonic beings was part of Hebrew thought in the earliest periods, but it appears not to have been a formative influence in the development of Hebrew religion. Angels appear in the significant notion of the court of Yahweh.[1] The only reference in pre-exilic prophecy is found in Hos. 12: 4, where the man of Gen. 32: 24, who wrestled with Jacob, has become an angel. The sons of God in Gen. 6: 2, who play so prominent a part in later thinking, seem to become angels through the influence of the translators of the LXX.[2] On the demonic side certain monsters such as Azazel (Lev. 16) and Lilith (Is. 34: 14) survive, but are only connected with a multitude of demons much later in the tradition.

During and after the exile there was considerable development of the concept. But even here in the canonical material angels and demons play a relatively small part. The heavenly court recurs in the prologue to Job and in the early parts of Ezekiel. The main function of an angel is still that of representing Yahweh, and often the two persons are confused. The prophet Zechariah, for example, never sees God himself, but only an angel. This book also provides the first reference to ranks of angels (2: 3ff), something that, like the few surviving associations of angels with stars, may reflect Babylonian influence. In Job 38: 7 angels and the stars seem to be identified, but the general absence of Babylonian beliefs in the Old Testament is remarkable. The prophets in general condescend to them in order only to reaffirm the primacy of Yahweh.[3] In the case of the demonic, however, there is greater development in the post-exilic period. The tendency is to avoid the attribution of evil to God, and this, coupled

with the direct encounter in the exile between the Jews and powerful
heathen gods and the loneliness of the journey across the desert, encouraged Hebrew thought to develop its conception of personal evil. The
demons that had been connected with physical evil are associated with
moral evil, a move that contained the seeds of a dualism that was never
far away.[4] It is generally noticeable, however, that this personalised evil is
mainly focused in one being rather than in a host of identifiable demonic
powers.

Thus, apart from Daniel, the canonical books provide little material
from which complicated angelologies and demonologies might develop.
Only in Daniel do the angels assume distinctive personalities. It is very
remarkable, however, that evil is progressively personalised into the Satan,
who gradually increases his independence from Yahweh, long before there
is any correspondingly good angel.[5] From this point on, during the Greek
period, the Jewish doctrine of angels grows apace and in total confusion.
Some literature abounds with these figures (Daniel and 1 Enoch), while
other books omit almost all reference (Maccabees, Wisdom and Ecclesi-
asticus). We turn, therefore, to systematic consideration of the three main
literary contributions, those of Daniel, 1 Enoch, and Jubilees.

(a) Daniel

In the first six chapters of Daniel the references to angels conform to those
generally found in the OT. Thus the fourth person in the fiery furnace is
'like a son of God' (3: 25), and God sends an angel to Daniel in the lions'
den (6: 22). These are both agents of Yahweh who function as extensions
of his presence. In 4: 10 a being comes to Nebuchadrezzar in a dream: $\dot{e}\hat{\iota}\rho$
$\kappa\alpha\dot{\iota}\,\ddot{\alpha}\gamma\iota o\varsigma\,\dot{\alpha}\pi'\,o\dot{\upsilon}\rho\alpha\nu o\hat{\upsilon}$. The second phrase seems to be an explanation of
the first, and demonstrates the usual use of $\ddot{\alpha}\gamma\iota o\varsigma$ (singular) in the book to
mean 'an angel'.[6] In chapter 7 God is described as surrounded by myriads
of beings, a view that is also common to 1 Enoch (e.g. 60: 1 and 71: 13)
and may reflect an association of the angels with the stars of heaven. In 7:
22, however, the term $\ddot{\alpha}\gamma\iota o\iota$ presents a problem that is of significance to
our argument in view of its connection with $\dot{\alpha}\rho\chi\alpha\dot{\iota}$ (7: 27). If the word
$\ddot{\alpha}\gamma\iota o\iota$ in the plural retains the meaning that it has in the singular in Daniel,
then it must refer to angels and the reference of $\dot{\alpha}\rho\chi\alpha\dot{\iota}$ is also to angelic
powers. The sentence then means that rule over the whole world will be
given to the angelic hosts, who will in turn hand it over to God. Alterna-
tively the plural term may refer to the people of God, in which case $\dot{\alpha}\rho\chi\alpha\dot{\iota}$
will be the authorities of the earthly kingdoms. A third possibility is that
$o\dot{\iota}\,\ddot{\alpha}\gamma\iota o\iota$ are angelic forces, who share with the people of God an attitude of
worship and obedience to the Most High. This view merely recognises an

ambiguity in ἅγιοι without attempting to resolve it.[7] The occurrence of ἀρχαί here, however, might give the clue. In normal Greek usage it means human authorities in the sense of the fact of authority rather than of its bearer.[8] The argument is not conclusive but it might reinforce the conclusion that here, as later in Paul generally, the term ἅγιοι refers to the human people of God.

There are two further references worthy of note. In 8: 8 the phrase δύναμις τοῦ οὐρανοῦ appears to mean 'the hosts of heaven'. The plural is not used, but the phrase stands in parallel with such a plural and the singular is probably to be taken in a collective sense. In 9: 21 Gabriel reappears (having first interpreted the dream in 8: 16), and he is called ἀνὴρ Γαβριήλ. This may be an example of the division of angels into the ordinary myriads, who are associated with the stars, and the higher angels, who are named and given human characteristics. One of the marks of the developing angelology of the intertestamental period is the way in which the higher angels are placed nearer to God, both in status and function, while the lesser relate increasingly to the world as fire, stars and the physical elements.

The highly significant 'angels of the nations' in chapter 10 will best be treated after consideration of 1 Enoch and Jubilees. They constitute a unique feature within the book of Daniel, the angelology of which is otherwise consonant with the general ideas of post-exilic Judaism. The tendency to personalisation may be observed as the unnamed and mysterious 'holy one from heaven' becomes Gabriel and, possibly, as 'one like a son of God' (3: 25) becomes the possibly more significant 'one like a son of man' (7: 13).

(b) 1 Enoch

The problems in 1 Enoch also concern the different strata within the book and their dating, particularly that of the Similitudes. Some place these in the first century B.C., but Hindley has offered cogent reasons for a time in the late first century A.D., and Milik has further proposed the third century A.D.[9] They seem to come from the Christian era and the angelology, although distinctive, clearly seems to have its origin in Jewish apocalyptic. The phrase 'Lord of the Spirits' is peculiar to the Similitudes, and there are two traditions about the fall of the angels. In the Noachic fragment the legend from Gen. 6 is employed, according to which the angels, led by Semjaza, lust after the daughters of men. In the list of chief angels that is given at this point, Azazel ranks tenth.[10] In chapter 9, however, he has become the leader of the rebellious angels who, having rebelled against God, are expelled from heaven. Again, in chapters 20–36 the Watchers are fallen angels. It is noticeable that they play no part in the Similitudes. 1 Enoch also associates the fall of the angels with the bringing of skills to men (8: 1ff), and with the myth that the demons issued from the giants at their death, these giants themselves being the offspring of the illicit union of angels with women (15: 8). But even here there is confusion: the giants are at first themselves demons, and later the demons are separated from them. There is no attempt to harmonise the different approaches into a unified angelology.[11]

The importance of this heterogeneous work is considerable. There is not only a large number of angels but there is also a growing importance attached to named angels, especially those of the throne – Michael, Uriel, Gabriel and Raphael (or Suriel). Of their functions, two in particular recur frequently in apocalyptic literature. The first is that of interceding for men (e.g. 60: 11 and 16: 2). Even in this the book presents confusion, since the intercessor may be Michael (60: 9) or Gabriel (60: 6) or even all the angels (39: 5). The second function is that of revealing the secrets of God to men (16: 2). As for demons, the whole book, including the Similitudes, depends upon the legend of Gen. 6 for the fall of the angels and the creation of the demons. This is a fundamental Jewish understanding that extends well into the Christian era. What is noteworthy, however, is the remarkably small role that demons play in the book. Their presence is acknowledged but their nature and function, especially when compared with those of the angels, is of little concern.

(c) Jubilees

The Book of Jubilees, also a composite volume, presents several curious factors about the spiritual world.[12] There is a firm association of angels with the world of nature (2: 2ff). The spirits of forces in the world were created on the first day. It is notable, however, that according to 2: 8 the sun, moon and stars were created without any ruling spirit, and the passage implies that the angels are not to be identified with these bodies. This may be an expression of the anti-hellenistic stance of the book. Within the angelic hierarchy there are two highest grades of angels who share the secrets and the plans of God. These are the Angels of the Presence and the Angels of the Sanctity (2: 18). These emphasise their holiness in proximity to God by worship, Sabbath observance, and even circumcision. One of the aims of the writer of Jubilees is to reaffirm the significance of the covenant of God with his holy people (10: 22f; 27: 21) and this hyperbolic description of the angels is part of this affirmation. The angels mediate between God and men, although on occasions God himself descends with his angels. This confusion reflects that of the oldest traditions, whereby the angels are often almost identified with Yahweh. In addition the angels guide men in the right way (4: 15*b*) and render an account to God of man's behaviour. In this regard they replace before God the now discredited Satan. The exact status of the angels is left open. They are not equated with God, but neither are they treated as men. Described in strongly anthropomorphic terms (even to the extent of circumcision), they are very close to God, having an unexplained existence within their own hierarchy.

The demonic ideas are also confused. The myth of the giants and the demons is recounted in 5: 15ff, and is followed by the fall of man and the flood (49: 2). The demons have a chief who is usually called Mastema, although in 1: 20 Beliar appears and in 10: 11 he is Satan. Yet it is also noticeable here that the angelic hierarchy is being worked out in terms of names and offices but the demons have only one leader. It should also be noted that the demonology is practically limited to chapter 10, which may be a fragment of the Apocalypse of Noah. In this their role is described as threefold: they corrupt and destroy men; they hurt and harm with sickness; and they obey Mastema. In 22: 17 the connection of idols with demons, which became so important later, is made and idolatry is firmly condemned.

Apart from chapter 10 little prominence is given to supernatural beings in Jubilees. They are not essential to the argument of the book.[13] In this composite work we have reflected two views of the spiritual world that found a place in Jewish thought in the second century B.C. On the one hand there was a growing awareness of the need to explain the physical world and God's relation to it. This was achieved, when necessary, by the development in the notions of angels and of demons. The book is to some extent anti-hellenistic, and the author, in order to come to terms with the Greek valuation of nature, offered a Jewish estimate in terms of angels, who relate both to God and to the world, but who need be identified with neither. On the other hand, in the latter part of the book we find the struggle with the problems of nature and of evil taken up without recourse to the device of angels and demons. The book is, therefore, in itself an important reminder that whilst Jewish angelology developed considerably during the second century B.C., it was by no means an all-pervasive belief. Many managed to adjust to the world without interpreting it in terms of spiritual beings. Unfortunately, lacking the Greek text of Jubilees, we are unable to determine the exact language and terminology that the writer used of these spiritual powers.

(d) The angels of the nations

After this brief consideration of these three books, we must turn to a more detailed examination of the concept of the angels of the nations. The idea, as with so many in this area, was revived by Dibelius, and has received considerable attention in recent studies of the NT.[14] Cullmann, with whom this development is chiefly associated, writes:

'We must regard the late Jewish teaching concerning the angels and especially concerning the angels of the peoples as belonging to the solid content of the faith of the NT. *The abundantly attested late Jewish belief* that all peoples are ruled through angels is present particularly in the Book of Daniel, in the Wisdom of Jesus, Son of Sirach, and in the Book of Enoch, and it can be shown to be present also in the Talmud and Midrash.'[15]

This widespread assumption itself needs careful examination.

The evidence for the angelic powers and the nations in Judaism is mainly derived from Daniel, 1 Enoch and Jubilees, but all probably reflect the thought of Deut. 32: 8: 'When the Most High gave to the nations their inheritance, when he separated the sons of men, he fixed the bounds of the people according to the number of the sons of God.' Most commentators regard this poem as an early composition, although von Rad in particular puts it into the time of the exile.[16] Since there is no obvious sign of Persian or Greek influence, it may be that we have here an example of the springing into life of an hitherto obscure idea.[17] It is clear, however, that the problem to which this verse in Deuteronomy addresses itself, namely the uniqueness of Israel in relation to the world as evidence of the mighty work of Yahweh, is that to which the later literature on this theme also turned. The tension inherent in Israel's monotheism and intense nationalism became increasingly apparent after the exile, and it is not surprising that the main references to the idea expressed in Deut. 32: 8 are post-exilic. Indeed most Jewish angelology dates also from this period, less because of intimate acquaintance with Babylonian religion than because of the problem posed to Jewish faith by the experience of exile.[18] The remoteness of God tends to be overcome by the development of intermediaries, and the problem of evil and suffering itself is met by a gradual increase in the significance accorded to Satan, who steadily alters his role from that of God's agent to that of an independent hostile being.

The main source for the notion of the angels of the nations is Dan. 10: 13ff. Here is an explicit reference to 'the princes of the nations', who are certainly not merely human rulers and who are introduced without explanation. This might suggest that the concept was not a new one. A correspondence of heaven and earth is found in Is. 34: 21 and, in the judgement of some, also in Ecclus. 17: 17: 'In the division of the nations of the whole earth he set a ruler over every people: but Israel is the Lord's portion.'[19] This verse, however, merits further investigation. Its context is that of the goodness of God to all men and the possibility of their discovering the wonders of God (17: 1-9). All men know the divine laws (verses 10-14) and God sees all that occurs (verse 15). Then follows the line ἑκάστῳ ἔθνει κατέστηοεν ἡγούμενον, καὶ μέρις κυρίου Ἰσραηλ ἐστίν, after which further comment is made on the openness of man's wickedness before God. The word ἡγούμενος is used again in the book in 41: 17, where it undoubtedly refers simply to a human prince. There is no obvious reason why it should not also do so in 17: 17. Indeed the writer's emphasis upon God's direct awareness of man's behaviour would seem to discount the need for intermediaries. Civil order, which is conducive to good morals, is the gift of God, and Israel, being a theocracy, has God as its king. There is no reference here to an angel of the nation.

When we return to Dan. 10 we note that the Prince of Persia is given no name and that he, together with the Prince of Greece, are the only two national angels mentioned for heathen empires. When further history is recounted in chapter 11 the wars are described merely in human terms. Thus, for example, the Kittim in 11: 30, who are presumably the Romans, are not described in terms of any 'Prince of Rome'. Again in 11: 5 the prince who is mentioned appears certainly to be human – i.e. Ptolemy – and in 11: 22 the 'prince of the covenant' is probably the High Priest. The use of the word ἄρχων in an angelic sense is not only restricted to this section of the book, but is even further limited.[20] The significance of this we shall draw out after consideration of the evidence from 1 Enoch and Jubilees.

In 1 Enoch 89: 59f and 90: 22f there are references that are often taken as a primary source for the concept of national angels. This is the story of the seventy shepherds, who are given charge by God over the sheep, to number or to destroy them according to his will. In 90: 20ff there occurs God's judgement of the shepherds, who are brought forward by the seven archangels. The question of who are the shepherds is difficult. R. H. Charles has reasonably established that they are angelic figures rather than human.[21] God, it appears, as true Shepherd of Israel, handed her over in her apostasy to the seventy shepherds, who, instead of fulfilling their commission, failed in their trust. The sufferings of Israel are to be laid at their feet rather than at those of God, for by the permissive will of God they have acted *ultra vires* and are therefore judged. It seems very unlikely that the shepherds are to be associated with the seventy nations. Charles himself links them with the seventy years of Jeremiah. What is certainly illegitimate is the solution that is exemplified by D. S. Russell, who recalls Is. 24: 21ff and remarks: 'This order of judgement – first the angels and then the earthly rulers – is the same order as that in 1 Enoch and reflects the general belief that before God judges any nation or ruler he first judges the guardian angel whose charge they are.'[22] But behind Is. 24: 22 lies not a belief in angels but the apocalyptic concept of the universality of God's judgement. The explicit reference is to the Babylonian cult of the stars and planets: on the day of doom the eclipse will be a terror to all.[23] That the emphasis is upon the universal nature of divine judgement is explicit in verse 23, in which the catastrophe that upsets the universe is accompanied by God's session on Mount Zion. The judgement of the fallen angels is a regular part of apocalyptic mythology, but it is nowhere clear that this judgement extends to a specific class of angels of the nations. Indeed close examination of the passage in 1 Enoch 89 argues exactly the reverse. For if we accept Charles' argument in favour of an angelic interpretation of the shepherds, then not only is a straightforward earthly reference excluded, but also any treatment of the shepherds as national angels. For the function of these shepherds is to protect the sheep, who are explicitly Israel and not the nations. The nations are characterised as lions and tigers (89: 66). Rather the shepherds are God's vicegerents, and in this sense they act as normal angelic ministers, who in their fall are to be judged alongside all fallen angels. It is a mistake, therefore, to associate them with any concept of national angels and to link them with the princes of Dan. 10.

Jub. 15: 31f is a further major passage. In a clear reference to the uniqueness of Israel and God's exclusive covenant with his people, which is based on the sign of circumcision, appears reference to the many nations who are God's: 'and over all he has placed spirits in authority to lead them astray from him'. It is not clear who these spirits are, particularly as elsewhere in the book the function of leading people astray is reserved for demons. We have here an example of that convention which treats the ultimate result of God's action as his immediate purpose. The writer is stressing that in spite of God's direct government of Israel the people will go astray. We are here perhaps on the fringe of the thought by which Yahweh moves from being the God of Israel to being the only God. The realities of existence demand that some sense is given to the religions of other nations, and these are gradually interpreted as the product of false spirits, who remain the appointees of Yahweh, the only God. There is within the passage a confusion in the claim that God did not appoint an angel over Israel but that he will also require Israel at the hands of his

angels. From such a position the notion of angels of the nations might
have developed, but although, as will be seen, hints towards such a belief
can be found, it still cannot be said to have become an accepted and
fundamental tenet of Judaism.

In these passages two distinct views may be discerned. On the one hand,
there is an attempt to ensure that the whole world is understood to be
under God's control. Anything less creates problems about his omnipotence
and thus ultimately about his existence. On the other hand, there is a concern to evaluate the special position of Israel in relation to God. Thus the
suffering of the people is explained either in terms of their apostasy (in
which case it is deserved and there is no forgiveness - Jub. 15: 34) or
through the permission of God, by which intermediaries have exceeded
their authority. The passages concerning the seventy shepherds seem in
fact to be the less usual thought, since God is more generally perceived as
being in direct relation to his people.

In Daniel, Michael is the Prince of Israel because, as chief archangel, he
is as near to God as it is possible to be. Thus when he appears it is as
though God himself were acting. These roles of Guardian and Intercessor
for Israel are attributed to him also in Test. Lev. 5: 6 and Test. Dan. 6: 1.[24]
In Ass. Mos. 10: 1 there is a vision of the day of the Lord's kingdom on
which the 'hand of the angel shall be filled', the angel presumably being
Michael, who will avenge Israel of her enemies. Again in the Testament of
Naphtali, which may be ancient, Abraham serves God whilst the seventy
nations prefer to serve their angels. The interest of all these passages, however, is not in the angels that the nations served but in the contrast between
those nations that are not God's and Israel, which is the Lord's people. In
the rabbinic writings Israel also either has her own prince, usually Michael,
or, more often, relates directly to God. A fairly common tradition finds
expression in Ruth R. Proem 1: 1:

'R. Johanan said: "Hear, O My people" in this world; "and I will
speak" in the world to come, in order that I may have retort to the
princes of the nations of the world, who are destined to act as their
prosecutors before me, and say, "Lord of the Universe, they have
served idols and we have served idols; they have been guilty of immorality and we have been guilty of immorality; they have shed blood and
we have shed blood. Why do they go to the Garden of Eden and we
descend to Gehenna?" In that moment the Defender of Israel keeps
silent . . . and the Holy One, blessed be He, says to him, "Dost thou
stand silent and hast no defence to offer for my people? By thy life, I
will speak righteousness and save my people."'

Thus Michael and God are brought together, but it is explicitly the direct relation between God and Israel that is emphasised. This is the context in which the concept of the angels of the nations appears. They do not function to connect heavenly events with earthly, but to ensure God's involvement with the whole world in such a way as to affirm his universal authority and his distinctive and personal care for Israel.[25] It is, therefore, misleading to speak of the angels of the nations as if they were a special class. It would be more accurate to recognise that angels in general are the agents of God and to realise that as such some will have dealings with the nations. This is confirmed by an examination of the rabbinic understanding of the state. So far as I can discover, there is no rabbinic writing on the state that makes use of the concept of angels of the nations. In addition, when each Midrash on the obvious texts concerning princes in the Psalms is examined, any angelic interpretation is always avoided. Only on Ps. 81 is heaven mentioned by application of Is. 24: 21, yet even here there is no doctrine of angels of the nations. The Midrash may be influenced by gnostic exegesis and its use of ἄρχων or it may reflect the style of Alexandrian Judaism, where Philo, for example, uses the term ἄρχοντες within a hierarchical picture of the cosmos in a passage that only on a superficial reading might appear to justify an angelic meaning.[26] There is in fact no evidence for Cullmann's commonly accepted claim that the evidence weighs heavily that this simultaneous use of the same word for demonic and earthly rulers is attested in the Jewish sources.[27]

Finally we must return to Dan. 10 and the princes of the nations. Whether the concept derives from Greek or Persian thought is of little importance. Angelic watchers are hinted at in Hesiod, but the evidence, such as it is, suggests that the origins for the connection of angels and people lie within Judaism.[28] Here two major factors are worthy of note. The first is generally recognised to have been the exile, an event that raised many imponderable questions for the Jewish faith. The second factor is less often perceived but in many ways was equally important. It was the influence of Alexander the Great. The twelve and a half years of his rule cannot be over-estimated in their significance. 'He lifted the civilised world out of one groove and set it in another; he started a new epoch; nothing could be again as it had been.'[29] Lacking any distinctive religion of its own, the Macedonian Empire recognised no one God behind events but allowed all religious interpretations under the umbrella of mere fickle Fortune. The type of thinking that is found about Cyrus in Deutero-Isaiah was inadequate for the world dimension of events to which the Jews were now being exposed. The exile could be interpreted as God's punishment for sin; the captors could be regarded as instruments of God's wrath. But as the whole world changed its pattern of life and thought under Alexander and was shaken by the subsequent internecine strife of the Diadochoi, a larger vision of divine purpose was required. Not all these events directly affected Israel, so that explanations that ultimately related to the people of God as the pivotal nation of the world were wanting in substance. It seems likely that this dilemma, coupled with the anti-dualistic develop-ment of the Jewish understanding of divine transcendence, produced the Danielic concept of 'the princes of the nations'. If this was so, it also may explain the difference between these princes in Daniel and the angels/spirits involved with the nations in 1 Enoch and Jubilees. In the latter two works the concern was domestic: the wars are the Maccabaean wars viewed within the context of Jewish experience. The author of Daniel, however, saw things not in this local perspective but in a world view. His under-standing was conditioned by the effect of the life and work of Alexander, and in no other Jewish writing are the princes of the nations such mighty figures. The Jewish tradition through to the rabbinic era tends to develop from 1 Enoch and Jubilees.[30] Daniel alone sees the uniqueness of Israel in terms of international events rather than in terms of local peoples. The doctrine that behind each nation there stands an angel is found in Judaism, but it is far from being a central concept. It was a means on occasion of asserting and preserving theologically the national identity of Israel in a world that paid little attention to her. This uniqueness was defined by reference to her status before God, and the social and political realities of the time were related to God's omnipotence and to Israel's impotence by spiritualising the problem in terms of angels. These beings never have any-thing to do with the concrete acts or persons of government. Indeed even in Daniel they relate only to past empires, and are only a device for explaining history.

In the light of this discussion it would appear that the significance of the angels of the nations has been misunderstood and misapplied in general, especially by Dibelius and Cullmann and their successors. The concept is one that represents one development of the normal understanding of angels and divine emissaries. It tends to come to the fore when there is little hope of Israel's asserting her identity as the sole people of God in the face of world events, and the so-called dual view by which earthly rulers and nations are believed to have personal angels appointed by God cannot be sustained.

(e) Jewish angelology and demonology in the first century B.C.

Rabbinic tradition derived the naming of angels from Babylon and in so doing was probably correct.[31] Certainly the experience of the exile itself, rather than the fact that Babylon was the place of exile, seems to have created a sense of the transcendence and absence of God that demanded response. This response may be seen in the development of a doctrine of intermediaries. Yet at no time were these beings allowed to infringe the omnipresence of God himself.[32] Angels were not an alien idea imported into Judaism; they seem to have been an aspect of popular belief. The religion of Babylon, however, was associated with the stars and planets. It is not surprising, therefore, that there are a few references that connect angels with stars. What is, however, remarkable is the almost total absence in the extant writings of any mention of astral religion within the Jewish culture. Yet if, as it appears, Judaism remained comparatively immune to foreign ideas when in such close contact with a vital foreign religion, it is to be expected that it would remain so also in later times.[33]

In the apocryphal literature the angels are given names. The giving of personalities to lesser angels proceeds apace, so that by the end of the first century B.C. they were legion.[34] Stress is always laid upon their intimacy with God and their consequent purity. There is also a distinctive group of Watchers, who may reflect some astrological influence (1 En. 39: 12; 18: 13). They function in divine worship, bringing messages to men, and interceding for men with God. Occasionally they deal with the souls of the dead (1 En. 62: 11). At the same time demonological ideas develop even more dramatically, chiefly we may suspect because there being less material to hand there was more scope for inventiveness. Even so the subject remains of comparatively little importance in the apocryphal writings. Satan gradually loses his angelic origin and the Greek term διάβολος becomes his proper name rather than a description of his function, until he is ultimately associated with the serpent in the Garden of Eden. He is also connected with the myth of the rebellion of the angels in heaven, which replaces the story of their lusting after the daughters of men as the chief cause of their fall, but this idea is of limited significance in Jewish thought.[35] Rather the fall of the angels through lust increases in significance in late Jewish writings and plays an important part in Christian thinking in the early years of the Church. It should also be noted that the rationalising of demons in terms of psychological experience is on the whole not part of Jewish thought in the first century B.C. Even in the writings of Qumran, which on angels and demons are fundamentally traditional rather than innovative, the spiritualising of particular demons can only come about because of the building-up of the one figure of Belial. Apart from this being, evil is not personalised.[36]

In the period prior to the Christian era, then, there was an abundance of ideas concerning the world of angels and of demons. Some of this was the product of experience and of the encounter of Jewish belief with foreign deities. Some was simply a broadening and development of those points of growth that had lain dormant in the OT. Indeed, the distinctive mark of much demonology and angelology was the way in which it was controlled by the fundamental concepts of the OT. It rarely ran rampant on its own. It should also be observed that there was a clear preference for angelology. By contrast with this development evil was concentrated in the one figure of Satan, Belial or Mastema. His minions, however, were neither named nor individualised. On the other hand, angels received names and the ramifications of the heavenly hierarchy were studied and developed. It is also significant that Yahweh's greatness at this point in Jewish history was not expressed by the number of his defeated enemies but by the number of his obedient and worshipping angels.

We may conclude this section by examining the various terms used in the OT on the subject of angels and demons. We are, however, limiting this examination to the language of ἀρχαὶ καὶ ἐξουσίαι, which Paul uses in the NT, in order to discern whether there is anything in common between this and Jewish terminology. Only a few of the terms used by Paul and in the deutero-Pauline literature are also found in the LXX. κυριότητες and κοσμοκράτωρ do not occur; ὄνομα is never used absolutely in a personal sense, but only in a qualified form;[37] στοιχεῖα occurs in three places and clearly refers only to the physical elements of this world (Wis. 7: 17; 19: 18; 4 Macc. 12: 13). The absolute occurrence of θρόνοι in Dan. 7: 9ff constitutes a problem that was much discussed by the rabbis. The thrones are introduced into this passage without qualification. Although later interpreters tended to put a messianic construction on them, it appears that the thrones of the council of God are in mind.[38] It is interesting to note that three of Paul's terms appear together in Dan. 7 - θρόνοι (9), ἐξουσία (singular, 27), and ἀρχαί (27) - but the passage, although probably of significance to some early Christians, is not used by Paul. Three key terms are common both to the Jewish writings and to Paul's - ἀρχαί, ἐξουσίαι and δυνάμεις.[39]

It is convenient to begin with δυνάμεις in view of its frequent use in the LXX for *sabaoth*. The translators of the LXX use κύριος τῶν δυνάμεων for 'Lord of hosts', i.e. 'Lord of the armies of heaven'. Dodd has pointed out that the word that we might expect, στρατίων, is avoided. This suggests to him that the translators were trying to substitute the notion of intermediaries for that of soldiers. He notes that in the Hermetic writings δυνάμεις are quasi-personal beings, and then compares the tendency in hellenistic Judaism, notably in Philo, to rationalise angels in terms of δυνάμεις.[40] This view, however, seems not to explain adequately the use of δυνάμεις as a translation of *sabaoth*. In the first place it embraces too long an historical perspective. Secondly the translators of the LXX may have avoided στρατίαι less with a desire to remove any military ideas and substitute intermediaries than because *sabaoth* did not seem to them to have military significance. The concept of the council of Yahweh is in the OT ambivalent. It may refer to a military company or to a consultative body, and it is possible that the latter understanding prevailed in the minds of the translators. Thirdly, angels can only be rationalised in terms of δυνάμεις after their general acceptance in mythical terms, but prior to this there is no reason to rationalise. In this respect it is a mistake to introduce Philo. For although it is commonly claimed that Philo rationalises Jewish thought in terms of his hellenistic outlook, this view does insufficient justice to his complex thinking on angels and powers.

It is exceedingly difficult to determine the place of δυνάμεις in Philo's thought. Probably his developed use of the term derives from the plurals used of God in the OT and from a growing sense of divine ineffability. In addition, the term enables him to dynamise his otherwise rather static concept of God, Θεός, for which he infers an etymology from τίθημι (*de conf. ling.* 137; cf. Herodotus, 2. 52). The Logos is to be associated with these δυνάμεις (*de fug.* 94ff), and this, together with the identification of the Logos with Michael (*Quis div. rer. haer.* 42) suggests that the δυνάμεις are regarded both as archangelic figures and as extensions of the godhead. In this sense Philo does not so much rationalise the OT as adopt its confusions. He also has a concept of angels that is differentiated from that of the powers, but his ideas are also remote from the Jewish apocalypses. For he has no names for angels, no relation between them and the physical world, no connection of them with death, and, above all, no evil angels.[41] By his own confession his angelology is fundamentally Greek and is derived from the neo-Platonic concept of δαίμονες (*de gig.* 6 and 16). This is not the result of rationalisation of Jewish mythology but a conscious Hebraising of Greek ideas.[42] Philo is of little relevance for the development of the Jewish concept of δυνάμεις and will not bear the weight that Dodd wishes to place on him.

The most probable explanation of the use of δυνάμεις as a translation of *sabaoth* lies in its connection of the plural names for Yahweh (something which the LXX generally heightens) with the attribution of δύναμις as a characteristic to God himself. The process is discernible in Dan. 8: 10, where δύναμις is used as a collective singular. The words ἀπὸ τῶν ἄστρων are epexegetic on ἀπὸ τῆς δυνάμεως, and it is only a slight step from here to conceptualising δυνάμεις as independent hypostases.[43]

Since 1 Enoch and Jubilees have not survived in Greek, there is always the problem whether the word translated 'Powers' was originally δυνάμεις. If, however, we allow this, it is clear that any statement of Jewish thought in the face of hellenism would find the term δυνάμεις ideal. For it would be both a way of associating God with the physical world without making an identification that might lead to some form of pantheism and at the same time a device for avoiding confusion between God and any demons. We have here a position complementary to that of Philo. Whereas he was attempting to read current Greek thought into the Jewish scriptures, the writers of Jubilees and 1 Enoch were attempting to provide a Jewish way of looking at the world, which both met the demands of hellenistic thought and safeguarded the sovereignty of Yahweh. This may have been achieved by using δυνάμεις as personal extensions of God in his universe.

The strength, then, of the word lies in its imprecision. This is also the mark of its use in early Christian thought. It is a less personal term than ἄγγελοι, and because of the characterising of God as δύναμις it allows for the extension of Yahweh into the world without diminution either of his transcendence or of his person. Later Judaism did rationalise angels in this language, but this was based upon the original adoption of the term in the LXX. Indeed, the angels at times become angels not of God but of the powers.[44] But this is part of later and more precise angelologies, whereby the δυνάμεις are associated only with the higher angels, the archangels.

The term ἀρχαί in the LXX depends upon the basic sense of the singular, which, Delling remarks, 'always signifies "primacy", whether in time . . . or in rank'. The only significant use in the LXX is in Dan. 7: 27. Delling also suggests that this verse makes a connection between human authorities and angelic powers. Following Dibelius he treats ἀρχαί and ἄρχοντες in Daniel as synonyms and argues that Paul adapted an angelic sense for ἀρχαί through the influence of Diaspora Judaism. Unlike the Jews, Paul, according to this argument, had no reason to associate ἀρχαί with national angels, since for him the people of God are not coterminous with the Jewish nation. He therefore widened the scope of the term.[45]

This view, however, cannot stand. We have already noted the specific use of ἄρχοντες in Daniel and that ἀρχαί convincingly makes sense in its usual meaning of human rulers. It is also in the light of our investigations unclear why the Jews of the Diaspora of all people should interpret ἀρχαί in terms of national angels, and why they should even have such a concept. Indeed, the Jews in the Diaspora tended not to think in national terms, but held their identity rather through a religious unity. Their attitude, for example, to the two Jewish wars with Rome is instructive. When it was a matter of national pride and rebellion, as in A.D. 66, they remained uninterested. The rising of Bar Kochba, however, had a religious reason behind it and the Jews of the Diaspora responded to this threat to the religious unity of all Jews. The use of the term ἀρχαί for angelic beings cannot have developed in this way.[46]

Clearly it has such a connection by the time of its coupling with ἄγγελοι by Paul in Rom. 8: 38. The probable explanation is similar to that offered for δυνάμεις. The singular word ἀρχή is only used as a definition or name for God in some Stoic thought, and a development of the plural in Jewish angelology cannot depend upon this.[47] The clue lies rather in the exegesis of Gen. 1: 1 through Prov. 8: 22. The hypostatisation of ἀρχή as an extension of God provided just the starting point for an angelic hierarchy of ἀρχαί. There is a fascinating example of such a shift in Clement of Alexandria's exegesis of Rom. 8: 38, although for him the ἀρχή is the Devil rather than God.[48] Without accepting the detailed application of Burney's thesis on *bereshith*, his argument that there was in Jewish thought an exegesis of the ἀρχή of God is convincing. The ἀρχαί, therefore, as angelic beings most probably developed from this hypostatised ἀρχή.[49] The beginnings of such an extension may be discerned in 1 En. 6: 8 where, if the surviving fragment of the Greek text may be trusted, the leaders of the angels are described as ἀρχαὶ αὐτῶν οἱ δέκα.

There is little to add concerning the ἐξουσίαι. Foerster suggests that Paul's use combines a Jewish perception of the powers as the ruling forces of nature with a hellenistic idea of a nexus of human destiny, εἱμαρμένη, which embraces the whole cosmos. This seems improbable, particularly in its rather rigid concept of fate, which is more appropriate to Egypt and the East than to the Greek world, in which the term may simply mean 'religious devotion'.[50] There is only one parallel to Paul's use of ἐξουσίαι that might antedate him, and that occurs in 1 En. 61: 10: 'And he will summon all the hosts of heaven and all the holy ones above, and the host of God the Cherubim, Seraphim, and Ophannim, and all the angels of power and all the angels of principalities.'[51] This reference seems similar to Paul's otherwise exclusive couplet αἱ ἀρχαὶ καὶ αἱ ἐξουσίαι, but in general Paul's use of ἐξουσίαι is scarcely paralleled prior to the Christian era and we are probably justified in surmising a development similar to that which we have noted for the other two terms.

2 The angels of paganism

The language that is used in the Jewish writing of the period immediately prior to the Christian era thus provides some clues to Paul's usage, but it is a wholly inadequate foundation for his theology. Before any conclusions are drawn, however, we should examine the possibility that his language and thought owes something to the pagan conception of angels. There is far more angelological speculation in the world of Asia and Greece than is sometimes realised. The chief problems are those of dating and of estimating the extent to which Jewish and Christian influences are at work. It is one of the merits of Dibelius' work that he recognised the existence of this material.[52]

In a number of inscriptions in Asia, especially from the area of Stratonicaea-Lagina, the term ὕψιστος is coupled with ἄγγελος. The details of the concept of Hypsistos are not here relevant. It seems to have been a title that was sufficiently vague to be used of pagan gods as well as by Jews of Yahweh. Although Kraabel has argued strongly against the usual supposition of an overlap between pagan piety and Judaism in Anatolia, the vagueness of the term seems to leave the question at least open.[53] The occurrence of 'The Angel' is of similar unimportance for Paul's thought. The concept is highly local and the references are to one angel rather than to an order of beings. A similar single angel is referred to in inscriptions from Thera. The balance of opinion, however, seems to be that these are wholly Christian, and, even if not, they probably betray Jewish influence.[54]

The plural ἄγγελοι is found in curses, in which ἄγγελοι καταχθόνιοι are linked with the divinities of the underworld. These texts however are mainly to be dated to the Christian era and are the product of a mixing of Greek and Jewish or Judaeo-Christian ideas.[55] An interesting inscription from Delos, which probably dates from the beginning of the first century B.C., is an early example of the tendency of Jews in the Diaspora to mix their religious terminology with that of their pagan contemporaries. It is noticeable, however, that the two references to spirits and angels are fully in line with the Jewish angelology of the second century B.C. The phrase τὸν κύριον τῶν πνευμάτων in line 2 is found in Num. 16: 22 and 27: 16 (LXX), and lines 9–10 recall the traditional direct association of God with his angels.[56]

A final area of interest is that of astrology and astral mysticism. The association of angels and spirits with the planets and the stars might suggest that this approach by the pagan world might have provided a source for Paul's language concerning the powers. The view that astrological terms appear in Rom. 8: 38f is discussed and rejected below, where it will be argued that Paul displays no obvious acquaintance with this topic. Such language gained in importance in the West from the end of the first century A.D.[57] It is interesting to note that as astrology developed in the form of astral mysticism, the fundamental experience of fatalistic astrology became clearer. It was less a relationship with stars, star gods, and powers, than to one God, whose sovereignty was witnessed to by the regular movement of the stars and planets. At first the god might be Zeus or Jupiter, but later sun mysticism increased and Helios or Sol usurped the position. This religion in the West is, however, too late a development to have influenced Paul's thinking, and amid the wide variety of language of astral mysticism, the distinctively Pauline configuration ἀρχαὶ καὶ ἐξουσίαι is not found.[58]

This brief survey shows that while angels did play a role in paganism in Asia, Greece and the West, this role was too localised and too indefinite for it to have influenced Paul or his readers. None of the churches to which Paul writes or to which the deutero-Pauline letters are allegedly addressed are in an area that evidences a concern with ἄγγελος or with ἄγγελοι. Most of the evidence for such beliefs dates from the post-Pauline period, in which there was a cross-fertilisation of ideas between pagans, Jews and Christians. Above all there is the argument from terminology. None of the Pauline phraseology for the powers occurs in paganism. There is only one example of the couplet ἀρχαὶ καὶ ἐξουσίαι, and this is found in Plato (*Alc.* 1. 135AB), where the reference is clearly to the civil government, as is that in Luke 12: 11. For the sake of completeness Plato, *Leg.* 10. 903B should be noted. The term ἄρχοντες here seems to mean 'personified laws of nature', but it is very difficult to determine Plato's intention in view of the uniqueness of this passage.[59] The unimportance of this text for the study of the NT is shown by the fact that nothing appears to have developed from it, even in the neo-Platonic literature, although it might be considered promising material.

3 Conclusion

From this survey of the evidence from pre-Christian Jewish and pagan thought concerning the spiritual world several significant points of considerable consequence for the study of Paul's thought emerge. During the period of the second century B.C. and onwards Jewish angelology developed, becoming increasingly complex as the intermediaries were progressively personalised. This was less the conscious elaboration of the doctrine of angels than the adaptation and extension of ideas from the OT of which the significance was heightened by the translators of the LXX. It was also primarily a development of indigenous religion. Although there are problems of language, the terms that are characteristic of the Pauline literature are on the whole insignificant in Jewish literature. Only δύναμις and its extension in the plural may confidently be traced. Parallel to this development is that of a demonology. Compared with the number of names of and terms for angels, however, the terminology for the demonic is notably limited. In particular demons are not given names, except for the mighty figure of Satan, Mastema, Belial or the Devil. At Qumran, too, there is no major change in this overall position.

The language of ἀρχαί, ἐξουσίαι and δυνάμεις, when it does occur in Jewish writings, seems not to be found in the distinctively Pauline configuration of ἀρχαὶ καὶ ἐξουσίαι. More significant, however, is the fact that the words are confined to the angels and archangels of Yahweh, and never are used of demonic forces. Interestingly Philo, too, follows this tradition, although in his work the alignment of the angels of God with the δαίμονες (in their original Greek sense) also appears. Such references as there are in paganism to angels and powers are found only in specific contexts and localities and have no clear point of contact with Paul's work.

The conclusion from all this evidence is that the concept of mighty forces that are hostile to man, from which he sought relief, was not prevalent in the thought world of the first century A.D. Such a conclusion requires that we re-examine the particularly Pauline evidence on this subject by exegesis of the relevant texts.

PART 2

Exegesis of Pauline texts

3

THE POWERS AND CHRIST TRIUMPHANT

1 Colossians

(a) Background

Much of the evidence for Paul's concept of αἱ ἀρχαὶ καὶ αἱ ἐξουσίαι is derived from the epistle to the Colossians, and the interpretation of Col. 2: 15 has been determinative in many understandings of the world of the powers. It is therefore the obvious place with which to begin the exegetical study of the NT texts. This is, however, a most difficult epistle to use in any assessment of a Pauline theme. Not only is the nature of the error that the writer opposes unclear, but the authorship of the letter and its destination are both doubtful.

On the question of authorship the arguments have been well rehearsed in the standard introductions and commentaries.[1] I accept the epistle as from the hand of Paul. The matter of the destination, however, is of particular importance for our study. For although Colossae, one of three destinations for this letter (4: 13), was a place of little significance in itself, from the point of view of the development of Christianity in that region of Asia Minor it may have been most important. The three cities of Colossae, Laodicea and Hierapolis were set in the Lycus Valley, where Caria, Lydia and Phrygia meet. In addition, the road system created by the natural barriers made this a key intersection. It was a meeting point of two cultures, with Colossae on the eastern side, open both to the West (Rome and the Greek cities of the plain) and to the East (the uplands of Anatolia). The place was also naturally numinous with its streams and mountains. In particular, the strange hot springs at Hierapolis were world famous and invested with mystery.[2] All of this contributed to the religious environment in which the particular situation that demanded Paul's letter arose. This letter, then, was written by Paul and addressed to the congregations of cities on the borderlands between the Greek West and the Anatolian East. In order fully to understand Paul's thinking this geography must be held in mind.

(b) 1: 16

In addition to the reference at 2: 15, ἀρχαὶ καὶ ἐξουσίαι are mentioned in 1: 16 and 2: 10. Angels are the subject of discussion at 2: 18 and there are two important references to τὰ στοιχεῖα in 2: 8 and 2: 20. We begin with an examination of 1: 16. A vast literature relates to 1: 15–20, in which many exegetes perceive a fragment of a hymn.[3] This, however, is not immediately a matter for study here, for whether this be a non-Pauline composition or a Pauline composition incorporated into the text, it certainly is the case that Paul here writes some word that presumably conveyed sense to the Colossians. The argument of the passage as it stands is relevant to the situation at Colossae and is valid evidence for Paul's thought.

Several of the main themes of the epistle are found in this section, notably, in addition to αἱ ἀρχαὶ καὶ αἱ ἐξουσίαι, the contrast of heaven and earth (1: 16, 20; cf. 3: 2), and of seen and unseen (1: 16; cf. 2: 18). Both themes are expressed in language that is unique to Paul.[4] The details of the description of the thrones and authorities are usually disregarded by those who treat 1: 15ff, or at best they are dismissed as epexegetic on τὰ ὁρατὰ καὶ τὰ ἀόρατα. One of the many conjectural divisions of the verses, however, affects the understanding of these powers and must therefore be scrutinised. E. Bammel has argued that there is a chiasmus in which verse 16 is arranged thus:

A	ἐν τοῖς οὐρανοῖς
B	καὶ ἐπὶ τῆς γῆς
B	τὰ ὁρατὰ
A	καὶ τὰ ἀόρατα
B′	εἴτε θρόνοι
A′	εἴτε κυριότητες
A′	εἴτε ἀρχαὶ
B′	εἴτε ἐξουσίαι.

The unseen world consists of κυριότητες and ἀρχαί, and is situated in the heavens; the visible world, which is on earth, is composed of θρόνοι and ἐξουσίαι. This suggestion is supported by a statistical survey of the occurrence of these terms.[5] The proposal has the merit of attending to the individual words of the phrase, but it must be rejected. Not only is it part of an unsuccessful arrangement of a presumed hymn, but it is also based upon statistics that are inevitably too few to be conclusive. More seriously it seems perverse to split the one phrase in the passage that is found complete elsewhere – ἀρχαὶ καὶ ἐξουσίαι.[6] Bammel's study, however, makes clear the need for the careful study of each term in the list, for this list is also unique in Paul's writing: it contains all his terminology concerning the powers, except δυνάμεις.

The word θρόνοι is used here either in a wholly unique sense 'angelic powers', or, as is more probable, by metonymy for the angels of God's presence.[7] The only existing parallel in Greek occurs in Test. Lev. 3: 8: θρόνοι, ἐξουσίαι, ἐν ᾧ [sc. οὐρανῷ] ὕμνοι τῷ θεῷ προσφέρονται. Another example, which appears not to have been noticed by commentators, occurs in Asc. Is. 8: 18: 'the Elect One to whose voice the heavens and the thrones give answer', and according to 2 En. 20: 1 there are in the seventh heaven 'a very great light, and fiery troops of great archangels, incorporeal forces and dominions, orders and governments, cherubim and seraphin, thrones, many-eyed ones etc.' It is just possible that these three works might have been known to Paul, but they are more likely to post-date him and be written under Christian influence. Their value for determining his meaning is negligible, for nowhere in Paul do we find the elaborate angelologies that characterise these books, nor even a hint that he was familiar with such complexities.

In the NT, θρόνος refers exclusively to the throne of God or of Christ. Whenever it refers to some other throne it is qualified and the reference is explained. In Rev. 4: 4 the twenty-four elders sit upon thrones. The only evil throne is that of Satan in Rev. 13: 2 and 16: 10. It is noteworthy that even in the Jewish mystic tradition the throne remains that of God alone. Whenever reference is made to Satan's throne or to that of Metatron, the qualification is without exception made clear. It would therefore appear impossible for the term θρόνοι, when used absolutely, to refer to anything other than the heavenly court, which sits with God and worships him. This conclusion would seem to be consonant with Dan. 7: 9ff, and interestingly is also expounded in Asc. Is. 7: 14–35. There each of the first five heavens contains a throne surrounded by angels. In the seventh heaven thrones are stored up for the righteous, who shall receive them from Christ on his return to heaven, when they too shall be members of the council of God. It is impossible that the term could be used of evil powers or angels, or even of civil governments.

Little may be said about κυριότητες. All the evidence for its use post-dates Colossians, although there might be a mention in 1 En. 61: 10 and 2 En. 20: 1. But both references are too late for comparison with anything Pauline. The term in both instances, however, occurs in a list similar to that in Colossians, and together with θρόνοι suggests beings who stand as part of the heavenly hierarchy and worship God.

ἀρχαί only occurs twice in the NT without ἐξουσίαι and ἐξουσίαι only twice without ἀρχαί.[8] The phrase is almost a stereotype and its distribution is notable. It occurs only in Colossians and Ephesians, and possibly in Tit. 3: 1.[9] In 1 Cor. 15: 24 the collective singular form is found - πᾶσαν ἀρχὴν καὶ πᾶσαν ἐξουσίαν. There is also the curious occurrence in Luke 12: 11, where a purely human political sense is undoubtedly to be understood. The possible derivation of the plural sense from the singular has already been discussed, and it may receive some slight confirmation from this passage in Colossians, where the plural (verse 16) is brought into proximity with the singular as a description of Christ (verse 18). When the static notion of ἀρχή is so dynamised with the biblical idea of God as the active source of all creation, it is no great step to pluralising this source in some way or other. In Rev. 3: 14 this concept is transferred very clearly to Christ.[10]

In the NT, ἐξουσία in the singular is usually so qualified that its point of reference is clear. This conforms to the standard usage in classical Greek.[11] A problem arises, however, with the plural, of which, apart from the connection with ἀρχαί, there are only two examples. In Rom. 13: 1 the word is qualified with ὑπερεχούσαις, and will be discussed later. There remains a significant reference in 1 Pet. 3: 22, which requires investigation. The order of terms there is exactly that in Asc. Is. 1: 3, which, however, may be directly dependent upon the text in 1 Peter.[12] Bigg has pointed to the similarity with 1 En. 60: 10, and suggests that it should be translated 'angels both of authorities and powers'.[13] He works on two assumptions: first that the powers are hostile to Christ and secondly that the author of 1 Peter would have been familiar with 1 Enoch. The first assumption is unwarranted from the language alone. As has been demonstrated, clear evidence of the hostility of the powers must be found in the context of any specific use of the language. Secondly, the assumption of the relation between 1 Peter and 1 Enoch turns upon the dating of the Similitudes. There are possible links between the two books, but they are not sufficiently firm to argue for direct dependence of the one on the other.[14]

The surmise that 1 Pet. 3: 18-22 contains a liturgical fragment on the ascension and heavenly session of Christ has recently received a measure of support.[15] The prominent ideas from Ps. 110: 1 and Ps. 8: 4f are found in verses 19 and 22. It has been suggested that in verse 19 there is a development of a Jewish tradition, which is also represented in 1 Enoch, according to which victory is proclaimed to the fallen powers, while in verse 22 there is contained a tradition of the hellenistic Church. There are problems here. In the first place there is the question of whether τὰ πνεύματα in verse 19 are to be understood as the souls of the departed or as those spiritual beings whose disobedience is recorded in Gen. 6 and the derived traditions. It is also difficult to understand ἐκήρυξεν in the unusual sense of 'proclaimed a victory'.[16] Such examples as there are in the NT of κηρύσσειν in a neutral sense (= κραυγάζειν) are very rare.[17] In no passage in which Christ is the subject is the content of the proclamation not the Kingdom of God or some equivalent, and the word normally refers to the proclamation of the gospel. Those who wish to interpret it here in terms of the proclaiming of Christ's victory usually argue that the gospel is proclaimed with a view to conversion and drawing men into the Kingdom of God, but that this cannot be the present sense, since the reference is to the subjection of the powers, not to their conversion. This may, however, be a misunderstanding. For if we take ἐκήρυξεν in its normal sense and the participle πορευθείς in both verse 19 and verse 22 to stand for the ascension of Christ, we have a picture of Christ on his ascension preaching to the spirit world.[18] Indeed the content of the preaching and the act of ascension are one, namely the reconciliation of earth and heaven and the vindication of the Lordship of Christ. This is also the theme of Col. 1: 15ff and, most interestingly, Eph. 3: 10, according to which God makes known his wisdom and power to the heavenly places through the witness of the Church. The key in 1 Pet. 3: 19 to the relation of Christ and the powers lies in the participle ὑποταγέντων. Through the influence of Ps. 8: 6 (LXX) the word is found in several Christological texts of the NT. Its other regular use is of the personal relationships that are to obtain between Christians. This moral sense is clearly related to the Christological, particularly in the thinking of the author of 1 Peter (2: 18; 3: 1, 5). In 1 Cor. 16: 16 it is used of the attitude that Christians are to adopt towards their fellow workers, their equals in Christ, and is rightly translated 'give due position to' (NEB).[19] ὑποταγέντων, therefore, in verse 22 is the exact opposite of ἀπειθήσασιν in verse 20. Those who were once disobedient and stood on their rights by refusing to acknowledge God, now, having heard Christ's proclamation of the gospel on his ascension, pay him the respect and obedience due to him.[20] The aorist passive would imply the meaning 'being brought into a state of obedience by the preaching of the gospel'.

This passage, then, does not refer to Christ's victory over malevolent powers. The ἐξουσίαι have no direct effect on the lives of Christians, and it is difficult to see on what grounds the writer would here have introduced the concept of hostile powers. It is not that the persecutors of the Church are envisaged in demonic terms. In this letter the persecutors are understood in moral terms and the alignment of the Christians with Christ is in terms of suffering (3: 17f). It is the ultimate achievement of this suffering Christ in preaching (3: 19) and in his vindication by God (3: 22) that creates the demand on the Christians for faithfulness, together with the promise of their own final vindication. The power of the gospel, which sustains Christians in persecution, is available for all who were disobedient to God, even of old. The context is placed in the context of the baptismal image of Noah's flood (the past) and the hope of God's final consummation. Nothing is said of the destruction of enemies. This, as will be shown, conforms to other parts of the NT, especially Pauline thought.

We may conclude that the terms θρόνοι, κυριότητες, ἀρχαί, and ἐξουσίαι, far from conveying to the Colossians the idea of hostile forces of the universe or of malevolent spirits, would have at most described beings whose status was neutral, requiring definite signs from the context to be interpreted in an evil sense. Indeed most uses of this language made these beings the angelic host of God, who are mentioned in order to establish God's awesome majesty and power. There is no suggestion in Col. 1: 15ff that these creatures impinge upon the lives of men. Nor are the heavenly places with their angelic inhabitants the locus of Christ's work. In view here is only the majesty of Christ as Lord. Moule rightly concludes that 'the cumulative effect of this catalogue of powers is to emphasise the immeasurable superiority of Christ over whatever rivals might, by the false teachers, be suggested. He himself is the agent and the place of their creation and their very *raison d'être*.'[21] It is doubtful, as we shall see, whether the false teachers were proposing rivals to Christ, but the full significance of this list, understood as angelic rather than demonic beings, cannot be developed until the other occurrences of the language of the powers in this epistle have been investigated.

(c) 2: 14f

In turning to the next reference, 2: 15, we move to the text that is usually regarded as the key to Paul's thought.[22] The whole passage from verse 13 onwards is full of difficulties and there are few points at which scholars show any consensus. The argument is concerned with the Colossian error (2: 9) and offers part of Paul's counter to it. It is worth setting the text out in full.

13c χαρισάμενος ἡμῖν πάντα τὰ παραπτώματα·

14 ἐξαλείψας τὸ καθ᾽ ἡμῶν χειρόγραφον
   [τοῖς δόγμασιν ὃ ἦν ὑπεναντίον ἡμῖν],
   καὶ αὐτὸ ἦρκεν ἐκ τοῦ μέσου,
   προσηλώσας αὐτὸ τῷ σταυρῷ·

15 ἀπεκδυσάμενος τὰς ἀρχὰς καὶ τὰς ἐξουσίας
   ἐδειγμάτισεν ἐν παρρησίᾳ,
   θριαμβεύσας αὐτοὺς ἐν αὐτῷ.

The structural parallelism of the two verses, two main clauses each with two dependent participial phrases, leads Lohse to accept the suggestion that verses 14-15 contain a fragment of a hymn, which has been taken over by the author of Colossians.[23] Final decision on this hypothesis will have to await detailed examination of the text. Certainly the parallelism is striking. If these verses do constitute a unit, the connection of forgiveness and the act of Christ is interestingly similar to the linking of forgiveness and redemption in 1: 14.

In 2: 14 the word χαρίζεσθαι appears in a context that requires not the usual meaning, 'to grant as a gift', but the less familiar 'to forgive'. It rarely has such a sense in Paul, although we may instance 2 Cor. 2: 7, 10. Indeed, explicit use of the concept of forgiveness is unusual in Paul, for the notion is usually implicit in his doctrine of justification. We shall return to this point later. Clearly, however, the key to verse 14 is the meaning assigned to τὸ χειρόγραφον. Four main views may be discerned among the commentators.[24]

Abbott, Prat and Wambacq support the understanding of χειρόγραφον as referring to the Mosaic Law. It is, however, impossible to see how Paul, even in a violent metaphor, could have spoken himself or cited another concerning the Law in such drastic terms – 'tossed aside and nailed to the cross'. It is also a reasonable supposition that the Colossian Church was mainly composed of Gentiles who did not naturally feel the Law as a burden to be removed.[25] The essential concept in χειρόγραφον is that of 'autograph', something written by one's own hand to authenticate an agreement. This can hardly be applied to the Law. A second view, proposed by G. Megas and espoused by Lohmeyer, is that the cheirograph is a covenant between Adam and the Devil. This idea appears in the Fathers, but the evidence adduced for it is all much later than Paul.[26]

The currently most popular interpretation is that the cheirograph is an I.O.U. from mankind to God. Schlatter, Dibelius, Percy, Masson, Hugédé, Moule and Lohse are among its supporters. The cheirograph is a certificate of debt, created by man's sins and therefore autographed by him. This interpretation also has ancient attestation in the Fathers and there is much to be said in favour of it. It exactly fits what is known of the normal use of the word in secular Greek. In addition the vision of mankind in debt to God would have been immediately perceptible by a Gentile congregation. But this interpretation is not without problems. With such a strikingly original image we might legitimately have expected from Paul a fuller exposition, unless it was one already familiar to the Colossians. More to the point is the question: Who wrote the cheirograph? Is it the autograph of all men or only of those who have been forgiven? J. A. T. Robinson has argued that our subscription to the ordinances of God, which as men we have signed, is erased; that καθ' ἡμῶν should therefore be taken simply as 'in our name'; and that the cheirograph has stood in our name since Ex. 24: 3, and is now against us to prove our guilt.[27] This interpretation does attempt to solve an otherwise pointless repetition in ὑπεναντίον ἡμῖν, but the proposed use of κατά with the genitive is only found in contexts of swearing and oaths, and the direction back to the OT removes its obvious immediacy in Colossians.

Finally the interpretation of the cheirograph as the Heavenly Book has gained recent support through the work of Daniélou. It turns upon Od. Sol. 23: 11 and perhaps the Gospel of Truth 19: 17, with an appearance in Rev. 5: 1ff. The Book of the Secrets of History and of God's redemptive plan is said to be available to the visionary to read on his ascent to heaven. A mention of such a book with the cross occurs in the Odes of Solomon, where the wheel and the cross are used as apocalyptic weapons. A similar connection is made in the Gospel of Truth. It is suggested that implicit in these references is a Judaeo-Christian exegesis of Col. 2: 14, according to which the Heavenly Book is identified with Christ. Blanchette has developed the idea fully.[28] He argues that the verse is an aside on soteriology. But if the cheirograph is Christ, how may it be described as 'against us'? And if Christ is the revelation of the Father, how can it be eradicated just as it is being made known? Blanchette refers to Paul's other allusions to Christ: in 2 Cor. 5: 21 he became sin for us; in Gal. 3: 13 he became a curse for us; so in Col. 2: 14 he becomes the bond for us. In these other instances, however, Paul is being explicit and does not adopt the allusive style implied in Colossians. In addition, this view requires that τοῖς δόγμασιν are taken as 'evangelical ordinances', which again is allusive and difficult. Above all, the transition of thought from the Heavenly Book to Christ and thence to the abolition of the book is too severe; it makes impossible demands upon the reader. Nor is this difficulty alleviated if the book is taken as that of condemnation.[29] If this is the case we might just understand the nailing of Christ to the cross as a public display of the divine plan of redemption, but it is not easy.[30]

This variety of interpretation reflects the two major difficulties in χειρόγραφον. The first is that there is no specific background for the use of the term in its Christian usage. It does not come from the OT, and the secular use merely points to the sense of 'an autograph'. This leads to the second problem, namely, to what is it an autograph? The sentence τοῖς δόγμασιν κ.τ.λ., although apparently explicative of χειρόγραφον, only confuses the issue, not only by what it says, but also by the way in which it breaks the apparent parallelism of the verses. There are therefore two

essentials to any interpretation of the cheirograph: the notion of personal
autograph must be obvious and the effect of the signature must be to con-
demn the signatory.[31] The basic idea of an I.O.U. needs the reinforcement
of the nature of this personal involvement, i.e. some sort of confession.

Writers of the Roman period regularly note as an aspect of eastern
religion the public confession of guilt. The literary evidence is considerable.[32] Mere public confession of guilt is inadequate as content for
χειρόγραφον. This need, however, seems to be supplied by epigraphical
evidence from Asia Minor.[33] There is a series of penitential *stelae* that have
five main characteristics. In the first place they are all cultic. Those who
have offended and in consequence have set up the *stele* are in some way
holy. Set apart for cultic functions for a period of time they have failed in
their religious duties. Secondly, they use as a key concept ἁμαρτία, a
failure in duty or some sin of impurity, by which they have fallen short of
the ritual requirement. This, thirdly, forms the substance of the confession.
In several examples the term [ἐξ]ομολογεῖσθαι appears, but always the
emphasis is upon publicity for the crime. The fourth mark is that the deity
concerned has demonstrated his acceptance of the confession of guilt. This
is proved by the punishment that the sinner received, which is included in
the inscription. The guilty man gladly accepts his suffering as a sign of
divine forgiveness. Finally, the *stele* is set up as a record of events and as a
warning to others not to trifle with holy things. In several examples a word
formed upon γράφω occurs, usually στηλογραφέω, although the actual
word χειρογραφέω is not found. The aim in setting up the inscription is to
call passers-by to acknowledge the majesty of the god concerned and to
function as a warning to any who may be tempted to sin. These five marks
are not explicit in every inscription, although a much restored example
from Sardis does include each:

ω]ν Ἀριστ[/]θεὶς καὶ ἀμ[αρ/τήσας κα]ταπίπτω
εἰς[ἀσ-/θενειάν κ]αὶ ὁμολογῶ τ[ὸ/ἀμάρτη]μα Μηνὶ
Ἀξιω[τ/τηνῷ καὶ στηλ]ογ[ραφῶ.[34]

These *stelae* were placed in the temple area of the cult that had been
infringed. Their significance for the religion of Asia Minor has been examined at length by the editors of the inscriptions. Their function, however,
is of little concern here; it is the fact of their existence that is interesting,
for they incorporate exactly the requirements of the term χειρόγραφον in
Col. 2: 14.

The dating of the evidence is very difficult. Most of the texts undoubtedly come from the second and third centuries of the Christian era. In the
light of the evidence for the growth of individual religion in Asia during

this period, this is not surprising. The earliest extant example dates from A.D. 126 according to Ramsay and comes from Satala.[35] The practice of public confession, however, is well attested at a much earlier date than this. The religious thought and general ignorance of Greek in the inscriptions suggests that they represent something at the root of religion in Phrygia and Lydia. The literary evidence from Ovid and Juvenal, who between them span the first century, suggests that the Graeco-Roman world was familiar with the practice of public confession. It would not seem therefore impossible that written versions of such confessions were part of the religious life of Asia in that period of the first century when Paul was travelling there.

There is a second problem. Could Paul have known of these inscriptions? This assumes that this present passage in Colossians is a Pauline composition or that it derives from Asian Christianity. There is no obstacle in the way of this latter view, for, as will be seen when the verse as a whole is examined, the images of the section are totally un-Jewish. Paul's travels certainly took him to that area of Asia where these *stelae* have been found and where this public confession flourished. Paul's possible use, therefore, would occasion no surprise. Yet there is also the requirement that the Colossians would have understood the reference without explanation. As has been noted, the city was situated at the point of intersection of Anatolian and Aegean cultures, and it is highly probable that the religious language and style of Phrygia and Lydia would have been familiar to the recipients of the letter. It is therefore possible that a background for χειρόγραφον might be found in a local religious practice. Before concluding this investigation, however, the term τοῖς δόγμασιν and the whole sentence needs further examination.

There is much to be said for the omission of the line τοῖς δόγμασιν, ὃ ἦν ὑπεναντίον ἡμῖν. It disturbs an apparent parallelism and reads like an inadequate attempt at explaining χειρόγραφον. There is nothing, however, in the textual tradition to warrant the excision of these words, and the possibilities of interpretation need to be presented. The attempt to understand γεγραμμένον from χειρόγραφον depends upon the interpretation of the cheirograph as the Mosaic Law, and therefore is to be discounted.[36] If we take the dative as instrumental, the meaning will be 'having cancelled the bond by keeping God's decrees'. Although consonant with Paul's emphasis upon the obedience of Christ, it is difficult to extract this from a simple dative. The alternative translation – 'having cancelled the bond by means of the decrees' – invites the question of which decrees are meant. The solution of the Greek commentators is that they are the evangelical ordinances of the gospel, and this is currently argued by Blanchette and

Kittel. There is, however, no evidence in the NT for such a sense for δόγμα. The word always means a decree or decision, and never the gospel. Light-foot hints that the unanimity of the Greek Fathers at this point is due less to their greater understanding of the word than to their reading of it with Eph. 2: 15 in an age of credal battles.[37] In any case, the separation of τοῖς δόγμασιν from δογματίζεσθε in verse 20 is unfortunate. To take the dative causally, as Percy suggests, has the advantage of treating the repetition of thought in καθ᾽ ἡμῶν and ὑπεναντίον ἡμῖν seriously: the cheirograph opposed to us because of (or by means of) its adverse decrees. Yet it makes a harsh sentence even harsher, and it is impossible to take τοῖς δόγμασιν in this sense when it stands before the relative. None of the parallels that Percy offers really applies to this passage.

A further alternative is to take the dative as associative. Lohse takes the decrees to be the commands of God, a use that he describes as 'Hellenistic-Jewish'. He also regards it as an insertion into an existing hymnic text. Bruce also treats the dative in this manner, although he does not under-stand the provenance of the thought nor its place in the text in the same way as Lohse, and offers as the translation 'the bond, decrees and all'. This has the merit of being about as loose a construction in English as is the Greek, yet it may be doubted whether the Law is to be associated with the cheirograph in this manner. For this must fundamentally refer to man's responsibility rather than to God's. The suggestion of Robinson, which is endorsed by Moule, that δόγμασιν might be implied in the action of a verb 'to subscribe to', which lies behind χειρόγραφον, is attractive.[38] The mean-ing would then be 'our subscription to the ordinances'. However, it does not meet the basic requirement of the term χειρόγραφον and is therefore inadequate.

There are two essential points to this verse in its context, which must be satisfactorily dealt with in any exegesis. First, the general context is that of forgiveness – the relationship of God with sinners (13c); secondly, the personal importance of man's cheirograph, something created and autographed by man himself, is prominent. This is not at all the context into which to throw an aside about false teaching. In addition, if the reference of ὃ ἦν ὑπεναντίον ἡμῖν is to δόγμασιν, the past tense is not easily explicable since it is all too clear that the error was flourishing as Paul wrote.

If the text is retained, possibly the best of these interpretations is that of Lohse and Bruce, which takes δόγμασιν as an associative dative with χειρόγραφον. Against them, however, we should remove any reference to the Mosaic Law. If the importance of the cheirograph as an autograph is stressed, τοῖς δόγμασιν are associated with it in the sense of 'our autograph

of self-condemnation in all its detail of personal decisions'. δόγμα is fundamentally a personal decision or belief, whether of the individual or, more
usually, of a corporation or government. The problem of ὃ ἦν ὑπεναντίον
ἡμῖν remains, and the solution of a slip from ἅ to ὃ is attractive, yet
without evidence. If δόγμασιν are allowed to stand thus closely with the
personal autograph of a man's sins before God, there is no problem in
understanding the same basic notion in δογματίζεσθε as referring to pre-
scriptions. For a decision to wrongful action is an ordinance or prescrip-
tion for the carrying out of the deed. Therefore to bind oneself with
ordinances of one's own making (δογματίζεσθε) is a specific example of
writing one's own χειρόγραφον τοῖς δόγμασιν.[39] The divine act corresponding to this act of man's autograph is found in that forgiveness which is
related wholly to the cross. The phrase ἦρκεν ἐκ τοῦ μέσου means 'threw
away for good', and this total abolition was achieved through the cross.
The crucifixion may be seen as the most serious crime of which man is
guilty. In that sense it is the final line of man's cheirograph, his penitential
stele, on which are listed all his crimes and the dismal history of his
punishment. It is his ultimate decision, his δόγμα, which became the
decree of Christ's death. The complex of verse 14, then, is that of man, his
sin against God, and the cross. The cross, which was the ultimate line in
man's listed confession is paradoxically the way of destruction for that
indictment of guilt. The thought is a familiar one in Paul. A similarly para-
doxical interpretation of the cross occurs in Gal. 6: 14. The key to Col. 2:
14 lies in the unusual metaphor of the cheirograph, which Christ has
removed. As a background for the term, it is difficult to find anything
that fits more exactly than the penitential *stelae* of Phrygia and Lydia,
provided that the detail is not pressed. The removal of the cheirograph is
described by two participles – ἐξαλείψας and προσηλώσας. It might be
urged that the idea of Christ or God nailing a stone to the cross is absurd,
but such an objection is excessively literalistic. Whatever the background
of the metaphor, none will stand such treatment. The chief notion that is
here expressed is that of man's personal responsibility before God and his
historic failure to meet that responsibility. The history of mankind since
Adam is written in terms of the guilt and punishment for this failure, and
it is for all to see, set up upon the χειρόγραφον. The message of the gospel
is that this dismal record is now by Christ's death obliterated and tossed
away.

It is in the context of this discussion that we should read 2: 15, and
not, as so often, in isolation from it. The same structure is presented –
three clauses, two of them participial around the main clause. There are
also considerable problems, not least that of the subject of the verbs. In

general the commentators on this passage take it to be God, arguing that, although the structure of the whole section is grammatically loose, nevertheless God must be the subject in 13*a* and that he is also therefore the subject of the following verbs.[40] Lightfoot on the contrary remarked that 'no grammatical meaning can be assigned to ἀπεκδυσάμενος by which it could be understood of God the Father' and concluded that Christ becomes the subject, probably with the verb ἧρκεν.[41] This solution highlights the problem: the question of the subject is raised most acutely by verse 15, yet if verses 14–15 are treated as a unit, it is difficult to conceive a change of subject at the beginning of verse 15. In order to preserve the apparent parallelism of the participles and main verbs, the change, if there is one, must occur with ἐξαλείψας. The ascension motif in the NT is, for obvious reasons, applied to Christ. In this passage, verses 14 and 15 mention both the cross and the triumph, which themes together form part of the ascension theme in the NT. It is therefore most natural to take Christ as the subject of these verses. Whilst it may be true, as Moule notes,[42] that the work of God and that of Christ tend to be identified in the NT, what we have here is a transition of subject because of the incorporation into Paul's thought of a familiar theme, which he uses as a semi-doxological conclusion to this section. He often employs a doxological conclusion to sections of his argument (e.g. Rom. 8: 38f; 11: 33). In the present passage the conclusion is semi-doxological because, while the imagery and content are of a style to invite adoration, the verbs are indicative. That it is not in detail integral with verses 16ff, but rather forms a conclusion to the foregoing section, is implied by οὖν, which seems to resume the argument from verse 13*a*. A complete solution to the question of the subject of these verbs must await full consideration of verse 15. There is, however, a reasonable presumption that the subject could as well be Christ as God.

ἀπεκδυσάμενος occurs in the NT only in this epistle. Indeed, it seems not to occur in Greek prior to its use by Paul, and it would appear possible that it is an intensitive Pauline construct, perhaps like ἀποκαταλάσσω in 1: 20. Most interpretations of the word assume an active sense for it, but although such a usage is not unknown, there seems strong reason in the first place to try to understand it in a middle sense. The writers of the NT are usually quite careful about such things. In Paul, apart from two uses of the middle of τίθημι in an active sense in 1 Cor. 12: 28 and 1 Thess. 5: 9 (and this particular use seems to have been accepted by the time of Paul), ἀπεκδυσάμενος is the only example.[43] Certainly the translation 'having disarmed', with the powers as the object of the participle, is quite impossible. Jerome's substitution of *exspolians* for the *exuens se* of the Vetus Latina is responsible for this.[44] The metaphor is not one of despoiling but of undressing.[45] This is certain from the other use of the word in Colossians at 3: 9 (cf. Eph. 4: 22f), where the picture is that of the total removal of clothes. If this sense is retained here it would imply that Christ is the subject and the middle voice carries its full meaning, i.e. 'having stripped off from himself'. The intensified form of the verb may refer either to a total undressing or possibly to a violent movement – 'having ripped off'.

The question, therefore, is what was ripped off. The argument of the Greek Fathers that the object is the powers of evil 'which had clung like a Nessus robe about his humanity' is resumed by Lightfoot.[46] This involves the assumption that the powers are evil and hostile, but also is subject to the telling objection that is articulated by Abbott: 'If it was only by putting off his human body on the cross that he could put off from himself the powers of evil that beset his humanity, this would not be a victory but retreat.'[47] There is something also slightly bizarre in the notion that Christ went through the world clothed in hostile powers, although it is found in Origen, *contra Cels.* 2. 64. An alternative view is to understand τὴν σαρκά as the object of ἀπεκδυσάμενος. This, 'the common interpretation of the Latin Fathers', has been revived by Robinson, who argues that ἀπεκδυσάμενος refers to τὴν σαρκά and that τὰς ἀρχὰς καὶ τὰς ἐξουσίας are solely the object of ἐδειγμάτισεν.[48] This is perhaps reinforced by the association in 2: 11 of σάρξ with ἔκδυσις, but against it is the difficulty of assuming τὴν σαρκά in a context where it is not obviously in view. In 2 Cor. 5: 4 the simple form ἐκδύομαι is used absolutely of the putting-off of the body, but in that context there is no difficulty in supplying this object.

If we view verses 14 and 15 together, understanding the theme of the first to be man, sin and the cross, the parallelism appears thus:

VERSE 14	VERSE 15
ἐξαλείψας	ἀπεκδυσάμενος
wiping out the autograph	stripping off from himself (?)
ἦρκεν ἐκ τοῦ μέσου	ἐδειγμάτισεν ἐν παρρησίᾳ
totally removed	publicly displayed
προσηλώσας	θριαμβεύσας ἐν αὐτῷ
nailing to the cross	celebrating in triumph

There is an obvious contrast in the ideas expressed in the main verbs, the second of which wholly counteracts the first. Around these the participles seem to expound the cross almost in chiasmic form. The violent metaphor of the human side of the cross, the wiping out of the cheirograph of man's sin and its achievement, is parallel with the second violent metaphor of triumph. The removal of the cheirograph is achieved by the nailing of it to the cross; the legitimate assumption, then, would be that the sense of ἀπεκδυσάμενος is to be found in terms of the triumph of Christ. If the cheirograph gives the clue to verse 14, the dominant motif in 15 is undoubtedly that of triumph.

It is worth noting that if our interpretation of χειρόγραφον is correct it represents a non-Jewish metaphor that has been exploited in the interests of Christian thinking. The same could well be true of θριαμβεύσας: it is a Roman triumph that provides the imagery.[49] This is certainly the main attested sense of the word. Lohmeyer has suggested that the imagery is drawn from the coronation of an oriental monarch and takes θριαμβεύειν to mean 'win a victory'.[50] This is not, as will be seen, the meaning of the term. In addition there is no obvious oriental background to Colossians, yet in view of the influence of Rome and her armies on Asia in this period there is some reason for thinking that the imagery associated with a Roman triumph was not unfamiliar. In a triumph there were several important events, each of which carried its own symbolism. Among these was the putting-off of the old clothes of the victor and the putting-on of the ceremonial dress of a *triumphator*. The change of dress was of central importance, although its historical significance remains unclear. This *vestis triumphalis* marked out the *triumphator* and, most notably, indicated his rank in relation to other leading magistrates. In all the ancient references to a triumph it is the *tunica palmata, toga picta* and *corona laurea* that are mentioned as constituting the definitive marks of a triumph.[51] In this context, then, θριαμβεύσας would appear exactly to describe the first stage of the triumph as the *triumphator* divests himself of his battle dress. In the case of Christ this battle dress is probably to be taken as the flesh that he had in life and in which he achieved the victory of the cross. There is no need, however, to assume an unexpressed reference to τὴν σαρκά, for ἀπεκδυσάμενος used absolutely in so defined a context as here could mean simply 'preparing himself'. The simple word ἐκδύομαι is found with this sense used absolutely in other Greek writing. The further occurrences of the root ἀπεκδυ- in Colossians also contain the idea of preparation for a purpose: baptism in preparation for resurrection and the removal of the old in preparation for the new. Under the dominance of the metaphor of a triumph in θριαμβεύσας the new robe of the *triumphator* is assumed to be adopted in exchange for the old. This also matches certain Old Testament pictures, such as that of Joshua in Zech. 3: 1ff and God in Ps. 92: 1 (LXX).

The metaphor of the triumph is rare in the NT, although the heavenly session of the victorious Lord is not. Apart from the present passage, θριαμβεύω occurs only at 2 Cor. 2: 14 in the NT, and it is not common in Greek as a whole. The key theme of a triumph is not that of winning a victory; it refers to the subsequent acclamation of the victor and the celebration.[52] θριαμβεύειν later came to mean 'to display publicly for abuse', but this is after the first century and may well be under the influence of Col. 2: 15. In a recent study R. B. Egan has revived F. Field's proposal, which dates from 1899, that the word merely means 'to publicise' or 'to make manifest'. Any particular reference to a Roman triumph is not merely unnecessary but is not implicit in the use of the term. Several of his suggestions for the exegesis of Col. 2: 15 and 2 Cor. 2: 14 commend themselves, but his view does not carry overall conviction. His minimal sense for θριαμβεύσας does not allow for the word ἐδειγμάτισεν in Col. 2: 15, and in both this passage and 2 Cor. 2: 14 there is an abundance of metaphor that Egan overlooks. His translation of Col. 2: 15 seems, for example, very weak, especially in the light of the parallelism that we have noted in structure with verse 14: 'Uncovering the principalities and powers, He [God] displayed them openly, making them known in Him [i.e. Christ]'. There is also no reason to doubt the acquaintance of the Colossians and the Corinthians with the essentially Roman concept of a triumph – for which θριαμβεύω is the word – in view of the strong influence that Rome was exercising on Greece and Asia in the mid-first century.[53]

There are only two possible interpretations of the word in the NT and elsewhere at the time of Paul: it is used of the *triumphator* either leading his victorious army to the plaudits of the crowd or driving his captives and booty before him. As the triumphal procession moved through the streets, the prisoners were driven before the *triumphator*, who rode with his family, the lictors, the magistrates and the senators, whilst behind came the army that had fought the campaign, together with any Romans who had been liberated, wearing the *pileus*. The army called out bawdy jokes at the general (*ioci militares*) and sang 'Io triumphe!' Outside the NT several occurrences of θριαμβεύω refer to the victor driving his defeated foes before him, but the meaning is usually ambiguous. In view of the rarity of the term in Paul it is worth looking at its occurrence in 2 Cor. 2: 14 to see if any guidance may be found to the Pauline usage.

The context is that of the steady movement of the apostles through the world (verses 12f). As they advance, led by God, they spread the good news of the gospel. This is here described as τὴν ὀσμὴν τῆς γνώσεως αὐτοῦ. This, in the context of a triumphal metaphor, immediately suggests that Paul is describing himself and the other apostles as the army of God rather than as his prisoners. For in the triumphal procession men walked beside the chariot with censers, and the clouds of incense that arose were provided not by captives but by victorious soldiers. Indeed, according to Appian in an interesting account of a triumph (*Punica*, 66), the incense bearers, being closest to the *triumphator*, were among the most honoured participants. This idea, if known in full to Paul, would fit well with the concept of apostleship in this section of 2 Corinthians. Although the military metaphors in the NT tend to appear in those letters that are doubtfully Pauline, and although the apostle as slave is a Pauline concept, this need not prevent on this occasion the dominant metaphor of a triumph from carrying the necessary implication that the apostles are God's army. The evidence of the incense suggests a sharing by the apostles in Christ's celebration of his triumph.

The picture in Col. 2: 15, when viewed in this light, is of Christ leading his triumphant armies as they follow him crying 'Io triumphe!' However in this instance the armies are not the apostles; they can only be $\tau \grave{a} \varsigma \ \grave{a} \rho \chi \grave{a} \varsigma$ $\kappa a \grave{\iota} \ \tau \grave{a} \varsigma \ \grave{\epsilon} \xi o \upsilon \sigma \acute{\iota} a \varsigma$, the heavenly host who have already been mentioned in 1: 16. Christ was instrumental in their creation, they have always been his, and now they adore him, after his struggle, in the celebration of his splendour. The possible objection that this may suggest that the angelic host shared in the victory that Christ in fact won alone on the cross cannot be sustained. Indeed, in the face of so bold a metaphor as that of verses 14–15, it might be thought pedantic. The passage, however, is not about the battle, which is assumed without exposition, but about the triumphant Lord. And, as has been noted, $\theta \rho \iota a \mu \beta \epsilon \acute{\upsilon} \omega$ itself does not mean 'win a victory' but 'celebrate the consequences of the victory'. So far as the present passage is concerned, the achievement of Christ is covered in verse 14; its celebration alone appears in verse 15.

Once the concept of triumph is recognised as central, the remaining parts of the verse all contribute to the picture. $\grave{\epsilon} \delta \epsilon \iota \gamma \mu \acute{a} \tau \iota \sigma \epsilon \nu$ is found only here and at Matt. 1: 19, where the alternative is $\pi a \rho \epsilon \delta \epsilon \iota \gamma \mu \acute{a} \tau \iota \sigma \epsilon \nu$. It is a neutral word, meaning only 'to publicise' and is quite naturally used in the context of a triumph.[54] The phrase $\grave{\epsilon} \nu \ \pi a \rho \rho \eta \sigma \acute{\iota} a$ has caused commentators some problems, but on the present interpretation of the passage it takes its usual sense 'boldly', thus intensifying $\grave{\epsilon} \delta \epsilon \iota \gamma \mu \acute{a} \tau \iota \sigma \epsilon \nu$, an otherwise colourless word. The whole phrase $\grave{\epsilon} \delta \epsilon \iota \gamma \mu \acute{a} \tau \iota \sigma \epsilon \nu \ \grave{\epsilon} \nu \ \pi a \rho \rho \eta \sigma \acute{\iota} a$ thus contrasts precisely with $\mathring{\eta} \rho \kappa \epsilon \nu \ \grave{\epsilon} \kappa \ \tau o \mathring{\upsilon} \ \mu \acute{\epsilon} \sigma o \upsilon$ in verse 14. The work of Christ was to toss away and remove from sight man's guilt. Now in verse 15 his work is the subsequent display of his majesty as this mighty achievement is celebrated. In this case the question of $\grave{\epsilon} \nu \ a \mathring{\upsilon} \tau \mathring{\omega}$ must be resolved in favour of its being understood to refer to the cross: the very place to which the cheirograph of man's guilt was nailed as Christ died, has become the place where the glory of the Lord is publicly displayed. We should also note that this interpretation makes it impossible that God could be the subject of the verbs.

This glorification of Christ is achieved by the public recognition of him by the angels of heaven. If Paul is here attempting to describe the defeat of hostile powers, it is difficult to see why he did not employ language that refers to defeat or destruction. In the light of what is actually said the presumption must be that τὰς ἀρχὰς καὶ τὰς ἐξουσίας here are, as in 1: 16, Christ's heavenly host, which is pictured as his army. We might compare Matt. 26: 53 where the twelve legions of angels are mentioned at the point of Christ's lonely struggle without any hint that they were involved in the struggle. In Rev. 19: 14, too, there is a reference to τὰ στρατεύματα τὰ τῷ οὐρανῷ. Although these are sometimes taken to be armies of martyrs, it seems more likely that they are an angelic host. 'As the Lamb, Christ is followed by the saints; but as the Celestial Warrior, coming from heaven to earth upon a mission of judgement, he brings with him his angels.'[55] A similar, but not identical, idea, that the angels are available to share with the righteous in winning a victory, is found at Qumran.[56] Not one of these examples is directly parallel to Col. 2: 15 and they are not cited as such. They do, however, show that the notion of an angelic host attaching to the Lord Christ, without any suggestion that they are involved in his struggle directly, was not unknown or impossible in the first century, and the strange remark in Justin, *1 Apol.* 6. 1f, confirms the continuing power of this notion.

There are two other interpretations that require note. Daniélou has argued that when Christ was raised on the cross he came to grips with the demons that inhabit the lower air, and that this is the thought in Paul's mind.[57] Apart from the fact that the notion of ascent on the cross is not a Pauline understanding, there is also the fact that the belief in demons of the air as mighty forces is one that post-dates the thought of Paul. This development is considered below. In any case, as has been repeatedly noted above, the verse is not about the struggle on the cross, but about the celebration of a triumph. A similar objection is fatal to A. T. Hanson's theory that behind Col. 2: 14f there lies a reference to Num. 25: 1-5.[58] Arguing that there is a parallel between the hanging of the rulers as an act of atonement in Numbers and Paul's view here of the death of Christ, and from possible connections of Num. 25 with Deut. 21: 23, which Paul quotes in Gal. 3: 13, itself parallel to Col. 2: 14, Hanson concludes that the passage paradoxically proclaims that what appeared to be the victory of evil was the victory of Christ. The conclusion is unexceptional among modern commentators on the verse, but the way in which it is reached, although original, must be rejected. Apart from certain details, there are two underlying assumptions that must be questioned. The first is that the powers are evil and hostile and that θριαμβεύσας refers to their defeat in battle. Secondly, it is assumed that the terminology of the passage would recall in Asia Minor an obscure event in Num. 25. Hanson himself remarks that the very fact of the obscurity of the book suggests that Paul is talking about something that was very clear to the addressees. Yet on his argument the common ground between Christians in Asia and Paul would lie in familiarity with the OT text and various Midrashic expositions of it. Yet, as we have noted, the area was generally noted for its paganism and laxity among the Jews, and it is difficult therefore to imagine the Colossian Christians being so well grounded in Jewish ways.[59]

Col. 2: 14–15, then, is a meditation on the work and achievement of Christ. The preceding section from 2: 6 had been concerned with that fullness or completeness which, Paul argued, is to be found in union with Christ and not in any wisdom. That argument effectively is concluded in verse 13, with its affirmation of forgiveness and new life. The wonder of this leads Paul to pause in his discussion, which is formally resumed at verse 16, and to express praise at the incredibility of it all. This he does in what may well be language drawn from some liturgical expression of the humbling and exalting of Christ. Verse 14 deals with the humbling in terms of man's sin and the divine remedy; the expression of the exaltation follows. Yet in each verse the key metaphor is drawn from the Graeco-Roman world. This would mean that, if this passage is a liturgical or credal fragment, then it evidences the early development of Gentile Christian worship, which was independent of Jewish Christianity and the imagery of the OT. The support for so regarding the passage, however, is insufficient to warrant the elaboration of an hypothesis. The whole passage and both metaphors hinge on the cross. The place where the ultimate expression of man's guilt is finally written is also the place where Christ sheds his battle-dress and moves in triumph, surrounded by the armies of heaven. Perhaps we may best see the sense in a paraphrase, in which the pervasiveness of the two main metaphors – χειρόγραφον and θριαμβεύσας – becomes apparent:

'He obliterated our autographed self-condemnation
  (together with all our damning decisions on it);

He has removed it once and for all;

He nailed it to the cross.

He laid aside his battle-dress (his flesh);

He publicly paraded his army of the heavenly host;

He, there on the cross, led them in his triumphal procession.'

This interpretation of τὰς ἀρχὰς καὶ τὰς ἐξουσίας in Col. 2: 15 is wholly in agreement with that demanded by 1: 16 and indeed more generally by Jewish thought prior to Paul. This view, however, also implies that the spirit world was not the centre of the Colossian error, as is usually supposed. Before meeting this difficulty, however, there are two further passages that require exposition – the notoriously obscure verse in 2: 18 and the nature of τὰ στοιχεῖα τοῦ κόσμου.

(d) 2: 18

> μηδεὶς ὑμᾶς καταβραβευέτω θέλων ἐν ταπεινοφροσύνῃ καὶ θρησκείᾳ τῶν ἀγγέλων, ἃ ἑώρακεν ἐμβατεύων, εἰκῇ φυσιούμενος ὑπὸ τοῦ νοὸς τῆς σαρκὸς αὐτοῦ, καὶ οὐ κρατῶν τὴν κεφαλήν.

One of the most complex problems in the epistle lies in this verse, which is usually reckoned to provide the core of the mysterious error of the Colossians. In 2: 16 Paul turns specifically to the situation in the Church. The connective οὖν probably refers back over verses 14–15 (especially if they function in a semi-doxological way) to the thought of verses 10–13: 'You are complete in Christ, with whom God has made you alive . . . Do not, therefore, allow anyone to deceive you.' It is not necessary that the apparent legalism of the error as expressed in verses 16f should be associated directly with the powers, nor is there any need to associate these powers specifically with the angels in verse 18. When this is recognised, some of the problems of the so-called Colossian error are removed. The nature of this error is very open to debate. It may be seen as having elements of Jewishness and of non-Jewishness about it, which may even cross the boundaries of a natural reading of the language.[60] For the moment the question must be temporarily left open in order to allow a study of the central question of the angels.

The structure of verse 18 is obscure. The easiest interpretation of θέλων ἐν is as a semitism meaning 'taking delight in'. If this is not allowed, and the evidence for such a view is very slim, then the meaning may be 'of his own will', although this makes less sense.[61] ταπεινοφροσύνη and θρησκείᾳ are linked, both apparently governed by ἐν. There is also a rank of participles in asyndeton. As the present text stands ἐμβατεύων governs the noun clause ἃ ἑώρακεν, which presumably means ὁράματα, and φυσιούμενος is coupled with οὐ κρατῶν τὴν κεφαλήν, this being Paul's judgement on the situation.

θρησκεία τῶν ἀγγέλων is associated with ταπεινοφροσύνη, which elsewhere in this epistle (2: 12) is commended as a virtue. The meaning of the word, however, must be determined within its context. As a technical term of religious devotion, ταπεινοφροσύνη is often connected with movement, as e.g. in the hymn of Christ in Phil. 2. The voluntary descent of Christ is perhaps contrasted with the enforced descent of the dissident angels.[62] From the human point of view such humility of devotion may become the means of ascent to the heavens, and one technique for this is that of asceticism. The Jewish apocalyptic literature abounds with references to such rigorous asceticism as the prerequisite for the visionary's ascension, and the term for this is exactly ταπεινοφροσύνη.[63] A similar belief continued to flourish in early Christianity. In Hermas, *Sim.* 5.3, fasting leads to an understanding of the parables, while in *Vis.* 3.3.10, it leads to a vision of God. According to Tertullian, by devotional excess Moses saw God, Elijah met God and Daniel encountered an angel. Paul himself would not have been unfamiliar with such a desire, which may even have formed an aspect of his strict Pharisaical upbringing. In addition to the major reference in 2 Cor. 12: 2ff, several other references to visions may be discerned in Paul's writings.[64] ταπεινοφροσύνη, of which fasting is an aspect, is descriptive of this rigorous devotion and it appears in 2: 18 that, whatever the meaning of ἐμβατεύων and θρησκείᾳ, the term refers to some desire for vision or ecstasy of which Paul disapproved.[65]

If this is so, we should naturally also expect some mention of entering the heavenly places. That such is the reference of ἐμβατεύων has been suggested, and the word has been interpreted on analogy with initiation into the mysteries.[66] This theory dates from 1911, when Sir W. M. Ramsay presented an inscription from the Temple of Apollo at Claros that dates from the second century A.D. A large number of commentators have followed him, but there are fatal flaws in this view.[67] Nock has clearly demonstrated that ἐμβατεύων in this and similar inscriptions represents the second stage of initiation, at which the initiate entered upon all that he had just learned.[68] It is applied to the climax of the mysteries only when a further word of explanation is added.[69] Yet without this connection with the mysteries there appears to be little material with which to work in understanding the language used here. The main alternative theory, apart from emendation, is that offered by Percy. He notes 2 Macc. 2: 30 and Philo, *de plant.* 80, and suggests that the term means 'investigating everything'.[70] This view is developed by Preisker, who draws upon 2 Tim. 3: 7 as an analogy. But these uses of ἐμβατεύω do not occur in contexts similar to 2: 18, where religion, its cult and practice, is under discussion. S. Lyonnet has attempted to hold a middle position. Accepting both the evidence against a direct reference to the mysteries of Claros and the evidence adduced by Percy, he suggests that this is another example of Paul using language familiar to the Colossians from its employment at Claros and Pergamum, which he then interprets in his own way. There are, then, three possible translations: 'scrutinising what he has seen'; 'the things which he has seen in his contemplation'; or 'vainly puffed up by the experience of what he has seen in his contemplation'.[71] None of these, however, is satisfactory, and the resort to conjecture becomes attractive. Most conjectures are based upon variations of κενεμβατεύω (Aristophanes, *Nub.* 225), but all are rightly rejected in the words of Dean J. W. Burgon as 'something which (if it means anything at all) may as well mean "proceeding on an airy foundation to offer an empty conjecture"'. Any textual confusion also must have occurred, if at all, at a very early date, since no trace survives. The intrusive μή into ἅ [μὴ] ἑώρακεν may be due to the influence of Ezek. 13: 3, together with a failure to understand Colossians. Recently F. O. Francis has made a further contribution to the study of this problem by pointing to the number of legal terms that appear in this section of the epistle – χειρόγραφον, καταβραβεύειν, κλῆρος, ἀνταπόδοσις, θησαυροί. He suggests that ἐμβατεύων is similarly used here, and brings papyrological evidence to bear. He links this with Euripides, *Heracleidae* 863–78, with which he compares Jos. 19: 49, 51, and proposes the meaning 'enter into possession'. This is an attractive theory, but it depends on the reader's abandoning a cultic context in favour of a legal one. If, however, our suggestion for the cheirograph is accepted and this is linked with the worship of the angels (very cultic language too), it would seem preferable to look for the sense of this obscure term in the language of religion.[72]

The inscriptions from Claros are late and represent a technical use of ἐμβατεύω. If, however, we return to the original use of the word by the classical writers from which this later use in the mysteries derives, we may find a clue to its meaning in Colossians. It is used mainly of a god entering a place that has been consecrated to him and implies less movement towards a place than presence in or movement on a spot. The best translation is usually 'to haunt'. It is used of Pan (Aeschylus, *Pers.* 449), Dionysus (Sophocles, *OC* 679), and of Apollo in Lydia (Ps.-Euripides, *Rhesos* 225). When used of mortals the same idea of association with a sacred place is preserved, the place usually being a man's homeland. Thus in Sophocles, *OT* 825, Oedipus lists among the things that he must forgo μηδ' ἐμβατεῦσαι πατρίδος, and the chorus in Euripides, *Electra* 595, prays τυχᾷ σοι, τυχᾷ κασίγνητον ἐμβατεῦσαι πόλιν. This use stresses the importance of a precious and religiously significant place upon which a man may place his feet. One of the marks of Phrygian religion was the pursuit of ecstasy, and this was never wholly eradicated from Asia Minor. E. R. Dodds has convincingly shown that the *Bacchae* of Euripides is a faithful account of a form of religion that survived, if occasionally in an attenuated form, until late in the Roman Empire.[73] Central to the ritual was *oreibasia*, the ecstatic dance of the Maenads. The error at Colossae is by no means to be thought of as a Dionysiac orgy, but there appears to be an underlying concern with what is elemental in religion. There are certain strange parallels with the *Bacchae* in this epistle. Col. 2: 18 shows a concern with visions and the encounter with the divine is the aim of religiousness. *Bacchae* 466ff also discusses this question, especially 469–70:

Pentheus   πότερα δὲ νύκτωρ σ᾽ ἢ κατ᾽ ὄμμ᾽ ἠνάγκασεν;
Dionysus   ὁρῶν ὁρῶντα, καὶ δίδωσιν ὄργια.

Knowledge of the god and the reception of his cult is by means of a face to face encounter and is no mediated experience. There is also at Colossae the matter of wisdom (2: 8), and one of the chief motifs of the *Bacchae*, which recurs throughout the play, is the contrast between true and false wisdom: 179, 186, 200, 203, 311, 332. The whole is summed up in 395: τὸ σοφὸν δ᾽ οὐ σοφία.

It appears possible, then, that ἐμβατεύων is used here not so much in reference to the language of oracles or of the mysteries, but as a word taken from the heart of the local religious tradition. This included questions of wisdom, ecstasy, dreams and visions, and dancing upon sacred mountains.[74] It certainly appears most probable that the error at Colossae had local roots, for there is no hint in the epistle of any intrusive group. Paul appears to use language that, whilst not explicitly used in our chief literary source for Bacchic religion – Euripides' *Bacchae* – nevertheless exactly fits the type of religion there displayed: excess and contradiction. ἐμβατεύων therefore should keep its essential sense of 'treading upon a religiously significant place'. The question of where this place is sited is in turn tied to the meaning of θρησκεία τῶν ἀγγέλων.

The cult of angels has usually been taken as the centre of that curious amalgam of thought and practice that is believed to characterise the error at Colossae. It is treated as complementary to ταπεινοφροσύνη, that humility in man which makes him feel unworthy to worship God. He therefore seeks the intercession of the angels. Certainly in apocryphal Judaism and indeed at Qumran the possession of the names and functions of the angels is so regarded. The chief problem raised by the present text, however, is that, if we are to understand the angels to which Paul refers in a Judaeo-Christian sense, it is impossible to find any evidence for the practice of worship of the angels by men. The occasions when a mortal falls in awe before a celestial being can scarcely be described as θρησκεία τῶν ἀγγέλων. The term θρησκεία is a cultic word and is not used to describe this personal response, which in any case is notably rare in the NT.[75] The notion that the Jews worshipped angels comes from the *Kerygma Petrou* as reported in Origen, from Heracleon, and Clement of Alexandria. There are also remarks in *contra Celsum* and a further allusion by Aristides. That the rabbis mention worship of angels is clear, but it is always in the context not of condemning a current practice so much as making it clear that for a Jew, however wayward, it is impossible to worship any being other than Yahweh, not even an angel.[76] It is, however, also clear that the Judaism of the Diaspora in Asia tended towards syncretism, and it might be that the remarks of the rabbis are irrelevant in this area. Yet the largest collection of literary and archaeological material that is relevant to the Diaspora hardly mentions angels and there is no hint of their worship.[77] Although all other conceivable aberrations within Judaism are evidenced, there is no suggestion of such a cult. In his eagerness to connect Diaspora Judaism with the worship of angels at Colossae, Goodenough assumes that it was not improbable within a Jewish milieu, but he offers no evidence. So far as may be seen, although the Jews were not above identifying Yahweh with a local god, they seem not to have moved towards a multiplicity of gods or angelic beings as the object of worship.[78]

It is equally difficult to find in contemporary pagan religion any practice that might be described as worship of angels. Reverence for intermediaries cannot be termed θρησκεία, and the suggestion of A. L. Williams that the hellenistic δαίμονες were assimilated with the Jewish ἄγγελοι cannot stand. The demons were not worshipped in cultic form, and the assimilation with Jewish angels occurred later than the beginning of the Christian era.[79] It therefore seems reasonably certain that Paul was not here referring to a pagan cultic act.

One other small piece of evidence is sometimes adduced. In the mid-fourth century, Christians were forbidden by the thirty-fifth canon of Laodicea to 'abandon the Church of God and invoke angels and hold conventicles'.[80] This is not a reference to worship of angels but to the naming of angels in magic. Canon 36, which is against priests being magicians, confirms this. In later times, in the environs of Colossae, there are found chapels dedicated to the Archangel Michael. This probably represents a Christianising of local deities during the period of the Church's expansion and is not a reflection of the Colossian error of the first century.[81]

There is, then, no direct evidence for a cult of angels either in Judaism, Christianity, or paganism in the first century, other than that which possibly appears in Col. 2: 18.[82] Yet in this context, with its language of strongly religious tendencies, it is difficult to imagine that Paul is simply listing an error in the phrase θρησκείᾳ τῶν ἀγγέλων. Many of the problems associated with the verse vanish if the genitive is taken not as

objective, as is assumed by most commentators, but as subjective. It is not
a question of worship being offered to angels, but of the worship offered
by angels.[83] Most of the references to the angels in the literature refer to
their worship of the Almighty, hymning his praise and doing his will. The
Christian traditions in e.g. Rev. 4 and 5; Asc. Is. 7: 13f; Test. Lev. 3: 4ff,
all represent the idea of a heavenly liturgy offered night and day to God.
The aim and desire of the visionary or ecstatic is to share in this worship
and the interpretation of θρησκείᾳ τῶν ἀγγέλων should therefore be in
terms of this heavenly court, in which the Colossian Christians wish to
share.

The whole verse may now be put together. Its structure does not, as it
is usually punctuated, depend upon an assumed parallelism of the two
nouns ταπεινοφροσύνῃ and θρησκείᾳ after ἐν. The parallelism lies between
the two participles θέλων and ἐμβατεύων. It may be set out thus in
tabular form for convenience:

μηδεὶς ὑμᾶς καταβραβευέτω
θέλων ἐν ταπεινοφροσύνῃ
καὶ
θρησκείᾳ τῶν ἀγγέλων (ἃ ἐώρακεν) ἐμβατεύων,
εἰκῆ φυσιουμενος ὑπὸ τοῦ νοὸς τῆς σαρκὸς αὐτοῦ
καὶ
οὐ κρατῶν τὴν κεφαλήν.

θέλων ἐν, therefore, governs only ταπεινοφροσύνῃ, for the dative θρησκείᾳ
follows from ἐμβατεύων. The difficult clause ἃ ἐώρακεν is parenthetical, a
pejorative aside on the claims of the visionary. The neuter plural is no real
problem since it virtually summarises both the rigorous devotion and the
sharing in worship. The simple dative with ἐμβατεύων is usual and here
emphasises presence in a place rather than any movement towards it. The
translation of the verse should therefore be: 'Let no one judge you unfit to
be a Christian with his personal wishes about religious excess and his
haunting the courts of heaven at worship with the angels, his so-called
visions, puffed up by his private, earthly imagination.' The objection that
the genitive τῶν ἀγγέλων cannot be subjective because of the occurrence
of ἐθελοθρησκεία in 2: 23 is not well founded.[84] Self-appointed worship',
if that is the correct translation of the term, is exactly the criticism that
Paul would wish to make of this attempt to share the courts of heaven. Far
from being caught up by the Spirit, these errorists were claiming to achieve
a place in heaven by sheer effort and self-aggrandisement. It was not, then,
notions from the mysteries nor a unique cult of the angels that was leading
the Colossians astray. The problem was the same as that found elsewhere:

claims to spiritual superiority were being validated by claims to higher religious experience through a mystical ascetical piety. The language of such religion, with its excesses of self-denial and its exaggerated assumptions of intimacy with the heavenly host, is contrasted by Paul with the fundamental Christian requirement of κρατῶν τὴν κεφαλήν. The angels of this passage are the very same beings as the powers in 1: 16 and 2: 15: they are therefore the hosts of God at worship. With their very exalted view of Christ, the Colossians were in danger of trying to exalt themselves along with him. They had succumbed to this temptation, using the only means they knew – rigorous asceticism. Paul here in the epistle puts the angels where they belong – around Christ in heaven – and reminds the Christians of their calling to the simple demand of holding to the head.

(e) τὰ στοιχεῖα τοῦ κόσμου

There are two references in Colossians to τὰ στοιχεῖα τοῦ κόσμου, which, on the general consensus of opinion among twentieth-century commentators, refer to spiritual forces. This view, as with so many in this field, derives in recent times from Everling through Dibelius, and today it is almost universally accepted. The word στοιχεῖα occurs in the NT only here; Gal. 4: 3, 9; Heb. 5: 12; and 2 Pet. 3: 10. The Pauline use is usually qualified by τοῦ κόσμου, and the omission of these words at Gal. 4: 9 suggests that the stress within the total phrase is on the ideas in τὰ στοιχεῖα rather than in τοῦ κοσμου, for clearly the reference in verse 9 is no different from that in verse 3.[85] In secular Greek the word is used in all periods. It is therefore important to attempt to isolate that meaning which it would have had for a congregation that received a letter from Paul in the middle of the first century A.D. The views of a writer like Simplicius from the sixth century can hardly be taken as evidence without extreme qualification, particularly with a word like στοιχεῖα, which undoubtedly changed its meaning in the course of time. Outside the NT there is a wide range of meanings, all of which derive from the basic concept of a primary, immanent component. The history is well set out by Delling and Burton.[86] It is clear that the two meanings 'elementary ideas' and 'elements of the universe' finally prevailed together by the end of the classical period. The connection to astral bodies followed. The earliest explicit use in this latter sense would seem to be in Test. Sal. 8: 2, which is quoted by Burton. The date of the work is uncertain, but it is certainly within the Christian era and possibly as late as the third century A.D. What is certain is that of the three possible meanings – 'elementary ideas', 'physical elements', and 'spiritual bodies' – only the first two are attested during Paul's time. That both Jews and pagans assigned angels or demons to various objects is well known. We cannot, however, automatically shift the meaning of στοιχεῖα from the objects to the angels or spirits. In the first place these angels are never simply described as στοιχεῖα, and secondly, as Delling points out, 'it is by no means obvious that the elements are understood as beings when religious modes of speech are used'.[87]

The use of στοιχεῖα for stars occurs first in the second century A.D., being found in Justin Martyr. Thus e.g. in *2 Apol.* 5. 2 the words refer to the sun and the moon, the planets that govern the seasons (cf. *Dial.* 23. 3), although to make this clear Justin had to add the adjective οὐράνια. Such a use perhaps represents a transitional phase in which the word began to be associated with the heavens. It has been suggested, in order to give a spiritual meaning to στοιχεῖα in the NT, that Paul had in mind the cult of the planets that rule the lives of men, these being the abode of the spiritual forces, i.e. τὰ στοιχεῖα. Again, however, it is significant to note that in no reference to reverence for the planets is the term used. It is quite illegitimate to move from the worship of the planets to the idea of the worship of angels.[88] In any case, as we have noted above, it was chiefly from the end of the first century that interest in the stars increased in the West. In astrology the number seven is of unusual importance, this being the ancient number of the planets, and it is quite possible that the later association of στοιχεῖα with the planets was in part due to the seven vowels.[89] Possibly of similar significance was the rise of the notion of the seven-day week, the importance of which began to increase as Christianity moved into the Mediterranean world.[90] What is clear is that the idea of angels or star spirits in connection with the term στοιχεῖα developed subsequently to the time of Paul.

Various commentators have found three main meanings for the word in Paul. Among the Fathers the sense 'elementary teaching' predominated, as the basic religious conviction either of Jews or of pagans. Clement of Alexandria and Origen associate the word with the elementary religious teaching of men prior to the coming of Christ. Some, however, did introduce the idea of physical elements or astral bodies – e.g. Chrysostom (*in Ep. Col.* 2. 6) and Augustine (*ad Gal.* 4. 1-3) – who associate τὰ στοιχεῖα, the one with the sun and the moon and the other with the gods of the Gentiles, although Augustine refuses to admit that these are personal beings. The caveat offered by Bandstra at this point is significant: 'If a Father holds that Paul is referring to heavenly bodies and goes on to say that Gentiles considered the heavenly bodies to be personal deities, it does not follow that he understood Paul to be referring to heavenly beings.'[91] He also lists the more recent commentators who have taken τὰ στοιχεῖα to mean 'elementary teaching'. R. M. Grant has made an interesting development of this interpretation, suggesting that the Christian use of 'abba' might lie behind it. The elementary instruction of the child leads him to say this childlike word and it thus symbolises elementary teaching. Perhaps, however, Paul is too disparaging about the word for this view to carry conviction.[92]

Few seem to have held that Paul is referring to the elements in a cosmological sense. More, like Delling, link this sense with the principal meaning: 'τὰ στοιχεῖα τοῦ κόσμου denote that whereon the existence of the world rests, that which constitutes man's being. Paul uses it in a transferred sense for that whereon man's existence rested before Christ, even and precisely in pre-Christian religion, that which is weak and impotent, that which enslaves man instead of freeing him.'[93] Even in the third interpretation, according to which the term is understood to mean personal beings, some wish to retain the association with the Law as that primitive binding force from which the Christian is freed. Appeal is made to the myth that Paul himself employs in Gal. 3: 19, that the angels were involved in the giving of the Law. Percy considers that Paul has coined the phrase to pass a negative judgement on his opponents.[94] The majority of commentators, however, take στοιχεῖα to be spiritual forces in the universe that are hostile to men. There are two views on this. The one regards the stars as inhabited by hostile spirits, thus keeping the connection of στοιχεῖα with stars. The other regards στοιχεῖα as spirits in general and therefore as directly comparable with the other Pauline phrase αἱ ἀρχαὶ καὶ αἱ ἐξουσίαι. The difference between these views is not important.[95] Although this is currently the dominant view, it must be rejected. Astrology and concern with the stars became a religion of the people from the end of the first century onwards, but it never became *the* religion. The increased interest in astrology paved the way for the later understanding of στοιχεῖα as astral elements, but at the time of Paul, there is no evidence to support this sense. The natural understanding of anyone hearing the epistles in the mid-first century A.D. would have been either as 'the elements that make up the world' or 'elementary teaching', and it is between these that a decision must be made for the intention of Paul.

Before considering the Pauline texts, however, mention should be made of the other occurrences in the NT. These are not very instructive. In Heb. 5: 12 the only possible meaning is 'elementary instruction'. 2 Pet. 3: 10 is more complex, with its language of violent, apocalyptic eschatology. τὰ στοιχεῖα here are probably the sun and the moon, the dissolution of which was an ingredient in the apocalyptic tradition. The two verbs associated with the term here are *termini technici*, and that τὰ στοιχεῖα are astral bodies is confirmed by their position in verse 10*b* between οὐρανοί and γῆ.

The alternative explanation that they are the physical elements, whilst not to be ruled out, seems dull and irrelevant in this context. In any case such elements are surely included in οὐρανοί and γῆ. Neither 2 Peter nor Jude (in which there is the only reference in the NT to the planets – verse 13) may be dated with certainty, but they are unlikely to have been much earlier than towards the end of the first century. In this case it is not surprising that στοιχεῖα might here refer to celestial bodies. If this is so, it is worth noting that this is the first evidence of such an absolute use of the word.[96]

Paul, however, alone has the phrase τὰ στοιχεῖα τοῦ κόσμου, which is scarcely paralleled elsewhere.[97] Wis. 7: 7 is near, but not very close, and the recurrence of this uniquely Pauline phrase in two separate epistles suggests that for him it has specific reference. The word κόσμος generally refers to the world of men in Paul, and this, although characterised at times as evil, is not necessarily evil or dispensable in the ecology of God. We may not therefore simply assume that through the addition of τοῦ κόσμου, τὰ στοιχεῖα immediately takes on a connotation of the powers of evil. In Gal. 4: 3 the context is that of the acceptance or reacceptance by the Galatian Christians of the imposition of the Law. The key contrast is between past and present. Before their conversion they were ignorant and innocent (νήπιοι), for whom τὰ στοιχεῖα were elementary teachings. These are ἀσθενῆ καὶ πτωχά (verse 9), elementary notions of man's religion, which Paul from a Christian position must reject. The remark is comparable with the radical comment in Rom. 8: 3: τὸ ἀδύνατον τοῦ νόμου. It would seem, then, that the definition offered by F. Prat is correct: τὰ στοιχεῖα τοῦ κόσμου are 'the rudimentary notions which are suited to the childhood of humanity, and which wise men – or God himself accommodating himself to its weakness – teach, like an alphabet, in order to prepare it for higher, maturer, and diviner teaching. The Law of Moses is included in this elementary institution.'[98]

If this is the sense in Galatians, we must ask whether the occurrences in Colossians are consistent with it. In 2: 8 τὰ στοιχεῖα τοῦ κόσμου are joined with τὴν παράδοσιν τῶν ἀνθρώπων and are opposed to Christ. It cannot be argued that because Christ is a person and is the second term of this disjunction, then the first half must equally have personal reference.[99] The tradition of men is a pejorative idea (cf. Col. 2: 22f) and it is with this that τὰ στοιχεῖα are identified. Similarly in 2: 20 the contrast is between the Christian's liberation from τὰ στοιχεῖα τοῦ κόσμου and his desire to return to the life of regulations. The στοιχεῖα are composed of the same things as the δόγματα, which are implicit in δογματίζεσθε. It is also noticeable that both in Galatians and in Colossians all references to στοιχεῖα are found 'in connection with a relapse from the freedom of Christianity into some dogmatic system'.[100] There is, therefore, no reference in τὰ στοιχεῖα τοῦ κόσμου to supernatural beings, spirits or angels. One final observation, which seems to have passed unnoticed in previous studies, appears to confirm this view. A key idea in Colossians is that of completion (πλήρωμα). In 2: 8 that completeness which is found in Christ is mentioned alongside the description of τὰ στοιχεῖα as the tradition of men. The contrast appears to be implicitly between the inadequacy or incompleteness of τὰ στοιχεῖα and the fullness of teaching in Christ. There is a similar collocation in Gal. 4: 3, where, however, the comparison is not of content but of time. The old age of slavery to the elementary teaching was incomplete until the dawning of the new age, πλήρωμα τοῦ χρόνου. There seems to be a contrast in Paul's mind between τὰ στοιχεῖα and τὸ πλήρωμα, the former carrying notions of that which is inadequate and incomplete in contrast to the latter, which stands for the fullness and completeness that is in Christ.

(f) Intermediate conclusions

Having now considered all the material relating to the principalities and powers in Colossians, we are in a position to draw some intermediate conclusions on Paul's understanding of the spirit world in this epistle and its significance for the recipients. Four conclusions present themselves.

1. τὰ στοιχεῖα τοῦ κόσμου are not spiritual beings. It is therefore misleading to translate the terms as 'elements', whether this signifies the spiritual beings behind the world or alludes rather more distantly to angels as givers of the Law. This term should be removed as a personal term from the vocabulary of Paul. Since there are no such beings they cannot be central to the Colossian error, and some other direction must be sought for its nature and content.

2. αἱ ἀρχαὶ καὶ αἱ ἐξουσίαι, together with the addition in 1: 16 of θρόνοι καὶ κυριότητες, are not mentioned for any intrinsic interest in them, either by Paul or by the Colossians. Both references occur in passages which, if not hymnic-credal fragments, nevertheless within the epistle function more as emotive descriptions of Christ and his work than as theological statements. The other use in 2: 10 also conforms to 1: 16 and 2: 15, and is considered further below. The reference to these powers is part of the demonstration of the completeness of Christ himself. He is genuinely Lord, his glory being witnessed by the worship of his hosts, both in creation and in his triumphal exaltation after his crucifixion.

3. The language that Paul employs has to some extent an obscure back-

ground. It is clear, however, that the principalities and powers are angel figures of the heaven of God, not demonic beings or fallen angels. Neither are they hostile to men. Indeed in this epistle they scarcely relate to men, their sole function being godward.

4. There was certainly no cult of angels at Colossae or anywhere else at this period. With this notion safely removed, the way is open for a re-assessment of the Colossian error, without making use of an unattested world of demonic powers and angel worshippers.

(g) The Colossian error

In order therefore finally to substantiate these interim conclusions, the nature of the Colossian error must be coherently presented. All interpretations to date, so far as I have discovered, have understood this in terms of fear of the demonic or worship of intermediaries. A recent article by M. D. Hooker comes near to abandoning these usual assumptions, although she too gives a prominent role to the powers and possibly allows too much significance to a possible role for Torah in Col. 1: 15–20.[101] Three key points stand out in the epistle, when its thought is compared with that elsewhere in Paul, and these provide the clue to the situation at Colossae. They are the use of the root πληρο-, especially in connection with the Christology of the epistle; the explicit use of and centrality of the concept of forgiveness; and the distinctive approach to Christian behaviour in the paraenesis. Each of these points requires examination.

There are seven occurrences of words derived from the root πληρο-, leaving aside the routine occurrence in 4: 17. πλήρωμα is used twice of Christ (1: 19 and 2: 9): πληροφορέω is used of Christians (4: 12) and the cognate noun in 2: 2. πληρόω is used in 1: 9; 1: 25; and 2: 10. Most of these uses are not unusual. It is in the context of the Christology of the epistle that these references become significant, the use of πλήρωμα being found in this sense only in Colossians and Ephesians. As will be demonstrated, while there is no change in the basic meaning of the word for Paul when he uses it in Colossians, it is a marked development of his thought to apply it to Christ and to draw consequences from this application.

The fundamental meaning of the word is 'that which fills' or 'that which completes', and hence also 'the completion that results'.[102] It is used of Christ in Colossians in 1: 19 and 2: 9, and on both occasions Paul accentuates the completeness of the πλήρωμα by the addition of τὸ πᾶν. In 2: 9 there is the explicit addition of τῆς θεότητος, but it seems likely that it is implied in 1: 19. Any attempt to relate this use of πλήρωμα to a gnostic use is in part refuted by Paul's use of θεότητος here. It is not the equivalent of θειότητος and πᾶν τὸ πλήρωμα τῆς θεότητος cannot possibly be translated 'the totality of divine beings'. Certainly the term πλήρωμα seems to have been a technical term in some gnostic teaching, but those who favour such a reference here have overlooked some important points. In the first place there is no evidence for its use in a technical sense in the mid-first century.[103] The word is found regularly in the LXX, and the presence in Colossians of a certain amount of Wisdom language may suggest that Paul was thinking in those categories in his use of πλήρωμα.[104] It is also argued that the Colossian error was a tendency to think of Christ as merely one among many beings, these being referred to as πλήρωμα. Yet this is not the meaning of the term even in explicitly gnostic systems. In the cosmogonic theory of Valentinian thought, for example, it was paired with τὸ ὅλον. It was not the collection of spiritual beings so much as the aggregate of the Aeons plus the Saviour plus the pre-existent Elect One, the disjunction within this πλήρωμα leading to the existence of the cosmos. It is therefore an abstract term expressing this totality, and the category of worship is not one within which to think of the πλήρωμα. In its own nature it was impersonal, non-spiritual, and represented a cosmogonic function.[105] Those who have attempted to interpret the term in Colossians in a gnostic sense have assumed that Paul is meeting the errorists on their own ground. This, however, is very doubtful, for, as Percy rightly argues, Paul gives no hint of any misuse at Colossae of what is for him a meaningful theological term.[106] The term is used distinctively by Paul. In 1: 19 it is related to the function of Christ as the agent of creation and head of the body, and as such he is the means of reconciliation for the universe. In 2: 9 there is the connection of κεφαλή and πλήρωμα as Christ is viewed functionally in relation to the Church.

In 1: 19, if πλήρωμα is taken to mean 'the fullness of God', there is very little difference between taking it as the subject of the verb or understanding θεός. It may be that the collocation of a neuter phrase and masculine participle is violent, but if in Paul's mind the fundamental thought is πᾶν τὸ πλήρωμα τῆς θεότητος, as in 2: 9, then the transition is not too difficult. Paul reaches the climax of this part of his discussion concerning the person and work of Christ through a functional reference to the incarnation as God's means of reconciling the universe. In 2: 9 there is a particular problem in the adverb σωματικῶς. The best solution here is perhaps to understand Paul to be referring to the totality of Godhead being found in Christ 'actually' and therefore also 'in bodily form'. Certainly we have here no academic argument about the incarnation, for the language, as in 1: 19, is functional. Just as the completion of the person of Christ on earth was the totality of God, so by incorporation in this Christ now the Colossian Christians find their own completeness: καὶ ἐστὲ ἐν αὐτῷ πεπληρωμένοι. This is a strict use of the perfect tense for what occurred once and is still the case.

The term πλήρωμα, then, in Colossians points to the centrality of Christ's function in redemption, whether in a liturgical style of language (1: 19) or when used as a theological weapon in the establishing of the Christian community (2: 9). This fact, coupled with the absence of any mention in the epistle of the Holy Spirit (except perhaps a conventional reference in 1: 8) suggests that the real trouble at Colossae lay in the understanding of Christ. There is no evidence of division or factions in the Church, nor of differing beliefs. The whole Church was failing to understand the concept of completion both in its Christology and in its moral outlook. The error appears to have been at heart an inadequate understanding of the connection between belief and behaviour, which for Paul evidences a fundamental misunderstanding of the relation of the Christian to Christ and to the Church. Thus in 2: 19 οὐ κρατῶν τὴν κεφαλήν means not that they do not recognise Jesus as Lord but that they do not keep a close enough grip on the nexus of Christ and Church.

The key to this error – for which the term 'confusion' might be a kinder and more accurate description – lies in 2: 6–7. The unusual compilation of Pauline ideas here points to the importance of the verse. παραλαμβάνω is a technical word for receiving the tradition that has been handed on. The mixture of metaphors in the participles points again to the question of maturity as the central issue. 'Christ Jesus the Lord' is seen as the content of the teaching received, the living Christ is himself the tradition. This unique title for Christ suggests that he is perceived as the Christ (the kerygmatic basis), the Christ Jesus (the historical foundation), and Jesus the Lord (the Christian confession, together with its moral implication).[107] That this is the key verse is shown by the structure of Paul's argument. Having encouraged the Colossians, he introduces the first mention of behaviour immediately before his excursus on the status of Christ. His prayer in 1: 9 is that the Colossians may have ἐπιγνῶσιν τοῦ θελήματος αὐτοῦ, i.e. that knowledge which issues in action, as is borne out in 1: 10. The main Christological ideas of the epistle occur within the framework of the exhortation in 1: 10 and the similar exhortation in 2: 6. From this section the conclusions are drawn that Christ is the head of the body, that in him dwells the πλήρωμα, and that he is the means of God's reconciliation of all things. This reconciliation is localised in terms of the life of the Colossians in 1: 21ff. The very difficult verse 24 connects this argument with that which is to follow concerning Paul's mission to the world to establish mature Christians (1: 28), which is then specifically related to the Colossians in 2: 1–5. In 2: 6 the position is made explicit, and after a warning in 2: 7, the question of the maturity of the Colossians is expounded in baptismal language, which leads to the semi-doxological conclusion of 2: 14f.

Throughout this section the unifying theme is that of completeness, this being expressed in words based upon the root πληρο-. In the case of Christ this involves the presence of the Godhead, and in the case of the Christians it involves their relation to their immediate head. Schematically the section and the words may be set out thus:

1: 9–12	Demands on the Colossians	9.	πληρωθῆτε.
1: 15–23	Person and work of Christ	19.	πᾶν τὸ πλήρωμα.
1: 24	(Connecting verse)	24.	ἀνταναπληρῶ.
1: 25–9	Paul's labours for God	25.	πληρῶσαι.
		(28.	τελεῖον)
2: 1–5	Paul's labours connected to Colossae	2.	πληροφορίας.
2: 6–15	The life in Christ	10.	πεπληρωμένοι.

This careful interrelating of belief and behaviour, of Christ and the Christians, makes sense of the relation between the opening remarks and the attack on the error. This apparent discontinuity is noted by most commentators and is usually explained either in terms of the importation by others of the Christ hymn or by reference to the fact that Paul was hesitant to launch into his theme as he did not know the Colossians personally. Neither explanation is satisfactory. In addition this structure also explains the oft noted phenomenon of the stress in this epistle upon Christ as the head of the body. The question of Christian maturity is not one of membership of a particular group, nor is it participation in divinity. It is rather a recognition of the relation of Christ to his people and a commitment to the implications of that relationship. Paul therefore does not stress participation in Christ, but participation in that body which is under the headship of Christ. This is a small modification in his thinking on the body, but one that was demanded by a particular situation. The structure also explains the absence of reference to the Holy Spirit. The danger of emphasising the nature of the Church as the body of Christ is that within the body there has to be an explanation of the relations between the various parts. When called upon for such an explanation Paul did it mainly with concepts that explain the immanence of God, namely the presence of the Holy Spirit. But, as Paul found at Corinth, the danger of connecting function within the Church with gifts of the Spirit is that of division, which detracts from the centrality of Christ. It leads in fact to a Christian religiosity in which success in the irrelevant is substituted for a simple grasp of the essentials. The questions of the Colossians seem to have been concerned with the apparent remoteness of Christ. The hopelessly corrupt sentence in 2: 23 seems to imply that the Colossian attitude was that they were alone, unless through rigorous religious practices they could seek and find Christ in the heavenly places. This attitude inevitably led to that excess of religion which Paul characterises as loss of the centre (2: 18f). His answer in ecclesiological terms is to tie the body to its head, its source and the source of everything.[108] The cosmological language serves to exalt the head and thus, by implication, to magnify the importance of the body (2: 10). The introduction into this situation of the simple concept of the body of Christ would confuse the issue. The heavenly aspect of Christ is accepted and then, in the Pauline manner, built on in a new and startling way (3: 1ff). The religious language of the Colossians has been Christianised.

This raises the question of the error from the Colossians' point of view. One aspect that is incontrovertible is the excessive religiosity, which showed itself in legalistic approaches to food and festivals, a religion of self-inflicted regulations, and above all a religion of self-denial in a manner that tended to devalue the material world. Asceticism is rarely an end in itself. It is a means to closer association with the divine, or, as Paul has it, an ecstatic experience of heaven (2: 18). Although, as we have demonstrated, hostile spiritual forces are absent from the epistle, the world of those spirits who share in the worship of God clearly held a fascination for the Colossians. Because of their longing for mystical experience of heaven these Christians needed to be reminded of the Lordship of Christ. This is especially brought out in the singular use of $\dot{\alpha}\rho\chi\dot{\eta}$ $\kappa\alpha\dot{\iota}$ $\dot{\epsilon}\xi o\upsilon\sigma\dot{\iota}\alpha$ in 2: 10. The angelological interpretation of the Colossian error has led most commentators to an immediate association of this verse with the references in the epistle to $\dot{\alpha}\rho\chi\alpha\dot{\iota}$ $\kappa\alpha\dot{\iota}$ $\dot{\epsilon}\xi o\upsilon\sigma\dot{\iota}\alpha\iota$, with the result that the connection of thought between $\kappa\epsilon\phi\alpha\lambda\dot{\eta}$ and $\pi\lambda\dot{\eta}\rho\omega\mu\alpha$ has been overlooked. This verse is not a simple statement of fact relating to Christ's supposed conquest of demonic forces. Indeed, if these beings and their defeat were so central, it is difficult to see why the references to them are so oblique. Verse 10 echoes the opening discussion on Christ, pointing not so much to the nature of the error as to the supremacy of Christ. Christ is the $\dot{\alpha}\rho\chi\dot{\eta}$ as both 'source' and 'ruler', and in this second sense he is also characterised as $\kappa\epsilon\phi\alpha\lambda\dot{\eta}$. The function of 2: 10 is to relate Christ (2: 8), who is the $\pi\lambda\dot{\eta}\rho\omega\mu\alpha$ (2: 9), to the Colossians, who are $\pi\epsilon\pi\lambda\eta\rho\omega\mu\dot{\epsilon}\nu o\iota$ through their incorporation in the head.

The desire for union with the divine as the aim of ecstatic religion was certainly present in Asia Minor in the first century A.D. Mithraic religion was just beginning its spread from the mountains of Anatolia. Similarly the

cult of Attis and Dionysiac religion both included union with the god. The
worship of Sabazius, which in the minds of some was confused with
aspects of Judaism, incorporated most facets of Asian religion, including
union with the divine. The means to such union included the use of food
and drink;[109] legal observances of festivals; ritual orders; and asceticism
leading to ecstasy. All of these customs characterise the Colossian confusion far too well for them to be overlooked. Yet at the same time care
must be taken not to interpret the situation wholly in terms of a mixture
of Asiatic cults.[110] For whatever language is employed by Christian congregations to express their faith, that faith, however wayward, is not merely a
syncretistic compilation, for its determinative influence will be the
kerygma. Nevertheless, the general laxity of religious conviction in Asia
Minor is well attested. Not only were all the cults syncretistic, but even
Judaism conformed to the pattern. In such a climate the first failure of the
Christian gospel could well have been a slide away from the implications of
the Christian profession, the divorce of creed from practice. This is suggested by the way in which Paul carefully associates knowledge with
actions from the very beginning of the letter – 1: 9f. Of particular interest
too is 3: 1ff, where it would appear that Paul takes the peculiarly Colossian
term τὰ ἄνω and reinterprets it so that it ceases to be a term of mystical
pietism and becomes one of moral force. The ground for this, as also in
2: 11ff, is Christian baptism. The completion of the Christians into full
maturity is to be found in Christ alone, whose incarnation brought that
completion within the range of men, who may themselves appropriate it
through baptism. The chief expression of this thinking in 2: 11 poses
problems. Perhaps the best interpretation is that which sees here the death
of Christ referred to as his circumcision, for in this way ἀπέκδυσις remains
strictly parallel to ἀπεκδυσάμενος in 2: 15. Yet however the verse is taken,
clearly it refers to the incorporation of Christians within Christian baptism.
In this event is to be found that maturity which Paul desires for his readers,
and with this firm base for the Christian life established, he is able to make
use of the otherwise dangerous language of the Colossians.[111] For them τὰ
ἄνω seems to have denoted a place to be reached through mystical piety.
Paul converts it confidently into a moral one, carefully avoiding any
encouragement to ecstatic experience. We note, for example, how
ταπεινοφροσύνη in 3: 12 becomes the Christian virtue of humility in contrast with its technical sense in the controversy of 2: 18. Paul can do this
since for him 'the things that are above' are firmly fixed in the person of
Christ in whom πᾶν τὸ πλήρωμα dwells and with whom the Christians are
associated through baptism. τὰ ἄνω can no longer be treated spatially or in
terms of aspiration, but only morally in terms of the baptismal life. There

is a comparable approach in Phil. 4: 19f, where the heavenly citizenship, a spatial metaphor, becomes the basis for moral exhortation.

The realised eschatology of 3: 1ff is to be explained in the same way. This has been taken as evidence for a form of proto-gnosticism at Colossae.[112] In addition Bornkamm has suggested that in 1: 5, 23 and 27 ἐλπίς has lost its future reference and has been realised into a present possession in an un-Pauline way.[113] This, however, is to assume that such a realised eschatology was a distinctive mark of gnostic systems. But much gnostic eschatology was similar to that which is frequent in the NT, holding a tension between the present and the future.[114] The variations in eschatological tension in the NT are due to the particular situations that faced the writer and to whether the body of Christians or an individual is in mind.[115] Ascetic and ecstatic religion strongly individualises faith and experience. In a Christian context the desire would be for the resurrection of the individual, i.e. a realisation now of the heavenly experience of the ascended Christ. In such circumstances the eschatological tension would be relaxed in favour of a realised eschatology. Paul turns such eschatological presuppositions back on the Colossians. He does not reprove, but through the aorist συνηγέρθητε (3: 1) and the particle οὖν he refers back to the occasion of initiation through baptism and emphasises the moral characteristics of the baptismal life. The aim is maturity, that the Christians, πεπληρωμένοι, may live a life of πληροφοφία. To that end Paul emphasises the supremacy of Christ as the one in whom, both in creation and redemption and in risen power, πᾶν τὸ πλήρωμα τῆς θεότητος dwells.

It is noted in all the commentaries that in this epistle there occurs the only specific use of the language of forgiveness in the Pauline literature. In 1: 14; 2: 13; and 3: 13 the term is found. Käsemann has suggested that 1: 15-20 contains a baptismal liturgy in which the notion of forgiveness would be important.[116] He puts it, however, in the context of a world enslaved by cosmic forces and suggests that the language of forgiveness would be inadequate. We have shown that such a supposition cannot be supported. In the epistle it is noteworthy that the language of forgiveness represents that view of the relation of God and man which carries the strongest moral overtones, whether of past sins forgiven or of the moral life now required. It is also interesting that in 1: 13, where Paul describes the Christian state in most unusual terms, he moves the discussion from the realm of authority into that of forgiveness.[117] The language of forgiveness also tends to point to an error at Colossae that involved moral behaviour rather than cosmological concern.

Lastly we may briefly look at the place of paraenesis in the epistle. There is a concern with behaviour almost from the beginning of the letter.

That this is evidence for a confusion among the Christians over belief and practice is perhaps confirmed by the interesting parallelism between 2: 13ff and 3: 5ff. The language with which Paul treats the situation of the Colossians through baptism and their subsequent error (2: 13ff) is wholly in his mind when he embarks upon his ethical exhortations in 3: 5ff. This is easily perceived in tabular form:

2: 15	ἀπεκδυσάμενος	3: 9	ἀπεκδυσάμενοι
2: 18	ταπεινοφροσύνη	3: 12	ταπεινοφροσύνη
2: 13	χαρισάμενος	3: 13	χαρισάμενοι
2: 18	καταβραβευέτω	3: 15	βραβευέτω
2: 19	πᾶν τὸ πλήρωμα	3: 15	ἐνὶ σώματι

and the two contrasts:

2: 20	τὰ στοιχεῖα τοῦ κόσμου	3: 16	ὁ λόγος τοῦ Χριστοῦ
2: 22	φθορά	3: 16	πλουσίως

This would appear to confirm our previous conclusions that in four areas Paul takes the Colossian religious position and language and creates out of it his complex of Christian faith and practice. He stresses the moral sense of τὰ ἄνω; he interprets baptism in terms of the dual relation of man with God and man with man; he understands the fullness of God in Christ; and finally he expounds the implications in moral terms of the Colossian emphasis on a realised eschatology.

The intention behind this section on the Colossian error has not been exhaustively to interpret the detail of the epistle, but simply to show that in the light of our intermediate conclusions on the meaning of αἱ ἀρχαὶ καὶ αἱ ἐξουσίαι in the letter the error becomes comprehensible without recourse to any cult of angels. It also avoids argument over Jewish or hellenistic elements in the error and certainly excludes a gnostic interpretation. The error is explained in terms of what is known of the religious situation in Asia Minor in the mid-first century A.D. This interpretation also accounts for the gentleness of Paul in the epistle. He was not countering a major Christological error, for which he surely would have used stronger language, but a confusion over the connection between religious experience and moral practice. For the purposes of this present study the intermediate conclusions are confirmed. The cosmic powers that have often been assumed to have dominated the lives of the Colossians are not mentioned in this letter, nor does Paul acknowledge their existence. Nor are angelic powers, worshipped as intermediaries between Christ and men, to be found here. Certainly there is no mention of a cosmic battle from which Christ emerged victorious to save men from the powers of this world. Since, however, for many the interpretation of Col. 2: 15 in terms of such a victory has been fundamental to their understanding of such powers elsewhere in the NT, the removal of the idea here has far-reaching consequences. Indeed it throws into question the whole notion of a cosmic background to Paul's thought.

2 Philippians 2: 10

We turn now to Phil. 2: 10 with its reference to the universal adoration of Jesus Christ as Lord. R. P. Martin has well summarised the variety of views that have been expressed on this text.[118] The three adjectives – ἐπουρανίων καὶ ἐπιγείων καὶ καταχθονίων – would appear to amplify the notion of Christ's universal Lordship, in terms of both demanding and receiving such worship. In this case the words are most naturally taken as neuters, thus aligning the concept with that expressed, for example, in Psalm 148.[119] To take them as masculine, referring respectively to spiritual forces in the heavens, men on earth, and the dead in Sheol, is a view based upon an understanding that at this stage of the Christian era is inappropriate. An alternative view, which is espoused by Dibelius and followed by many, is to make all three adjectives refer to demonic forces.[120] This interpretation has received a wide measure of support, but requires re-examination.

There is first the question of a threefold division of the universe under the control of mighty forces. This is strongly urged by Cullmann, who makes considerable play with Ignatius, *Trall.* 9. 1: ἐσταυρώθη καὶ ἀπέθανεν, βλεπόντων τῶν ἐπουρανίων καὶ ἐπιγείων καὶ ὑποχθονίων.[121] Martin, who follows Cullmann here, and adds references of his own from various magical papyri, summarises the view of the majority when he remarks:

> 'Ignatius seems to be saying that the reality of Christ's death was attested by three sets of foes: the first class are the principalities and powers which crucified him and were overthrown by that death (I Cor. ii. 8; Col. ii. 15); the second group are the enemies of the Lord on a human plane who brought about his death; while the third was "the strong man" whom Christ has now bound, so that He might "spoil his goods" and release from Hades the awaiting spirits of the righteous who were Christians "before the time".'[122]

This interpretation, common though it is, does not take sufficient account of the context of the remark. Ignatius is reciting a brief account of the faith against which the Trallians may test that docetist Christology which was infecting the life of their Church (10. 1). There is a need to witness the certainty of Christ's humanity, both in life and death, with its attendant suffering. The context is not that of triumph over enemies but of the universal attestation of the fact of real, actual and bodily death. In this context βλεπόντων is exactly the word: the whole inhabited universe saw Christ on the cross and saw him physically die. It would be a most irrelevant word in a discussion of struggle and defeat. In addition it should be noted that ἐπουράνιος and ἐπιγεῖος in the plural in Ignatius are usually neuter, as e.g. in *Trall.* 5.2, just prior to the present passage. Ignatius in fact wholly omits any reference to demonic forces. His world is one in which the sole power of evil is the ruler of this age. This Evil One is ever present and in function approximates to Belial in apocalyptic Judaism and at Qumran. When Ignatius claims knowledge of the heavenly places (*Trall.* 5.2) and of the rulers (*Smyrn.* 6.1), he regards them as the hosts of angels surrounding the throne of God. The argument in *Smyrn.* 6.1 is exactly that of Paul in 1 Cor. 6: 1ff. In any case, for Ignatius such knowledge is unimportant (*Trall.* 5.2), but he certainly shows no signs of an awareness of hostile forces against which Christ struggled, as will be argued in full below.

In a catena of texts Polycarp (*ad Phil.* 2.1) probably includes Phil. 2: 10. He interprets the adjectives as neuters, although he omits the third. He seems to limit the reference to man alone.

In the light of these uses it is reasonably certain that the three adjectives are neuter rather than masculine. In this case the reference is not so much to beings that inhabit the three regions as to the overall notion of universality of homage to God. The best parallel is Psalm 148 and although the personification of all creation in this way is not usual, within a highly poetical context such as Phil. 2: 10 there is no difficulty in so understanding it.

The arguments for Christ's victory over angel powers that are based upon 1 Pet. 3: 22 and 1 Tim. 3: 16 have been refuted above. Two passages from the early Fathers are adduced by Martin in this context. At first sight Justin, *Dial.* 85, might appear to provide a justification for this belief. Justin is trying to establish the equation of Jesus with the Lord of Hosts of Ps. 24, to whom all the angels offer their worship. As one might expect in a debate with Jews, Justin reflects a mixture of Jewish ideas, among them the identification of pagan gods with demons (79), the fall of the angels (79), and the power of the name of God in exorcism (80). In *Dial.* 85 he associates in particular the title 'Son of God' with exorcism, agreeing that any exorcism in the name of the God of Abraham, Isaac and Jacob works, but that those in the names of prophets and kings do not. Since exorcisms in the name of Jesus Christ are effective, he is clearly Son of God. This Lordship of the Son is recognised both by God and by the angels who surround him. There are two arguments in the chapter, and Justin does not confuse them. One is concerned with the efficacy of exorcism. The other is concerned with God's recognition of Christ. The power of the name in exorcism is not related to any idea of victory over the powers but to divine sonship. Paul himself says nothing about exorcism, and we may therefore conclude that the mention of the name of Jesus in Phil. 2: 9 has nothing to do with the defeat of demons and exorcism.

The citation of Irenaeus, *adv. haer.* 1.10.1 in this context refutes itself. Irenaeus is contemplating the wonder of the unity of the faith among the diversity of the Churches. A credal statement composed from the NT includes Phil. 2: 10. If he is thinking carefully at all – and in a passage of proof texts this is improbable – Irenaeus is excluding the notion of the demonic from τὰ ἐπουράνια κ. τ. λ. For having described the universal homage of all creation that is offered to Christ the Lord, he adds a statement of the judgement of the wicked spirits, who are notably separate from τὰ ἐπουράνια κ.τ.λ.

Since there is no mention in Phil. 2: 6ff of any conflict between Christ and his enemies, it appears that the emphasis here is upon the fact that there is no area of the universe that is beyond the sovereignty of the Lord of that universe. It has been further suggested that since the setting of the verses is that of an enthronement drama, the submission of the powers is implicit in it. Martin, who argues this, couples it with a new understanding of ἐξομολογεῖσθαι. Instead of its usual meaning of 'openly to declare' he suggests 'to own' or 'to recognise', and refers to the willing or unwilling recognition of the Lordship of Christ over the powers. That such a meaning may be given to the word is well attested, but it is less clear that it should be accepted in the present passage, especially when it is part of an argument that justifies this use of the word by a presumed enthronement scene. On this notion we should note that there is a difference between exaltation and enthronement. Exaltation is the raising of Christ by God to his right hand, and the emphasis is upon acceptance by God. Enthronement contains rather the raising-up of the king by his people and their acknowledgement of his rule. The difference is one of emphasis, but in the earliest Christian confessions this is always on Christ's acceptance by God. This is the force of the regular use of Ps. 110: 1, which, as will be argued in detail below, is less the enthronement of a triumphant victor than an acknowledgement by God of his co-regent. It should secondly be noted that enthronements were not a feature of the Jewish or western world in the first century A.D., although the language of the enthronement psalms may have affected Christian worship. The enthronement ritual of the divine king in Egypt also has apparent, but unreal, bearing on the question.[123] But the significance of the image for Christian thinking in the first century A.D. is far from certain.

The language of the worship offered, in particular the reference to the Lord Christ, suggests a clear link with the kerygma and the Christian confession rather than with any supposed subjection and admission of defeat by cosmic powers. There is abundant evidence for the belief that when worship takes place heaven and earth are linked.[124] In addition, when the passage is seen in the context of liturgy the unimportance of time-scales is clear.

Phil. 2: 10, therefore, is not to be set in the context of the defeat of angelic powers or of an enthronement ceremony for an exalted heavenly man, but rather in one of simple Christian worship of those whose confession is 'Jesus Christ is Lord.' Demonic forces and Christ's supposed conquest of them are not in the author's mind. The key lies in the worshipping Christian community, to which are linked all aspects of the creation.

3 'The enemies' in Psalm 110: 1

This verse is cited frequently in the NT and is also used regularly in the sub-apostolic period. It has been regarded, apart from the Messianic application, as supporting the idea of Christ's victory over demonic powers. Cullmann has clearly expounded this view: 'Nothing shows more clearly how the concept of the present Lordship of Christ and also of his consequent victory over the angel powers stands at the very centre of early Christian thought than the frequent citation of Ps. 110: 1, not only in isolated books, but in the entire NT.'[125] This position has gained widespread acceptance, although Cullmann's further identification of these powers with the 'ministering spirits' of Heb. 1: 14 has been on the whole rejected. On closer examination, however, the verse seems to say nothing about such powers nor about their defeat.

Of the twelve citations of the verse in the NT outside the Gospels, only three actually contain the reference to the enemies. In Acts 2: 34 the whole verse is quoted as Messianic testimony. Along with Ps. 16: 10 it is used to prove that Jesus is both Lord (Ps. 110) and Christ (Ps. 16). 1 Cor. 15: 25 cites the verse along with Ps. 8: 6, as also does Eph. 1: 20. This use is considered further below. The third mention of the enemies occurs in Heb. 10: 12–13. It is clear, however, that they are not the central interest in this passage, for, apart from the Devil, demonic forces do not feature in Hebrews. The text here, as with all the briefer citations in the NT, affirms the exaltation and vindication of Christ.

A significant fact, which appears to have been overlooked, is that all these references to the exaltation of Christ relate not to his supposed conquest of the demonic forces but always to Christ in direct relation to human need before God and to human experience. In Acts 5: 31 the exaltation of Christ becomes a call to Israel to repentance and the forgiveness of sins. In Rom. 8: 34 the heavenly session results in Christ's intercession for us. In Col. 3: 1 the resurrection and exaltation is the basis of a call to a higher moral life, and in Heb. 10: 12 and 12: 2 the work of Christ is also being viewed in its impact upon the life of man. Even Heb. 1: 3 and 8: 1, which appear to be wholly formulaic, use the text in the context of Christ's work for men in terms of God's forgiveness and acceptance of them. The primary use, then, of Ps. 110: 1 is to refer to the exaltation of Christ as the ground of God's acceptance of man, rather than to any conquest of demonic powers.[126] This conclusion has been reinforced in the study of this psalm and its use by D. M. Hay, who demonstrates that it is used 'to articulate the supreme glory, the divine transcendence of Jesus, through whom salvation was mediated. It was primarily used as a symbol not of his saving work but of his ultimate status.'[127]

When we turn to the sub-apostolic period the same usage survives. *1 Clem.* 36.5f expands upon the ideas in Hebrews, finally quoting Ps. 110: 1 with specific reference to the enemies. These enemies are not, however, demonic; they are purely human: οἱ φαῦλοι καὶ ἀντιτασσόμενοι τῷ θελήματι αὐτοῦ. Polycarp (*ad Phil.* 2) uses the text for moral exhortation, and Barnabas 12: 10 connects it with Is. 45: 1 as proof of Christ's Davidic Messiahship. For Justin, who makes considerable use of the text, one of the crucial arguments for the relationship of Christ to God lies in the effectiveness of the name 'Christ' in exorcism. Thus Ps. 110 provides Justin with a twofold proof, first in the matter of Christ's Messiahship and secondly in the conquest of demons. Nevertheless Justin holds to the original intention of the verse in which the subject of the verb θῶ is not Christ but God. Christ as an individual does not conquer any demonic forces. The point is that Christian exorcism in the names of Jesus evidences the unity of Christ with God.

There remains one verse in the NT in which Ps. 110: 1 is connected with conquest – 1 Cor. 15: 24f. The theme of the whole section is the Lordship of Christ. To this end Ps. 8: 6 is brought into connection with Ps. 110: 1, with the addition of πάντας. The verb that is used here, καταργέω, is used in a wide range of contexts in the NT, but it always retains the basic notion of 'render harmless' or 'make inoperative'. From this, of course, the idea of destruction and defeat may well follow, but the term itself is not one of battle or of victory. The subject of καταργήσῃ is probably Christ; that of θῇ is ambiguous; but the subject of ὑπέταξεν in verse 27, in the light of what follows, is God. If it were not, Paul would here be at clear variance with the usual use of the text in the NT. For the subject in the other citations is certainly God, as in the original context, who accepts the Lord at his right hand, where he sits until God finally makes his enemies his footstool. For this reason alone the verse would be inapt for any proof of a victory of Christ. Indeed the Midrash on the verse would confirm this: 'To the Messiah also will it be said: "And in mercy shall the throne be established; and he shall sit on it in truth in the tent of David, judging" [Is. xvi. 5]. That is, the Holy One, blessed be He, declared: "The Messiah shall sit, and I shall fight his battles."'[128] There is at least a very strong suggestion that $θῇ$ in verse 25 is the point at which the subject changes to God.

The context of 1 Cor. 15: 24 is that of the two Adams. In one other notable passage in Paul there is a similar collection of ideas – Adam, subjection, hope. This is Rom. 8: 18ff, where Paul relates the subjection of the creation by God to vanity, this being the characteristic mark of the story of Adam and the fall as used in Rom. 1: 18f.[129] In Romans the expectation is of the restoration of the right balance in the whole creation, part of which is man himself. This balance is witnessed by Ps. 8, as also the writer to the Hebrews realised. 1 Cor. 15: 24 is concerned with the same material, but instead of viewing it in terms of the first Adam and vanity, it looks at it from the perspective of the second Adam and the rule of God. Whereas in Romans the aim is that of the release of creation from bondage, in 1 Corinthians it is the removal of the final negation of God, i.e. the removal of death itself. The corollary of both expressions is the total affirmation of God and his creation.[130]

There are three points of note about the ultimate destruction of death according to 1 Cor. 15: 24ff and 54ff. In the first place the verb $καταργήσῃ$, the subject of which we have noted is Christ, is that which occurs in 1 Cor. 2: 6ff in connection with the rulers of this age. There, as is argued below, the rulers are the human leaders who carry responsibility for the death of Christ. Their power is being brought to nothing as a result of their encounter with the Lord of Glory. In the present passage Paul makes the same point. The list of those being brought to nought is a conventional one for power and authority of whatever sort. The terms are in the singular with the generalising addition of $πᾶσα$. The reference is to human authority of whatever sort and wherever located; there is no question of the relation of death to these authorities. Death is characterised as the last enemy. It is an adversary of God that functions within man's existence. It seems that Paul is personalising death here but within this apocalyptic conception the mythological element is reduced so that death itself is the last enemy and not the Devil. This is reaffirmed in verses 55f, where in a taunt this figure of death is connected not with any power of evil or the Devil, but with sin. We are therefore not in the realm of supernatural powers, but within the realm of history.[131] Thus the parallelism between 'all authority' and 'death' lies primarily in the historical sphere:

all human authority is being robbed of its power and ultimately even the relentless power of death itself will be reduced to impotence. This is confirmed by the way in which Paul ties his remarks in both verses 24ff and 54ff to immediate implications for the readers. The apocalyptic vision in verses 24ff leads to the practical question of baptism (ἔπει) and the taunt song in verses 54ff results in the severely practical call to holiness of living (ὥστε). It seems clear, therefore, that Paul here is not aligning death with a series of hostile beings that he believes Christ to have conquered. He is concerned with a correct perception of the relation of the risen Lord to God, so that the Christian community may develop an appropriate response in its life within the new order that God has created and will ultimately confirm.

'The enemies' in Ps. 110 play no significant part in the thought of the earliest Christians, and they appear not to be important to Paul. The testimony of the psalm expresses and confirms the exaltation of Christ and therefore defines his present relationship with God. Far from this being interpreted in terms of a cosmic myth the verse was used to relate the present status of Christ at the right hand of God to the human experience of Christians and the demand of the gospel upon them. Above all, the persistent emphasis in the psalm and its use in the NT upon God as the subject of all the verbs undermines all attempts to support the notion of the Lordship of Christ expressed in terms of his achievement of a victory rather than through God's acceptance of him.

4

THE POWERS AND THE SPIRITUAL WORLD

1 Ephesians

The problem of the authorship of Ephesians is far more acute than that of Colossians. The question may for the time being be left in doubt, but this cannot be made an excuse for the omission of the epistle from a study of Pauline thought on the powers. In dealing with any theme of Pauline theology attention should at least be given to any common ground between the recognised writings and Ephesians. The present approach, therefore, will be to consider the subject of the powers and connected ideas in this epistle and then to compare the findings with Paul's writings elsewhere.

The heavenly world is mentioned frequently in the letter. The terms αἱ ἀρχαὶ καὶ αἱ ἐξουσίαι occur in three passages, each of which is an exegetical difficulty. In addition, the Devil appears under several guises, and the widespread language of τὰ ἐπουράνια and of οἱ οὐρανοί demands careful investigation.

(a) The heavenly places

Two terms for the heavenly world occur in Ephesians: τὰ ἐπουράνια is found in 1: 3, 20; 2: 6; 3: 10; and 6: 12. οἱ οὐρανοί occurs in 1: 10; 3: 15; 4: 10; and 5: 9. The latter is used for the heavens when they are simply contrasted spatially with the earth. Thus in 1: 10 the earth is specifically mentioned, and in 3: 15, where the image of 'families in heaven and earth' is introduced, the discussion is less about the organisation of the heavenly world than about the universality of God's fatherhood. In 5: 9 the heavens as the dwelling-place of God are implicitly contrasted with the earth. Only in 4: 10 does the reference appear to be different, and this is discussed in full below.

The term τὰ ἐπουράνια is of greater significance in the epistle. One question, since the term only occurs in the genitive and dative, is whether the neuter should be read (as has been assumed so far) or the masculine. It is not a serious problem. If the word were masculine, with presumably τόποι understood, this would resolve the greater difficulty of the meaning of the idea that is expressed in the phrase, but, as we have seen, the term in Phil. 2: 10 is most likely neuter, and it is probably correct also to take it so in Ephesians. The second question is whether the term is to be understood in a spatial or a spiritualised sense, and therefore whether it differs in any way from οἱ οὐρανοί. Ignatius joins it with τὰς τοποθεσίας τὰς ἀγγελικάς (*Trall.* 5. 2), where a topographical sense predominates. The word τοποθεσία generally keeps this meaning, as, for example, in the astrological writings of Vettius Valens (e.g. 42.12), where the reference is to the lay-out of the heavens.[1] In *Smyrn.* 6, however, τὰ ἐπουράνια are associated with ἡ δόξα τῶν ἀγγέλων καὶ οἱ ἄρχοντες and there can be little doubt that some personal notions are included. Since the word is never linked with a clarificatory phrase in Ephesians it is difficult to determine its exact reference. Odeberg has argued for a difference between τὰ ἐπουράνια and οἱ οὐρανοί and that this distinction is deliberately employed by the author. Since the believer already knows life ἐν τοῖς ἐπουρανίοις (2: 6 and 6: 12), there is a spiritualising of the phrase, which designates both heaven and the spiritual life in which the Church shares on earth. Spiritual blessing and warfare are the consequences of the Church's being in the heavenlies (1: 3 and 6: 12). Thus Christian existence in the heavenlies is in the realm where Christ's Lordship is exercised.[2] Against this Percy has argued that there is no difference between the two phrases, τὰ ἐπουράνια perhaps being more solemn and therefore liturgical.[3] Schlier, following Dibelius closely, offers 'die Himmel des Daseins' as a translation of τὰ ἐπουράνια, an idea that seems remote both from the language and from the period of the epistle.[4]

In both 1: 3 and 2: 6 it is the Christians who are concerned with the heavenlies, and this affords a convenient starting point from which to investigate the term. Since the discoveries at Qumran, it has been noted that there are apparent associations between the thought of the scrolls and that of Ephesians. Kuhn, for example, has shown that stylistically Ephesians contains four times more frequent use of semitic syntax than any Pauline epistle, and this is also a characteristic of the liturgical language of Qumran.[5] Other parallels of thought and expression, going beyond a merely religious similarity, have been noted. One such example is found in 2: 18ff, where the Church is pictured as the eschatological temple in which there is access to the Father. Although a line of development may be traced through the recognised Pauline epistles, there are sufficient new features in the image in Ephesians to cause one to look for associated ideas elsewhere.[6] The overall imagery is particularly elaborate, especially in the way in which the temple is related to Christ and its celestial character is worked out. A comparison between this and the thought on the celestial temple in the DSS lies not so much in the content of the image as in its function in its context. In 2: 18 the fundamental notion is that of access to any association with God. The ἀγίων in verse 19 are almost certainly the Christian saints rather than angels, but whichever view is taken the emphasis is still on access to God. At Qumran also the association of the earthly community with the heavenly is well attested. The heavenly angels are united with the community on earth and the elect on earth participate in the heavenly liturgy.[7] This parallel clarifies the passage in 2: 6. The bond between the Christian, a member of the community of the elect, and Christ is stressed by the συν- compound words: συνεζωοποίησεν, συνήγειρεν, συνεκάθισεν. The link between the earthbound saints and the heavenly host is no gnostic wish, but reflects the aspirations of a worshipping community, whether Christian or at Qumran. 'The meaning is that in the Risen Christ in the Church and as the Church they have been admitted into the existent heavenly regions, which are identical with the eschatological temple sanctuary.'[8] Parallels are sometimes drawn with the description in Phil. 3: 20 of the Christian citizenship in heaven. This is, however, irrelevant to Ephesians. In the former the stress is laid upon Christ's presence in heaven and upon the saints' membership of heaven, from which they are temporarily absent. In Ephesians there is a different emphasis on the presence of the Christians with Christ in the heavenly places. This leads to a relaxing of the eschatological tension such as might be expected in any Christology that so closely links the present Church with the present Christ.

This connection between the Church and Christ is one that is regularly explored in the NT. In Ephesians there are several significant points to note in this regard. A dynamic understanding of the Spirit is largely lacking; it is difficult to understand the Spirit in terms of Christian experience.[9] Some commentators have viewed the letter in terms of baptismal homily, but they seem to have overlooked the way in which the Spirit functions in this epistle. For while the Spirit is certainly associated with baptism in 4: 1ff, on the whole it is institutionalised as an accepted part of the life of the Church and scarcely shows signs of being a dynamic force. A short comparison between 1: 14 and the similar but not identical view in 2 Cor. 1: 21 is instructive. In 2 Corinthians the personal agency of God in dealing with Christians and the sealing of the Spirit as an experience (N.B. ἐν ταῖς καρδίαις ἡμῶν) is emphasised. By contrast, in Eph. 1: 13f the language is institutionalised into the building-up of religious terms, which removes the whole passage from the context of immediate experience. If we then turn to the relation between the Christian and Christ as this is explained in Ephesians, we find a large number of phrases based upon ἐν Χριστῷ. Yet of these, few seem close to the distinctively Pauline use, and his experiential sense gives way to a simple instrumental or causal dative with ἐν.[10]

The epistle to the Ephesians, then, answers the question of the relation between the Christian and Christ in a distinctive way. The author links heaven and earth by means of the Church, which he regards as larger than the local congregation, though not wholly so. The sense of ἐκκλησία from the LXX as 'community of Israel' begins to dominate as the Church is viewed in increasingly universal terms. τὰ ἐπουράνια, when used of Christians, functions in a 'Christological–local' sense. The community is viewed in idealistic terms as the assembly of the righteous and, as at Qumran, this community has direct access to heaven. Whereas at Qumran, however, the association with God is achieved by means of the purity of the congregation and the presence of the angels of holiness, in Ephesians it is only possible through the grace of God and the work of Christ.[11] The importance of the purity of the congregation in maintaining this relationship is well brought out in the paraenesis of the epistle, which is directed at community holiness. Indeed Eph. 5: 3ff could almost be derived from Qumran.[12]

The world view of Ephesians appears, therefore, to be twofold. There is the simple division of heaven and earth and a further differentiation between the abode of God, to which the saints have access, and the earthly community, one of whose tasks is the maintenance of its sanctity. In this context Odeberg rightly saw that the function of τὰ ἐπουράνια is to avoid a metaphysical dualism and to help sustain a moral dualism.[13] This we find in Ephesians expressed most explicitly in its Christology, which is concerned above all with the creation and preserving of the relation between the holy God and the holy people. τὰ ἐπουράνια functions in a 'figuratively local meaning',[14] and the problems that relate to it are very similar to those concerning the phrase 'the kingdom of God' in the Gospels. The language is spatial and concerned with locality, but at the same time it expounds a view of spheres of influence or authority. The occurrences in 3: 10 and 6: 12 are considered in detail below. The questions that they raise, however, do not run counter to the figuratively local sense that is here proposed, but are rather concerned with the nature of the occupants of such space. This understanding of the term, however, does raise the question of the divisions of the universe as they appear in the epistle.

It is sometimes suggested that the author assumes a complicated view of the heavens, such as was available in the first century A.D., especially in his reference to the struggle (6: 12) and to the prince of the power of the air (2: 2). The most significant passage that deals with the topography of the heavens is that in 4: 8ff, which refers to journeyings between heaven and earth. The division of the universe that the author here assumes is twofold and not, as is sometimes argued, threefold. The journey of Christ to which reference is made is not his descent at the incarnation followed by his ascension at the end of the earthly ministry. Rather, as is made clear in verses 9–11, the emphasis is upon the ascent followed by the descent, which is associated with his giving of gifts to men.[15] It is in this context that the reference to captives must be read. Clearly there is a stress on a reversal of roles in the testimony from Ps. 68, but any detailed exegesis is here omitted. The text itself is only employed for the words ἀνέβη and ἔδωκεν, while the remaining words are not expounded and the reference to αἰχμαλωσίαν is not made explicit. That there is no reference in the mind of the author to any victory over demonic forces seems clear from two pieces of evidence over and above this silence. In the first place, the location of Christ's activity is the earth. The argument concerns Christ's ascension, which is from the earth. The phrase τὰ κατώτερα τῆς γῆς includes a genitive of apposition and means the earth which is 'lower' in contrast to the heavens.[16] Secondly, any demonic forces that might appear in the epistle, notably in 6: 12 which is discussed below at length, are not found on or under the earth but in the heavenly regions themselves.

Once it is realised that for the author of Ephesians the crucial division is between heaven and earth, then all discussion of whether there are many heavens and of their specific relation to men becomes irrelevant. The phrase ὑπεράνω πάντων τῶν οὐρανῶν in 4: 10 implies that the writer was aware of a multi-heavened cosmology, but the real point of note is that it plays no part in his theology. This observation is itself important, since it means that even when a writer was aware of contemporary cosmology and acknowledged it in passing, it was not necessarily normative for his thinking. The reason for this in the case of the author of Ephesians is undoubtedly because his main theme is that of the relation of the community to God, which may be expressed in terms of the earthly and the heavenly, and understood, as here in 4: 8ff, on the simple model of the work of Christ. It was this, expressed in terms of a twofold division of heaven (God) and earth (man), that determined the cosmology, rather than the cosmology that gave content to the work of Christ.

The key, therefore, to understanding τὰ ἐπουράνια in Ephesians is to be found in the recognition that the author begins from the fact of the ascended Christ and the fact of the Christian community on earth. With this twofold division and the relationship between the two parts goes a twofold division of the cosmos into the heavenlies, where Christ is, and the earth, where the Church must live. But because of the inseparability of

Christ and the Church, and of the heavenly host and the people of God, which is realised most fully in worship, τὰ ἐπουράνια are also the sphere in which Christians live their lives. This is what is meant by our definition of the term as 'figuratively local' or 'Christologically local'.[17] The implications of this for the angelology and demonology of the letter are considerable. For, just as the author, although apparently aware of cosmological theory, leaves it aside in favour of his Christologically determined world view, it would seem likely that any reference to angels or evil powers will function to achieve the same end alone, namely the glorification of Christ. The evidence must now be assessed.

(b) The powers

Specific references to αἱ ἀρχαὶ καὶ αἱ ἐξουσίαι occur in three passages. In 1: 21 a citation of Ps. 110: 1 is expanded, apparently to emphasise the glory of the exalted Christ, who is now seated at the right hand of God in the heavenly places. The usual plural phrase gives place to a collective singular, which should be translated 'above all rule, all authority, all power and lordship, above every name that may be named for all eternity'. There are four reasons for this. First, ὑπεράνω is an improper preposition that approximates to ὑπέρ. Although it clearly has a spatial sense in Heb. 9: 5 and also probably in Eph. 4: 10 (which are the only occurrences apart from the present context in the NT), its use in terms of rank and power is well attested. It does not mean that Christ is seated spatially above the powers of the lower heavens, which would be to assume an interest in cosmology that the epistle does not show, but that Christ's authority is greater than any other authority. Secondly, the collective singular with πᾶσα may legitimately mean either every principality in a personal sense or the abstract notion of all rule and authority. Thirdly, as has been demonstrated above, the heavenly session of Christ is not the same as a victory over opposing forces. Ps. 110: 1 is always used to stress the glorified presence of Christ with God, as here, and does not refer to some act of Christ in defeating his enemies. Lastly, the idea of the subjugation of all things to Christ is made explicit in this passage by the quotation of Ps. 8: 6 in verse 22. This is a second notion, distinct from the first, as is shown by the insertion of καί and by the development in verse 22 of the theme of τὰ πάντα, which is taken from Ps. 8. The sequence of thought, therefore, is twofold: the glory of Christ and his acceptance by God is expressed through the testimony of Ps. 110; the subjugation of all things to Christ is expressed by the development of Ps. 8. It would therefore appear unlikely that the reference here is to personalised spiritual powers.

There is no real parallel with Col. 1: 16, where the terms are both different and plural, as well as part of 'all things', in the creation of which Christ shared. The language in Eph. 1: 21 functions simply to contrast Christ's authority with all other authority. This thought may be paralleled in Col. 2: 10. If, however, some sort of personal sense is insisted upon in this context, we may only perceive in them, as in Colossians, the heavenly host. There is no mention of a victory by Christ or of a conquest of the powers. One final point, however, confirms that the personalised interpretation is improbable: the term ὄνομα is included. In the OT and NT the name, especially that of God or Christ, has its own power. Always, however, when the name is so understood there is an explanatory phrase attached to the word. When used absolutely, as here, it would appear to mean 'title' or 'dignity' in an abstract sense, and this would also encourage a similar abstract sense for the other terms in this list. Personality is not an obvious mark.[18]

The second occurrence, that in 3: 10, immediately calls to mind 1 Pet. 1: 10ff, especially 12. Many commentators remark on the similarities between the passages, although the only real parallel lies in the temporal contrast between past and present and the mention of spiritual beings – αἱ ἀρχαὶ καὶ αἱ ἐξουσίαι in Ephesians and ἄγγελοι in 1 Peter. Numerous parallels may be found in Jewish and Christian literature for the idea of the heavenly hosts looking with wonder upon the world of men and God's involvement in it.[19] It would seem, therefore, that the powers here are most likely to be the hosts of heaven. The expression here in any case is too gentle for the notion of hostility between on the one hand God and his Church and on the other the hosts of evil. The work of God has a gloriously intricate design (πολυποίκιλος), which becomes apparent to the watchers through the centre of the pattern, i.e. the redeemed people of God. ἐν τοῖς ἐπουρανίοις is probably used unusually here as a synonym for ἐν τοῖς οὐρανοῖς as the locus of God's dwelling, around which the angels stand. With the two prepositional phrases, however, it might be possible to take the phrase more closely with γνωρισθῇ, thus making it refer to the locus of the revelation itself. If so, we would maintain here the close link implicit in this phrase between the heavenly Christ and the earthly community, although this construction is perhaps a little difficult.

The third mention of the powers, that in 6: 12, will be discussed fully below. It offers a view that is unique in Ephesians, which otherwise in its language of the powers conforms to the use in Colossians. They are the hosts of God at worship and in adoration, and not hostile cosmic forces.

(c) The prince of the power of the air

The reference in 2: 2 is unique and so problematical that it deserves careful treatment in any study of the powers in Ephesians. The verse occurs in a description of the old way of life in which the Christians engaged before their conversion. Structurally the verse seems to be composed from three parallel phrases:

1.   κατὰ τὸν αἰῶνα τοῦ κόσμου τούτου
2.   κατὰ τὸν ἄρχοντα τῆς ἐξουσίας τοῦ ἀέρος
3.   τοῦ πνεύματος τοῦ νῦν ἐνεργοῦντος ἐν τοῖς υἱοῖς τῆς ἀπειθείας

The first two prepositional phrases flow together, and it might be argued that the meaning to be given to αἰών depends on that attributed to ἄρχων. Since the latter is clearly personal, it might be inferred that we have here a reference to a personal aeon, and the link is then sometimes made with the myth of Aeon.[20] This particular myth, however, dates from the second century A.D., and its occurrence here, which is unparalleled in the NT, would mean that Ephesians would have to be given a very late date.[21] The use of the word covers a wide range of meanings. 'Aion is a term of fluid sense, popular perhaps because of the vague suggestion of the unknowable.'[22] Its use in a philosophical and political sense is well attested, but evidence for a personal use is lacking. The boundary between hypostatisation and personification is often hard to define.[23]

In the NT there are two, possibly three, meanings for the word. There is the sense of a long, usually unlimited, period of time, in which the plural has no different connotation from the singular. There is a second sense in which it stands for an age of history, the meaning that is the most common Pauline use. The third possible use is that found in Heb. 1: 2 and 11: 3, where the plural seems to refer to the whole universe, as also perhaps in Ignatius, *Eph.* 19.2. The second meaning seems most apposite in Eph. 2: 2. The conjunction of αἰών and κόσμος recalls 1 Cor. 1: 20, where the words are synonyms. For Paul the contrast between the two ages cannot be separated from the moral implications of life in the coming age. This is clear in the paraenesis of the epistles, in which eschatology and ethics are inseparable. The temporal root of αἰών, then, is connected with the moral consequences of life in the two ages. It is into this area of thought that the first phrase in Eph. 2: 2 falls. The plural 'sins' suggests a reference to actual wrong-doing and moral failure, rather than a theological statement about man's status before God. This style of life was the characteristic of the first aeon. It is this that gives αἰών its meaning, which does not depend on the meaning or presence of ἄρχων in the second phrase. It should be noted that when one half of a parallel is personal, it does not follow that the other term must necessarily be so understood. We may instance Col. 2:8, where, as we have shown, τὰ στοιχεῖα are not to be taken as personal terms simply because they are contrasted with Christ.

The second phrase is much more difficult to interpret. The first question is how the double genitive is to be taken, and upon the answer to this depends in part how we take the following genitival phrase τοῦ πνεύματος κ.τ.λ. There appear to be four possibilities. First, ἐξουσία may be understood collectively as ἐξουσίαι, in which case τοῦ ἀέρος will express the area of their authority. There are examples of collective nouns being so used, but none in the case of a word like ἐξουσία, which is not obviously collective. The plural is so well attested that we must reckon that the author would have used it if he had so intended the phrase to be understood. An alternative is to take τῆς ἐξουσίας as a genitive in apposition to τὸν ἄρχοντα. In this case the latter would be intensified: 'the powerful ruler of the air'. This would divide the genitives from each other, which, if not impossible, does not give as impressive a sense as the Greek seems to imply. If, however, ἐξουσία were taken to mean not 'power' but 'sphere of authority', the phrase would translate thus: 'the ruler whose sphere of authority is the air', thus localising the power of this being. ἐξουσία will then be understood in a local sense, as, perhaps, in Col. 1:13. Lastly we may take the whole phrase τῆς ἐξουσίας τοῦ ἀέρος as a unit in genitival apposition to τὸν ἄρχοντα. The meaning then produced would be 'the ruler whose source of might is in the air'. There is not a great deal of difference between this and the previous suggestion. Before we attempt to decide between these, the word ἀέρος requires attention.

Many commentators claim that it was a commonplace of the age that the air was ruled by hostile demons. There is indeed considerable evidence for this, and Judaism increasingly shared this belief. But the actual nature of the belief requires careful attention.[24] Evidence for its existence in hellenistic Judaism is often assumed in Philo, *de gig.* 6: οὓς ἄλλοι φιλόσοφοι δαίμονας, ἀγγέλους Μωϋσῆς εἴωθεν ὀνομάζειν· ψυχαὶ δ᾽ εἰσιν κατὰ τὸν ἀέρα πετόμεναι. The context in Ephesians, however, is quite different from this. Philo is arguing that since each of the four physical elements contains life, it is obvious that the air itself must contain life, even though such life is invisible. This life consists of the souls that serve their Creator, and of all manner of good and bad souls and angels. If a man will accept this mixture, he may live a life free from fear. Philo's speculative deductions from his premise of life in each of the physical elements are very different from the notion of the hostile prince of the power of the air in Ephesians.

In 2 En. 29: 4 Satanael is described as flying continually in the air above the abyss.[25] Other instances that are commonly cited are of no value as evidence. In Test. Benj. 3 the reading is very doubtful: τὸν πλησίον ὑπὸ τοῦ ἀερίου πνεύματος τοῦ βελιάρ. Asc. Is. 7 contains the remark that 'we ascended into the firmament and there I beheld Samael and his powers'.[26] Both passages, however, are of uncertain date, and the possibility of their being interpretations of Ephesians cannot be ruled out. There is, finally, an association of the demon of the air with Fate in a Jewish magical papyrus in which Adam prays ὑπεράσπισόν μου πρὸς πᾶσαν ὑπεροχὴν ἐξουσίας δαίμονος ἀε[ρί]ου [καὶ εἰ] μαρμένης. It may be that this reflects a Zoroastrian idea that Fate is itself the air.[27] This text, however, certainly postdates Ephesians. This is the sum of the evidence for the concept of a kingdom of evil in the air in the first century A.D. There is certainly no evidence for a widespread Jewish belief.[28] Although the air was believed to be alive with life, this life was not considered to be hostile until later than the probable date of Ephesians. Despite the rich variety of Jewish and pagan demonology, there is no evidence for a belief in a kingdom of evil in the air, ruled over by its own powerful ruler. This expression in Ephesians, therefore, is unique, but we cannot expect it to yield its meaning if it is simply read as ὁ ἄρχων τοῦ ἀερος.

In many interpretations the idea of ἐξουσία as a collective noun has influenced the commentators. This has led to a hunt for spiritual forces in the air and parallels being drawn between 2: 2 and 6: 12. But the context of each passage is entirely different. In 2: 2 the author is describing the situation of men before their conversion. He has described this in the conventional Christian language of the two ages, but the enormity of the evil (παραπτώμασιν καὶ ἁμαρτίαις), which is very clear to him from his standpoint within the community of the holy elect, requires an awareness of its magnitude that may only be expressed in personal language. Of men this description occurs in 'the sons of disobedience', whilst of evil it is achieved in terms of a personalised power of evil. The DSS have already proved a fruitful area for parallel ideas to those in Ephesians. In the War Scroll we find a theological interpretation of war in terms of the two Spirits of Light and of Darkness. Evil is always associated with Belial, who is the chief adversary of the sons and angels of light. His function is threefold: he is God's adversary (IQS 2: 5); he is the tempter and seducer of men (IQS 3: 20); and he is the prince of the spirits (IQS 3: 23).[29] Similar ideas may be found in Jubilees, 2 Enoch and the Testaments of the Twelve Patriarchs. It is exactly this Belial who is described in Ephesians. He is God's adversary, who stirs men to disobedience, although this is not his most important function here. He is clearly the tempter and seducer of men (ἐνεργοῦντος), and he is, as ὁ ἄρχων, a prince, presumably of spirits.

In the light of this we may consider the third phrase. The doctrine of the two spirits from Qumran may illuminate this. At Qumran this doctrine is generally viewed less in cosmic than in psychological terms.[30] This we also find in Eph. 2: 2. Having viewed the world in terms of the two ages, and in terms of the power of evil, the author sums up with a reference to the psychological importance of evil. ἀπειθεία is something to which a man might be tempted, which produces a psychological state that issues in moral depravity. Possibly τοῦ πνεύματος is dependent upon τὸν ἄρχοντα, but this is difficult.[31] It is also strange to take it with τῆς ἐξουσίας or with τοῦ ἀέρος. Perhaps the best solution, which itself is not perfect, is to regard it as an unconscious assimilation to the preceding genitives. So understood, the phrase stands for a third interpretation of the evil way of life of the Ephesians before their conversion.

In attempting to find a meaning for the phrase 'the prince of the power of the air', it is important to recognise that the air is not the key to the verse. Certainly it cannot be taken as a spiritualised version of the Homeric meaning of 'darkness'.[32] Its importance lies in terms not of locality but of universality. This e.g. is for Philo the most significant aspect of the air when compared with the other three physical elements. Whereas they are always localised, the air, because it is unseen, is never so.[33] We should also recall that in Ephesians, as we have seen, there is no particular cosmological concern, and the air as the lowest of heavens would seem not to be in mind. The interpretation of this obscure phrase seems best against a Jewish background. There are two well-known instances when Satan is described in terms of his universal presence. In 2 En. 29: 4 Satanael flies to and fro over the earth, omnipresent and tempting man to evil. In Job 1: 7 the same point is made about Satan even earlier in his career. He emphasises before God his universal movement; he is inescapable. The phrase in Ephesians may represent a similar stress. Satan is often described as 'the ruler' in the NT and the genitive τῆς ἐξουσίας may define the nature of his rule. The addition of τοῦ ἀέρος, while no doubt clumsy, serves to define that power, but in so doing it does not confine it to the sphere of the physical air, but liberates it, as in the case of Satan and of Satanael, into universality. The translation then must be a paraphrase: 'The prince whose power is universal and inescapable'. The whole verse creates a total picture of the pre-conversion depravity of the Ephesians:

> 'You were dead in your trespasses and your sins. Once upon a time you lived your life in such sins according to the ways of the old age, the age of this world, according to the devil, the prince whose power is universal and inescapable, according to that spirit which is even now at work in the apostates and moral failures among us.'

Eph. 2: 2, then, does not conjure up a picture of a kingdom of evil forces in the air, ruled over by Satan. Rather it concentrates evil, when conceived in personal terms, in the one being. The description of him here is obscure, but on the whole it conforms to the figure of Belial at Qumran and similar figures in the Jewish apocryphal writings. There is certainly nothing specifically gnostic or non-Jewish in this description, which in its background accords with what has already been noted for the book, *viz.* that it has strong affinities with the style of Judaism evidenced in the DSS.

(d) The struggle

The passage in 6: 12ff abounds with problems and is in several ways remarkable. If the letter is taken to be Pauline, the use of the word διάβολος is unique, although it is common enough in the Gospels and deutero-Pauline epistles. It is also noteworthy that αἱ ἀρχαὶ καὶ αἱ ἐξουσίαι are undoubtedly malevolent, hostile powers here, and no alternative view is possible. The Christian has to struggle against them, which is itself a novel idea. The word κοσμοκράτορες also occurs for the only time in the NT. τὰ πνευματικὰ τῆς πονηρίας is a strange phrase; the genitive is not difficult, but one might have expected a noun, τὰ πνεύματα, instead of the adjective. τὰ ἐπουράνια as the area of effectiveness of these forces is wholly at variance with the other occurrences of the phrase in Ephesians. That this problem was felt at an early stage may be seen from the reading in the Peshitta, which must represent ὑπουρανίοις. The evidence of the third-century MS 𝔓⁴⁶ which omits the phrase, may simply be a mistake or an attempt by the scribe to correct an error.[34] Although not unparalleled (see Heb. 2: 14), the order of words in the phrase αἷμα καὶ σάρξ is unusual. Finally, the sudden appearance here in the NT of an otherwise rare description of the Christian life in military terms, and its equally sudden disappearance in the Apostolic Fathers, is noticeable. These peculiarities are of varying significance, but for so short a passage the list is notable.

There are several uses of the military metaphor in the NT, and it re-appears later in Origen, Tertullian and Cyprian. Significantly in Eph. 6: 11ff, however, the military picture is mixed with that of the struggle.[35] Normally the language of the soldier is restricted in the NT to the apostles and their immediate associates. Thus e.g. the metaphor in 2 Cor. 10: 3ff describes the work of an apostle in its totality. The agon-motif was common in the hellenistic world, especially in the Stoic writers, and it not surprisingly features in the NT. What is remarkable is that so little use is made of it. The reason for this possibly lies in two major weaknesses in the metaphor. In the first place, the standard application is to the self-sufficiency of the soldier.

'The image of the soldier is used in connection with the man who bears all the vicissitudes of fate in a manly fashion, who wages war with his passions resolutely, who even rejoices in misfortune like a soldier in war, who accepts all ordeals as orders, who bears all setbacks like a soldier does his wounds, and who is capable of such conduct because he has made his interior life an impregnable fortress.'[36]

Despite many obvious points of similarity between this call to endurance and the Christian vocation of perseverance, it is the last remark to which the Christian gospel might take greatest exception. Indeed, such self-sufficiency is expressly resisted in Eph. 6: 10, where the might of God as a source for Christian living is emphasised. The second weakness of the metaphor lies in the Jewish apocalyptic tradition, in which the struggle tends to be removed from a human plane to the cosmic. The consequence of this may be a relaxation of moral effort that would be particularly incompatible with the gospel. A clear illustration of this can be found in the Judaeo-Christian tradition of the *Mandates of Hermas*. In *Mand.* 5 the righteous and evil spirits are described as contending in man, while in *Mand.* 6 they have become two angels that contend in his heart. In *Mand.* 12, however, the two forces have been personalised and externalised, and the language becomes that of a battle. What was first seen psychologically has become cosmic, and therefore at the same time is less immediate to man.[37] From the point of view of the Christian gospel the struggle cannot be based upon man's self-sufficiency nor may it be removed to realms outside him. The military metaphor, therefore, may be dangerously misleading, and this probably explains why the writers of the NT avoid it.

Eph. 6: 11ff, then, is unique in its use of the metaphor. It is consistent with the rest of the NT, however, in that the warfare described is based upon Christ's victory through obedience, so that the concepts, both of an earthly battle and of a struggle between an isolated individual and the force of destiny, are excluded. The language employed reflects this; for, as has often been observed, the description of the soldier and his armour is given primarily in terms of defence and not of offence.[38] The emphasis is upon the endurance of the Christian in the face of all danger, and the context is not cosmical–magical, but ethical.[39] The battle that is described is a religious and moral contest, and is set in the context of God's strength (verse 10) and of prayer (verse 18). This is further brought out by citations from the OT regarding the divine warrior, in the light of which the phrase ἡ πανοπλία τοῦ θεοῦ should be interpreted as 'the armour which belongs to God'. The Christian is perceived to share the same armour as that worn by the divine champion. It is important to note, however, that although there

are affinities between this description and that of the divine warrior in Is.
59: 14ff and Wisd. 5: 17ff, there is a fundamental difference: the divine
warrior is an avenging presence, whose task it is to attack evil in the world;
the Christian, on the other hand, is to stand firm in defence. The passage,
then, does not directly depend upon these texts from the OT, but is
reminiscent of them. They have been taken over and given a new direction.
Thus e.g. Is. 9: 5 (LXX) is apposite to the matter of the girdle. This was
used as a messianic text, but here it is transferred to believers. Again, the
description of the boots in this context might be related to the Roman
caliga, although Is. 52: 7 refers to the light feet of the messenger.

In the context of these preliminary remarks, we may turn to the specific
problem of verse 12. The attack that the Christian is to withstand is, in the
first place, from the wiles of the Devil. The word $\mu\epsilon\theta o\delta\acute{\iota}a$ is found in the
NT only here and in 4: 14, where it is coupled with $\pi\lambda\acute{a}\nu\eta$. The clear
meaning there is 'insidious wiles', and this is to be retained in the present
passage. It is coupled with $\delta\iota\acute{a}\beta o\lambda o\varsigma$, a term found only here, at Eph. 4: 27,
and in the Pastorals, among the letters associated with Paul. If the back-
ground to Ephesians may be seen in the Qumranic type of thinking, the
interpretation of 'Devil' should first be attempted in the light of the figure
of Belial. There is a difficulty here in that, although the life of that community was to some extent seen as a struggle between the forces of evil
and of God, nowhere is there so detailed a description as that in Eph. 6.[40]
On the other hand, the various views of the Devil that are found in
Judaism and in Qumran mean that almost any meaning and function may
be ascribed to him in terms of evil.[41] $\acute{o}$ $\delta\iota\acute{a}\beta o\lambda o\varsigma$ here is probably the same
being as that in 2: 2. It would appear that his work as tempter and seducer
of men is emphasised by the addition of $\mu\epsilon\theta o\delta\acute{\iota}a\varsigma$, as also in 4: 27.

The comparative clarity of this and its connection with what precedes it
(verse 11) and with what follows (verses 13ff) only serve to highlight the
obscurity of verse 12. That during the transmission of the text various
difficulties have been felt is clear from the textual variants. There is a
change of subject temporarily from the second to the first person. Whereas
verses 6ff and 13ff constitute exhortations to the readers of the letter, the
text here moves to the first person. Not surprisingly, therefore, the alter-
native reading $\acute{v}\mu\^{\iota}\nu$ is supported in $\mathfrak{P}^{46}$ B D* G and the Peshitta. In
addition, the insertion of $\mu\epsilon\theta o\delta\acute{\iota}a\varsigma$ after $\acute{\epsilon}\xi o\upsilon\sigma\acute{\iota}a\varsigma$ in $\mathfrak{P}^{46}$ would appear to
be more than a slip of the pen. It may represent a weak attempt to
harmonise this verse with verse 11, although it is difficult to judge. In
K L P the insertion of $\tau o\^{\upsilon}$ $a\acute{\iota}\^{\omega}\nu o\varsigma$ after $\sigma\kappa\acute{o}\tau o\upsilon\varsigma$ is well attested, and the
intention would appear to be to make explicit in the verse the eschato-
logical nature of the conflict. Finally, $\mathfrak{P}^{46}$ omits $\acute{\epsilon}\nu$ $\tau o\^{\iota}\varsigma$ $\acute{\epsilon}\pi o\upsilon\rho a\nu\acute{\iota}o\iota\varsigma$,

perhaps finding it inconsistent with the other uses of the phrase in the epistle. Certain other readings suggest ὑπουρανίοις or ὑποκάτω τῶν οὐρανῶν, thus evidencing some uncertainty about the sense of the text.

This variety of readings alone suggests that the verse has long been a problem. If the struggle is one of the Christian standing firm in the face of the assaults of the Devil, then verse 12 must be regarded as an amplification of this idea. It does not represent the offensive aspect of the struggle, as compared with the defensive side, which is discussed in verse 11. The preposition πρός does not carry the concept of attack, but serves simply to introduce the opponent. A good example of such a use may be found in Philo, *de sobr.* 65: ὁ τὴν πρὸς πάθη πάλην γεγυμνασμένος.

There are further difficulties. We have already noted that the powers here are, for the only time in the Pauline and deutero-Pauline corpus, explicitly evil. It is also worth noting the absence of the copula, which suggests that this is not an example of the Pauline couplet. Also for the only time in the NT the word κοσμοκράτωρ occurs. The term is not found in the LXX or in Philo, although as a loan word it is found in the rabbinic writings.[42] There is very little evidence for its existence prior to the second century, when it appears in gnostic texts and astrological writings, in which it is applied to Zeus or to the Sun. The first use of this word for a human ruler does not occur until the third century, when it is applied to the Roman emperor. Certain gnostics used it to refer to Satan as the Demiurge, but they appear to have avoided the astrological sense.[43] Unless, then, we are to place Ephesians well into the second century, we here have apparently the earliest attested occurrence of the word. In this case it might be understood through its component parts on analogy with παντο-κράτωρ: κόσμος is the world without God, and κρατέω refers to the power of the forces ranged against the Christians.[44] It is contrasted with 'blood and flesh', a phrase that stresses the impotence of man.[45] The κοσμοκράτορες represent the seriousness of the situation and the terrifying power of the forces ranged against the believer.[46]

The final problem is τὰ πνευματικὰ τῆς πονηρίας. The use of τὰ πνευματικά in the sense of 'spiritual forces' is unique in the NT.[47] Equally unusual is the reference to evil in the heavenly places.[48] As it stands it is difficult to relate this reference to the heavens to those elsewhere in the epistle.[49] Abbott argues that τὰ πνευματικά is related not to πνεύματα but to πνεῦμα, and emphasises that the term must be strictly neuter, i.e. 'spiritual forces or elements' rather than 'spiritual armies or hosts'.[50] But in the context of such nouns as ἀρχαί, ἐξουσίαι and κοσμοκράτορες one wonders whether the point may be pressed. It may be that the phrase in this passage again indicates belief in the two spirits. In Hermas, *Mand.* 6.2

there is mention of ὁ ἄγγελος τῆς πονηρίας. It may be that τὰ πνευματικὰ τῆς πονηρίας means not 'a host of wicked beings' but 'the powers (impersonal) of the angel of wickedness', the angelic aspect being covered by the reference to the heavenly places. If this were so, τὰ ἐπουράνια would correspond to its use elsewhere in the epistle. There is an obvious emphasis on πονηρία in this section of the letter, as in τῇ ἡμέρα τῇ πονηρᾷ (13),[51] and τὰ βέλη τοῦ πονηροῦ (16). In the latter text the word is masculine, referring to the Devil.

It is of interest that the Christian's struggle against the forces of evil seems to play no part in the earliest understandings of the meaning of church membership. Eph. 6: 12 is quoted by Clement of Alexandria, but prior to this the nearest passage is perhaps Ignatius, *Eph.* 13.2, where he refers to a heavenly and an earthly warfare. This cannot be considered as a specific allusion to this verse in Ephesians, for the spiritual forces are significantly absent, although they intruded into the longer text.[52]

In view of the intrusive nature of verse 12 into the context of Ephesians 6 and in view of the numerous problems that it presents, which admit of no obvious or satisfactory solution, we are justified in asking whether it was part of the original text. The unique reference in the Pauline literature to the hostility of powers does not even fit into the epistle to the Ephesians. There is also no attempt to explain what these powers might be, and the assumption is that they are well known to the readers of the letter. Nor is the nature of the struggle clear. It might be argued that it reflects the Qumranic notion of a war between the sons of light and the sons of darkness, but in that war the struggle is between men and men and, on the spiritual plain, between the angels of God and of Belial. The community on earth does not fight the heavenly forces, but the angelic forces of heaven stand with the earthly community in its earthly struggle. In Ephesians, however, the Christians are on their own and depend upon God, while the exact nature of the struggle remains obscure. If, however, verse 12 were omitted, the struggle becomes part of the paraenesis, in which the faithful are called to holiness and warned against the wiles of the Evil One.

As has been noted, it is very hard to find a place in the first century for much of the language of this verse alone of all the epistle. The association of the ἀρχαὶ, ἐξουσίαι and κοσμοκράτορες with ὁ διάβολος is foreign to the NT and its background; the introduction of the κοσμοκράτορες is especially suspect. The nearest traceable occurrence of the word occurs in Irenaeus' account of the teaching of the Valentinians (*adv haer.* 1.5.4), which would appear to contain a direct reference to Eph. 6: 12. Not only does κοσμοκράτωρ occur, but it is also directly connected with τὰ πνευματικὰ τῆς πονηρίας. But it is specially worth noting that in the text from Irenaeus the problem of the presence of the ruler in the heavens is appreciated, and a more consistent arrangement is made, whereby he has his domain among men, while his creator, the Demiurge, inhabits the heavenly places. In this context the word κοσμοκράτωρ is understood from its parts: the Devil is the lord of the World. In the NT he is given exactly this title in Jn. 14: 30, but this singular use is quite different from the plural in Ephesians. Within the Judaeo-Christian tradition the application of this description to one maleficent being is not unusual. The plural, however, is another matter. In this respect and in view of the development of the word in pagan sources, Eph. 6: 12 gives the appearance of a later development of the identification of the one Devil in terms of κοσμοκράτωρ under the influence of pagan notions of pluriform evil in the world. There are, therefore, two possible solutions to the problem of this verse in Ephesians. On the one hand, if the Valentinians cited by Irenaeus were using Eph. 6: 12, the presupposition must be that the verse was in the text and its extraordinary and intractable nature must be acknowledged. There is, however, a second possibility, namely that the type of teaching that is characteristic of the Valentinian gnostics provides the source for the verse in Eph. 6: 12. The verse was accepted by Clement without difficulty at the end of the second century (e.g. *Strom.* 3.101.3; 5.93.2), but the language does not fit the first century. It is possible that the verse was interpolated into Ephesians at a time when the word κοσμοκράτορες was in use and when belief in the presence of hostile forces within man's environment was increasing and yet early enough for the verse to be settled in the text by the end of the second century. Some time about the middle of the second century or just prior to it fits exactly these requirements.

If the verse is omitted, Ephesians stands as a theological unity. The life of the Christian community is to be one of purity and holiness in unity, and this is based upon the function of the community to hold together the life of the heavens and life on earth. The unity is that of the one Spirit, not that of two (see 4: 3f), whereas the aim of the Devil and his wiles is to establish the fact of two spirits and thus disrupt this unity. If we attempt to explain 6: 12 in terms of a host of spiritual forces under the command of this Devil, we create all the problems that have been listed above. In particular, there is the problem of the Devil's independence of the κοσμο-κράτορες; for they are clearly seen as powers in their own right, neither having nor requiring according to the text any commander. And, as we have noted, the text in Irenaeus uses the word in the singular of the Devil himself, and even as late as the third century the κοσμοκράτορες are conceived as powers in their own right and not as subordinates.[53]

How such a verse came to be incorporated into the text of Ephesians at this point is, in the light of Irenaeus' account of Valentinianism, not difficult to explain. The thought is typical of second-century gnosticism and the way in which it developed this type of language. Without the verse, Ephesians may stand with ease in the first century. Indeed, if the relationship between the thought of the epistle and that of the DSS is as close as has been suggested, it is essential that the letter is placed somewhere in the lifetime of Paul himself or only slightly later.[54] Paul's understanding of the powers as the hosts of heaven was accepted without difficulty during his ministry, if our interpretation of Colossians is accurate. It conformed to the Jewish background against which Christianity began to understand itself and it was not capable of confusion with any pagan understanding of demons and the like. The very period, however, in which gnosticism developed within the Christian Church and in which the world began to interpret some of its experience in terms of the oppression of hostile forces, was the very period in which the letters of Paul were being read apart from their context and in which they appear to have exercised less influence than perhaps at any other time in their history.[55] The style and type of language that we find in Eph. 6: 12 began to develop from this time onwards and indeed the verse subsequently became a very popular description of the Christian life.

It is only with the greatest hesitation that one would suggest interpolation, especially without any strong textual support. However, in the light of the evidence produced we are justified in surmising that in this verse there is an early example of tendencies and thought that, though foreign to the first century, and certainly to Paul, are typical of the second century and were later of considerable significance. This verse was incorporated into Ephesians in the first half of the second century so that it was fully accepted by the end.[56]

(e) Conclusion

The tendency in Ephesians is towards a dualistic view of the world, which is both cosmological and moral. As has been noted, the Christology of Ephesians determines its cosmology, and so inevitably Christology is associated with ethics in a striking way. The twofold division of the world into heaven and earth corresponds to the division of life into two ways – the heavenly and the earthly. This thinking is expounded in particular in 4: 8ff, where the twofold division of the universe (4: 10), the activity and person of Christ (4: 8f), and the moral implications of this (4: 11ff, expecially verse 15), all interact. The heavenly does not become a way of escape from the earthly, but the two are linked through the association of

Christ and the Church. The community functions as the link between the exalted Christ in the heavens and the life of the saints on earth. Through the grace of God, a man, when he believes in Christ, is transferred from the earthly realm to the heavenly, through his membership of the body (e.g. 2: 6ff; 18ff; 3: 10). In this way the body itself becomes an earthly witness to the angelic hosts of the work of God among men at the same time as it associates with them and the exalted Christ in the heavens. Ephesians heightens this style of thought to a degree that is not elsewhere evidenced in the NT.

With regard to the understanding of the powers, only one writer appears to have noticed a crucial difference between the language of Colossians and Ephesians. D. E. Nineham has commented that whereas the powers in Colossians are morally neutral, at the end of Ephesians they are essentially evil in themselves.[57] Yet, as we have seen, the difficulties relating to the powers in Ephesians are all concentrated in 6: 12. Without this reference they function in a similar way to those in Colossians, i.e. they appear as the hosts of God, in Colossians rejoicing in the triumphal return of their Lord and in Ephesians gazing in admiration at the manifold wisdom of God. If this verse is regarded as integral to the epistle, however, many difficulties ensue. We are required to see two different meanings in the mere five occurrences of τὰ ἐπουράνια in the epistle. We also require two meanings for αἱ ἀρχαὶ καὶ αἱ ἐξουσίαι, for it is difficult in the light of the evidence to construe them consistently as evil in this letter. In this case, too, we must see in this aspect of the thought of the epistle a misunderstanding of Colossians. In Ephesians the powers are primarily conceived in Jewish terms. The twofold world view, the unity of which is focused in the community itself, is very similar to the ideas of the sectaries of Qumran. Looked at in this light the heavenlies, the Devil, the ruler of the power of the air, and the struggle, all fit well together. None of these notions necessarily has any origin in gnostic speculation, but all are rooted in Judaism. This survey, then, would encourage a date in the first century for the letter, providing only we allow the theory of interpolation in 6: 12. On the question of authorship there is nothing to add. While the internal evidence would allow a date within Paul's lifetime, some of the forms of expression and content still suggest non-Pauline authorship.

For our present study, however, Ephesians is useful in showing that the Pauline understanding of the powers may not have been confined to him alone at an early stage of Christian history. The development of these ideas, which we shall later examine further in detail, may perhaps already be discerned in 6: 12.

2 Romans 8: 38f

Apart from the reference to angels and powers, Rom. 8: 38f raises two questions on Paul's understanding of the spirit-world: the first is the meaning of δυνάμεις and the second the relevance of astrological language and thinking for him. The context of this text is significant. Paul, having worked through some of the implications of Christian experience and their meaning for the whole creation, concludes with a semi-doxological affirmation of the invincibility of God's love. In such a conclusion we should scarcely expect the introduction of new concepts. Rather we may assume that he is using ideas that were familiar to his readers and to which they could respond.

The catalogue of forces consists of four pairs into which the isolated δυνάμεις intrudes, which is summarised in the phrase 'no other creature'. The conjunction οὔτε is not disjunctive but correlative, and the pairs are piled together for cumulative effect.[58] Thus life and death stand for human experience when viewed in terms of its ultimates; angels and principalities cover aspects of God's relation to man;[59] the other two pairs cover the spatio-temporal dimensions. The conjunction, therefore, is of considerable significance; not only does it create the cumulative and not comparative list, but it also functions in the same way with each half of each pair. Life is not opposed to death, nor is the present contrasted with the future. Similarly the more controversial pairings of angels and powers and height and depth must be read in the same way, conjunctively and not disjunctively.

In addition to the pair of angels and powers, the term δυνάμεις is found floating in the tradition.[60] The textual variants are instructive. The usual Pauline couplet of ἀρχαὶ καὶ ἐξουσίαι has probably led to the intrusion of ἐξουσίαι in certain MSS and in Origen and Tertullian. Similarly the transposition of μέλλοντα and δυνάμεις in a few unimportant texts may be evidence of a tendency to associate them with powers as demonic forces. A particularly significant exegesis of this verse by Clement of Alexandria is discussed in detail later. Paul associates angels with the powers. It has been suggested that when in Paul the word ἄγγελοι appears in the plural but without the article it represents demonic angels, and when with the article it stands for holy angels.[61] This, however, is inaccurate, for Paul's use of the article with ἄγγελοι appears to be arbitrary. We may compare 1 Cor. 4: 9 with 1 Cor. 13: 1, where in each text the same comparison between men and angels is drawn, in the one case with and in the other without the article. There is, therefore, no immediate way of telling whether the angels in the present context are hostile or good, but in the

light of the evidence already presented concerning ἀρχαί, this term should
be taken in its normal Pauline sense as referring to important members of
the heavenly host.[62] The reference to angels as a possible means of separat-
ing man from God is a hyperbolic paradox, which may perhaps be paralleled in the reference to an angel in Gal. 1: 8.[63]

Before examining δυνάμεις we should look at the suggestion that in two
couplets are found astrological terms. οὔτε ἐνεστῶτα οὔτε μέλλοντα is
certainly not necessarily so. Even the later magical papyrus *PG* V, 295 uses
the couplet simply to refer to the present and the future. The same pair is
found in 1 Cor. 3: 22, where, although there might be reference to the two
ages, it seems more probable that the language is simply temporal. The
other phrase, οὔτε ὕψωμα οὔτε βάθος, has been far more the focus for an
astrological interpretation of the passage.[64] Certainly the words are found
in astrological writings, although the usual counterpart there to ὕψωμα is
ταπείνωμα.[65] The reference is to the areas above and below the horizon.
The word βάθος shares in Greek all the connotations, both literal and
metaphorical, that attach to 'depth' in English.[66] To some extent this is
also true of ὕψωμα, which in the LXX tends to mean 'pride', but is very
rare in the NT. A modification of the purely astrological interpretation is
that by which the term is regarded as standing for the area in which astral
beings hold sway.[67] This view, however, overlooks the direct connection of
the pair to create a unit of thought. Paul seems to be expressing an idea
similar to that found in Ps. 139: 8f, where spatial imagery is used to
explain how hard it is to escape the love of God. In Rom. 8: 38 Paul is
using another spatial metaphor to make the same point, which may also be
paralleled in Eph. 3: 18, where however four dimensions are included.[68]
We may confidently dismiss the astrological interpretation, not only on
lexicographical grounds but also as anachronistic, as has been demonstrated earlier.

The intrusion of δυνάμεις into the list poses a problem. Generally in
Paul the term means 'miracles', and usually those that are consequent
upon the relationship between man and God, although in one instance the
relationship is that between Satan and man. Certainly any demonic or
astrological sense is missing, and the NT generally exhibits a remarkable
reluctance so to use the word. In Mk 13: 25 there is a direct quotation of
Is. 34: 4 (LXX) where the word means 'stars', but apart from this there are
only the Pauline uses and the occurrence in 1 Pet. 3: 22, which has been
discussed above. Excluding the present text, the meaning 'miracles' is to be
assigned to twenty-three occurrences in the NT. The attempt to construe
this particular independent use within the Jewish apocalyptic tradition is
more difficult than is sometimes realised.[69] Not only is that use, as we

have seen, generally foreign to the NT, but the one recognised instance in which it occurs is in an avowedly apocalyptic passage (Mk 13: 25). Yet Romans 8 as a whole is remarkable for its non-apocalyptic eschatology.[70] The apocalyptic interpretation has been usually supported by the astrological interpretation of some other terms in the passage, but this, as we have seen, is not accurate.

In the earlier discussion of this word its vagueness was noted. Apart from its use in the phrase ὁ κύριος τῶν δυνάμεων, its meaning always depends upon its context. 1 Pet. 3: 22 is the only clear occasion in the NT when it is found in an indeterminate personal sense, which itself is very rare outside the LXX until late in antiquity.[71] The usual Pauline sense of 'miracles' may not be as foreign to the present context as at first appears.[72] Miracles are ambiguous: they may validate a Christian ministry (e.g. 2 Cor. 12: 12) or they may invalidate it as the work of Satan (e.g. 2 Thess. 2: 9). Possibly Paul is here arguing that even through the ambiguity of the experience of the miraculous and the human response to it, God will hold on to a man. The problem of δυνάμεις is not easily solved. There is little evidence for a stellar sense and none for a demonic one. The usual meaning of 'miracles', while not impossible, is difficult. But this is itself a reflection of the primary problem of the intrusion of this lone word into a list of pairs, so that it lacks the controlling influence of another noun, which would have hinted at its true interpretation.

Wishing to exhort the Romans to adoration and confidence in the love of God, Paul does not retire into the realm of astrological or spiritual forces, but in his choice of terms comprehends the whole range of human experience. This is confirmed by the summary of this list in τις κτίσις ἑτέρα. The argument in Rom. 8: 18ff has been concerned with Christian experience and the physical aspect of creation, its 'bondage to decay'. There is, therefore, a twofold thrust in the use of κτίσις in verse 39. Not only is it impossible for anything to separate the Christian from God, it is also, and more importantly, impossible that any aspect of man's existence should separate him from this love, for the totality of experience, which contributes to man's own being as a creature (that which is summed up in the list of pairs), is itself creature, i.e. the work of God.[73] There is then in Rom. 8: 38f no reference to a hostile spiritual or astral world. The mention of angelic beings refers to man's life in its religious aspect.

5

THE POWERS AND THE POLITICAL WORLD

1 Romans 13: 1–7

The teaching of Paul in Rom. 13: 1–7 has been a central problem for the Christian Church throughout its existence.[1] In the twentieth century, however, there has been a major revival of interest in the passage, partly through the influence of Dibelius and his thoughts on the angels of the nations and partly owing to the political upheavals in Europe, especially the problem caused in Germany by the rise of Hitler. The debate on the word ἐξουσίαι in Rom. 13: 1 has largely focused on the exegesis of Oscar Cullmann, to which attention must first be given.[2]

Dibelius proposed a double reference for the word, which, he claimed, referred both to the actual human authorities and to spiritual forces that stood behind them.[3] Cullmann has developed this and thus become the central figure in the debate. He expressed his views in *Christus und die Zeit* (1946) and *The State in the New Testament* (1956), with an important interim article, 'Die neuesten Diskussion über die ἐξουσίαι in Röm. 13: 1–7'. At the conclusion of this article he summarised his position:

> 'The twofold interpretation of the ἐξουσίαι in Rom. 13, 1 as referring to the state and to the angel powers which stand behind it, is thoroughly justified as an hypothesis, from the standpoints of philosophy, Judaistic concepts, and the early Christian and Pauline theology. It is an hypothesis, and naturally we can never say with final certainty that Paul has in mind not only the secular sense of the word ἐξουσίαι, but also the meaning which he attributes to it in all other passages. I can only wish, however, that all other hypotheses which we necessarily must use in the field of NT science were as well grounded as this one.'[4]

Four main arguments supported this view. (*a*) The plural use of ἐξουσία in Paul always signifies invisible angelic powers. This is distinctively Paul's understanding and use of the term. (*b*) The subjection of the powers is a central dogma of the primitive confession and therefore of Paul's thought.[5] (*c*) 1 Cor. 2: 8 is a strong ground for the double reference to both spiritual and human forces, and in 1 Cor. 6: 1ff the problem of Christian involvement in the civil courts is solved by treating those courts as agents of the angelic powers. (*d*) Early Christianity shared the view of late Judaism that invisible spiritual powers were at work behind the earthly phenomena; in particular there was a firm belief in the angels of the nations. On this basis a six-point theory of the state within redemptive history is developed: the powers were created by Christ (Col. 1: 16) and crucified him (1 Cor. 2: 8). Although overthrown by the resurrection (Col. 2: 15) they remain active (Eph. 6: 12) and will only be defeated at the end of time (1 Cor. 15: 24). For the present, 'the powers, so far as they are subject themselves to Christ's Kingdom, stand behind the legitimate political powers' as Christ's servants (Heb. 1: 14).[6] These arguments are first found in *Christ and Time* and are resumed in the later article, although by then Cullmann had conceded that there was no text that explicitly states that the powers are subject to Christ as his servants, although, he remarked, 'what other meaning could the defeated powers have for Christ exalted to the right hand of God . . . except that they are his servants?'[7]

Cullmann's arguments are very vulnerable. That based upon a suggested general meaning of ἐξουσίαι cannot stand, for the uniqueness of Rom. 13: 1 is clear from the mere fact alone that the word here appears without any of the terms that are usually associated with it.[8] Again, unlike the other passages in Paul that have reference to the powers, Rom. 13 is not explicitly concerned with the work of Christ. The recommissioning of the powers after their defeat is nowhere suggested in the NT, and, if followed logically, such an idea would suggest that in Christ the powers themselves rule the believer. In addition, Cullmann seems to rest too much on 1 Cor. 2: 8 and 1 Cor. 6: 1. Von Campenhausen points out that the association of the powers and political figures is not part of the Christian exegesis of this passage in the early tradition.[9] The first known quotation of Rom. 13 occurs in Irenaeus, *adv. haer.* 5.24.1, and the first serious use of the passage for its political sense is found when Theophilus of Antioch uses it at the end of the second century.[10] Cullmann claims that a double meaning for ἐξουσίαι is implicit in this passage. In fact, however, closer examination suggests that Irenaeus is arguing against those who use an angelic interpretation of ἐξουσίαι in order to escape the earthly consequences of obedience to human rulers. He therefore emphasises not some implicit meaning but a realistic and natural sense of 'human rulers'.

The debate had reached a stage where two major questions could be discerned, and these were formulated by C. D. Morrison in his important monograph. First, was the concept of a close relationship between spiritual powers and the civil government restricted to the area of the Jewish angels of the nations? Secondly, did the doctrine of the state, when conceived in terms of the powers and the Lordship of Christ, underlie Paul's communication to the Romans in chapter 13?[11] Morrison's contribution in 1960 consisted of three parts. He first emphasised that Paul's words must be understood as communication rather than simply as imparting something. He was writing on the basis of common presuppositions, which meant that 'Paul presumed that the Roman saints would understand "God" because they were Christians and that they would understand ἐξουσίαι because they were citizens of the Graeco-Roman world.'[12] This is a useful observation, excluding, for example, fanciful ideas that this might be a piece of pure Judaism that has no real place in the NT. Morrison secondly offered a long study of the Graeco-Roman understanding of the state, in which he argued that the whole of life, including the state, was perceived in cosmic terms, the boundary between the spirit world and humanity being fluid and sometimes imperceptible. Thirdly, the work of Christ in relation to the powers was summed up in two propositions: the realm of Christ's authority is 'all things from the beginning', and the locus of Christ's victory is the Church alone. 'Although his relationship to the state brought the Christian into contact with the *exousiai* in their most aweful and majestic form, it rested on the same basis as his everyday life, mature manhood in Christ. As a man in Christ, his conscience alone would determine his subjection to the state or his non-compliance with its demands.'[13]

Morrison's arguments deserve longer consideration than is possible here. However, his suggestions must be rejected on three grounds – historical, exegetical and logical. His evidence for the cosmic understanding of the state is derived from early Egyptian ideas through to the third century A.D. He himself admits that most of his material is 'relatively late for our purposes'. It is in fact too late, not making any attempt to focus on the distinctive period of the mid-first century A.D. The exegetical failure lies in his attempt to limit the work of Christ to the sphere of the believer. The apparently cosmic Christology of Col. 2: 15 and Eph. 1: 21, for example, on the traditional understanding that he adopts, is more profound and universal than he allows. The final failure, that of logic, lies in his conclusion that Christians obey the state for the sake of conscience, a conscience liberated by Christ. But this notion is suddenly introduced at the end of the book without argument and without preparation, and the connection of the conclusion with the preceding argument is not at all clear.[14]

Since Morrison's book there have been various other works, all of them to varying degrees moving within the confines of the debate that have been outlined above. A complete exegesis of Rom. 13: 1–7 lies beyond the immediate scope of this work, but the question of the meaning of ἐξουσίαι in verse 1 requires attention. The notion of the angels of the nations has been fully treated earlier and shown to have no significance for Paul. We must, however, examine the two Pauline texts that are frequently used in writings on the powers and the political world – 1 Cor. 2: 8 and 1 Cor. 6: 1ff.

2 1 Corinthians 2: 6–8[15]

The phrase in 1 Cor. 2: 6ff, οἱ ἄρχοντες τοῦ αἰῶνος τούτου, is unique in Paul. Since earliest times opinions have been sharply divided on whether Paul meant some supernatural beings that control the world or simply those human authorities who crucified Jesus. Within these general bounds there are also numerous variations of interpretation. Without doubt the usual interpretation at present is that the rulers are demonic spiritual forces, and this is mainly due to Everling's recovery of the idea. It has, however, a long pedigree, being found in Origen and Marcion, and is currently supported by, among others, Bultmann, Lietzmann, Delling, Schlier and Barrett.[16] Two standards of argument are used to support this view. One is related to the myth of the divine redeemer, according to which the angelic forces fail to recognise the Lord of Glory. The second argument is well outlined by Héring.[17] In Col. 2: 15 and Rom. 8: 38 αἱ ἀρχαί are mentioned as being likely to hinder the work of redemption, and these are to be identified with the ἄρχοντες. The Roman Empire was for Paul beneficent (Rom. 13) and he therefore could not have written these words about human rulers. The word καταργέω is a technical astrological term for the nullifying of a superior power. And, finally, the rulers dispense a wisdom, something that is not characteristic of human political forces. Héring concludes that these powers may be gnostic, although we know little about them. Nothing is said of their motives for killing Christ, but simply that their domination was threatened by the love of God.

An allied view is that the rulers are both human and spiritual forces. This is supported by Dibelius, Leivestad, Wendland, Dehn, Caird, and especially Cullmann.[18] This view makes use of some of the above arguments, but is heavily dependent in particular on the theory of the angels of the nations, which we have already shown to be mistaken. As for Héring's arguments in favour of the demonic meaning, they fail to establish this. In the first place Col. 2: 15, as we have seen, does not bear the interpretation required and, in any case, the identification of ἀρχαί and ἄρχοντες is not necessarily accurate. The fact, secondly, that a Roman governor crucified Jesus, however beneficent the Roman Empire in general, could not escape the notice of Paul when thinking about the cross. Thirdly, the term καταργέω is well attested in a non-technical sense of 'render of none effect', without recourse to astrology. Indeed, it is difficult to find evidence that it was in fact a technical astrological term. The most powerful argument for Héring's interpretation, however, is the fourth, namely that earthly rulers do not dispense wisdom, until one asks what point it is that Paul was making. Clearly according to this verse the rulers did not have a wisdom, for they acted in ignorance. The argument is not based on a presumed angelic wisdom, but on a parallel between the wisdom of this age in 2: 6 and the wisdom of this world in 1: 10. It is the wisdom of God that is refused by men. Further clarification of this point follows from the suggestion of Feuillet, which is outlined later.

The third possible view, that the rulers are human, has received little recent support, apart from a notable argument by Schniewind.[19] This is doubly strong, since he himself argues for an all-pervading demonic world in Pauline thought, but refuses to acknowledge its relevance in this particular passage. He argues that 1: 20 - 2: 16 is a unit, within which the wisdom of this age and of this world are identical. The wisdom of God is refused by this world, and that refusal is connected with men in their various callings in 1: 20. These callings are all marks of involvement in the real world of men. There are four main arguments in favour of the rulers being similarly viewed as humans. The antithesis in 1 Cor. 2 is similar to that in 1 Cor. 1: it is between the men who accept and those who refuse, and not between men and angelic powers. Again, in the Gospel tradition the demons and Satan are not in fact ignorant but do recognise Christ, who in the present passage is regarded as the wisdom of God (1: 24, 30). 1 Cor. 2: 6ff is a piece of early Christian missionary preaching, perhaps even the earliest commentary on the kerygmatic phrase in Acts 3: 17: 'And now, my brothers, I know that you acted in ignorance, as also did your rulers' (οἱ ἄρχοντες ὑμῶν). There is a similar reference to rulers and their ignorance, with a specific mention of Pilate, in Acts 13: 27. This is a most important observation, for it brings the use of ἄρχοντες here into line with that elsewhere in the NT and in Greek in general. In addition it is significant to observe that the cross is central in itself and not merely as an example of the ignorance of the powers. This fact suggests that we are dealing with the world of historical events and not with cosmic mythology, and therefore also with historical rulers. Whatever Paul is confronting at Corinth it is clear that he confronts it with 'the word of the cross' (1: 18, and see 2: 2).[20] In this context it would seem that if he wishes to reinterpret the resurrection historically as the divine interpretation of the cross, then he cannot at this point of his argument risk mythological speculation on the crucifixion. There is, therefore, every reason for expecting in the phrase οἱ ἄρχοντες τοῦ αἰῶνος τούτου a reference to Pilate and Caiaphas.

An additional perspective on the problem is offered by A. Feuillet, who looks to the OT as a source for Paul's language.[21] In 1: 20 there is a citation from Is. 33: 18 and 19: 11, in which the term ἄρχοντες occurs. Even more close to Paul's phrase, however, is Bar. 3: 9 – 4: 4, in which 'the rulers of the peoples' appear (3: 16). Developing a hint from Thackeray, Feuillet connects Bar. 3: 9ff with Jer. 9: 22 (cf. 1 Cor. 1: 31), and argues that we have here a reminiscence of a sermon for the 9th Ab.[22] A reminiscence of such a sermon could well explain the comparative isolation of the idea of wisdom in this section of the Pauline correspondence. The question remains, however, as to what would have been communicated to the Corinthians. The evidence of the use of ἄρχοντες in contemporary Greek will only allow the conclusion that it would have been taken to refer to the human rulers who contrived the crucifixion of Jesus. The mention of the rulers in 2: 6 before the explanation of who they are in verse 8 may well be due to Paul's thought running on the lines of the sermon and thus also running ahead of himself. There is no need to assume that this was the substance of a sermon that Paul himself preached. Indeed all that need be allowed is that the language of Baruch and Jeremiah should be in the forefront of his mind as he wrote this part of 1 Corinthians. If this is recognised, Munck's wholly justified objection to seeing a Pauline sermon in this section loses its force.[23]

There are, then, no grounds for seeing in these rulers any demonic powers, and therefore this passage ceases to be evidence for an angelological interpretation of the powers in Rom. 13: 1, whether simply or in the double form.

3 1 Corinthians 6: 1ff

This passage seems of very doubtful significance as evidence for an early Christian belief in spiritual rulers. Paul is dealing with a concrete situation in which the Corinthians are taking one another to court, but he argues not in terms of the nature of the courts and their authority, but in terms of the expected standards of Christian behaviour.[24] The contrast is not between morally good and morally bad persons, but between Christian saints and the non-Christian world. The chief contact between this passage and Rom. 13: 1ff would seem to be in common agreement that appearances matter. Paul offers two arguments against the Corinthians' practice. First, if the Christians are worthy to judge the world, they are clearly worthy to judge their own small disputes. That the saints will judge the world in the Messianic age is an ingredient of the Jewish apocalypses. In addition the association of the Twelve with Jesus in judgement would have perhaps conveyed this view to the early Christians independently of the

Jewish writings. The second argument moves from the status of Christians as judges to the object of their judgement. If in the last day they are to judge angels, then they are certainly capable in the present of dealing with the small matters of everyday life, τὰ βιωτικά.[25] The judgement of the angels is also part of the apocalyptic tradition. It is possible that the reference here is to the condemnation of Satan and the fallen angels: if the saints can handle these massive spiritual evils, then they are indeed competent to deal with their own trifles. It is, however, more likely that this is an hyperbole and the reference is to all angels, good and bad alike. The particle μήτί γε has the effect of very strong comparison.[26] It is also significant that there is no article with ἀγγέλους. There are five anarthrous occurrences of ἄγγελοι (plural) in the Pauline and deutero-Pauline literature. Of these 1 Tim. 3: 16 occurs in a possibly hymnic context. 2 Thess. 1: 7 is a problem, but the word, which must here refer to specific angels, may be anarthrous because of the anarthrous nature of the whole passage.[27] The three remaining passages are Rom. 8: 38; Gal. 3: 19; and 1 Cor. 4: 9. In each of these the angels are not mentioned because of any interest in them for their own sakes, but simply because mention of them provides the spiritual dimension to the context in hand. In Rom. 8: 38 no angelic force can separate man from God; in Gal. 3: 19 the Law was given not by God but by any spiritual agency you care to mention. But the clearest parallel to 1 Cor. 6: 1ff lies in 1 Cor. 4: 9, where the phrase ἀγγέλοις καὶ ἀνθρώποις means 'the whole universe of intelligent beings'. So in this present passage Paul does not refer to angels in terms of their function and status, but directs attention to the extent of the Christian's power and authority in judgement.[28] In the light of this, every matter must be handled within the community in order to avoid unseemly behaviour.[29] This passage will not take the weight that the angelological theory of the state sometimes seeks to put on it, and it has nothing to say to the interpretation of Rom. 13: 1.

4 Conclusion

By this stage in this work we have examined all the evidence that has been produced for an angelological interpretation of ἐξουσίαι in Rom. 13: 1 and have found it to be wanting. In particular there is no evidence for the significance of the angels of the nations for which Dibelius and Cullmann in particular have argued, nor can the so-called 'double' interpretation of the powers be sustained on the basis of 1 Cor. 2: 6–8. There is no difficulty in interpreting Rom. 13: 1–7 if the term ἐξουσίαι is taken to refer simply to human authorities, which, after all, is the normal Greek sense of the word.

CONCLUSION TO PART 2

The aim of this section of NT exegesis has been to investigate the use of the language of the powers as it occurs in the Pauline literature. Because the interpretation of these powers that is here offered runs counter to much that has been written and assumed about them, the attempt has been made also to show in each case that the fundamental understanding by Paul of αἱ ἀρχαὶ καὶ αἱ ἐξουσίαι *in bonam partem* is consistent with a realistic understanding of the particular errors and teaching in each letter. At this point we may enumerate the conclusions.

The use by Paul of the language of the powers and associated terms conforms to basic Jewish usage. The understanding of the spiritual world generally at this time produced multiplication of spiritual beings in relation to God, while evil was limited to one being, the Devil, together with some demons. The terms used for the powers, however, are not applied to the demons, and what language there is of demons in Paul is very scarce and conforms to the traditional Jewish association of them with idols. These terms from Paul's Jewish background would also have conveyed to Gentiles notions of power and authority that are associated not with hostile forces but with God. For in general the pagan use of these terms is for the authority and power of rulers in the secular world. The exact historical situation of Paul needs to be appreciated before any attempt is made to understand the meaning of his teaching on this subject. Around A.D. 70 a most important change took place in the outlook of the whole world, not just the Jewish world, which makes it exceedingly dangerous to derive ideas from the post-Pauline world and impose them on his thought.

The OT and Jewish background for Paul's teaching on the powers that is sometimes discerned in Ps. 110: 1 and in the concept of the angels of the nations are irrelevant to his teaching. The term ἄρχοντες is purely a human term in Paul and has no connection with the later gnostic use. And in Romans 13 there is no mythology of an angelologically determined state, but a paraenetical realism, which is typical of Paul. The phrase αἱ ἀρχαὶ καὶ αἱ ἐξουσίαι that occurs in Colossians and Ephesians contributes to the Christology, not by pointing to any achievement of Christ in battle against hostile powers, but by associating him with God as the one who receives the recognition and worship of the heavenly host. The term δυνάμεις by its very rarity and fluidity is a difficulty, but if the reference is to spiritual powers, it should be aligned with αἱ ἀρχαὶ καὶ αἱ ἐξουσίαι as the angelic host. The final problem that was noted was that of Eph. 6: 12, which, whatever view is taken of the powers, seems to reflect an understanding that should be dated to the second century A.D. If, however, our argument for interpolation is sound, then it represents exactly the type of development that took place in Christian thinking on the powers after the time of Paul. To this development we shall now turn.

PART 3

The post-Pauline development

6

TEXTS WITHIN THE NEW TESTAMENT

The interpretation of the work of Christ in terms of hostile powers and their defeat is certainly found in Christian thought by the end of the second century. The question must therefore be asked as to how Paul's language of the powers came to be so interpreted. Within the NT, outside the Pauline literature, the angelic powers are chiefly mentioned in Revelation, 2 Peter and Jude. These three books require discussion, but this does not imply that they represent developments upon a Pauline theme. They are, however, all most probably assignable to a period of Christian history subsequent to Paul and give valuable instances of thinking that was found in the Church.

1 The Revelation of Saint John the Divine

Accepting that this book was written towards the end of the first century, we may observe in it how the language and attitudes of Jewish apocalyptic remain constant within a definitely Christian tradition that is found in Asia Minor. There are no points of direct connection between Pauline literature and Revelation.

Angels are understood in three main ways in the book. They function simply as heralds of God (1: 1; 5: 2 etc.). Sometimes the epithet ἰσχυρός is applied (10: 1; 18: 21), which may suggest a class of ἰσχυροί. Within the conventions of apocalyptic this should not occasion surprise, and it might be an exact parallel to that extension of God as δύναμις through the creation of δυνάμεις, which we have already noted.[1] Indeed ἰσχύς is a particular attribute of God in 5: 12 and 7: 12. The angels, secondly, form together the host of God at worship, and the various classes of angels that are common in Jewish apocalyptic also appear. The third use, however, is rather different: the seven letters to the Seven Churches are addressed to an angel for each Church. These cannot be bishops or Church leaders, for the word ἄγγελος is without exception otherwise used in Revelation for a heavenly being. Nor may they be associated with the idea of guardian angels, for John himself denies this.[2] In 1: 20 he says that Christ holds the seven stars and the seven lampstands, and that the stars are the angels of the Seven Churches, while the lampstands are the Churches themselves. The key here lies not in a one-to-one connection but in the perfection of the number seven, which implies that the letters, while addressed to specific Churches, are in fact addressed to the whole Church of God. This is made explicit in the refrain at the end of each letter. The writer seems to be expressing through the concrete circumstances of known congregations that cosmological perspective, with its double direction of both time and space, which typifies the whole book.[3] Just as the specific, historical, temporal victory of the Lamb is now the subject of the atemporal, heavenly worship of the hosts of God (5: 9), so the temporal, and at times corrupt and deficient, existence of the Christian congregations on earth is identified with the eternal existence of those same congregations with their Lord in the heavens. The temporal and spatial dimensions are mixed. There is also the important consideration that by this means the pastoral requirement of a call to repentance may be made to Churches whose life is now estimated and judged *sub specie aeternitatis*, there being contained within that *aeternitas* both spatial and temporal notions. For this reason the letters are addressed to an angel, for it is the means of linking this spatio-temporal concept of the Church and its eternal aspect.

There are also several references to the forces of evil in Revelation. Two points may be noted. First, these forces are focused on the one figure of Satan, the Dragon, or Beliar. In this John reflects that Jewish apocalyptic tradition which we have also noted in Paul. Secondly, Michael and his angels appear in a guise similar to that of the ἄρχοντες in Daniel in 12: 7ff. Fighting the Dragon, Michael is conceived as the protector of the people of God, which now is not Israel but the Christian Church. The writer, however, shares with the author of Daniel a universal perspective. The sufferings of the Churches are not simply local but are part of a world-wide catastrophe. Whereas, however, Daniel used the princes to represent the empires of the world, John is in a more immediate situation and the only empire to be reckoned with is that of Rome. The struggle, therefore, is characterised not as between the prince of God and the prince of Rome, but as simply between Michael and the Beast.[4] Revelation is orientated to the past and to present experience as a basis for future hope. The Danielic hope on the other hand is based solely upon the evidence of history without the obvious reinforcement of present experience. Apart from this struggle between Michael and the Beast, demonic forces are comparatively rare in Revelation and, when they do appear, are conceived in primitive apocalyptic categories and not as present powers in their own right.

Revelation adds little to our understanding of the early Christian approach to the spirit world. It is noteworthy that there is no reference to any hostile powers and principalities. This is because the writer simply adopts the Jewish imagery that was available to him and redeploys it in a Christian context. This imagery lacks much reference to hostile demonic forces in the universe, apart from the tendency to concentrate all evil in one being, Satan or the Devil. His origins are not discussed in the book, although his hostility to God continues the development of the idea of his pristine rebellion, a view that became predominantly the Christian view during the second century. The angels, however, fully conform to the Jewish background to the book. They are a great multitude, although individual angels are also the messengers of Yahweh, and their chief function is to worship and praise God.

2 The Epistle of Jude

Within its short compass the Epistle of Jude shows a remarkable interest in angels. It may be taken as composed prior to 2 Peter and is probably a product of the late first century. It reflects within a Christian tradition that Jewish thinking on the angels which is derived from the type of teaching found in 1 Enoch.[5] In verse 6 the fall of the angels who failed to keep their ἀρχή is recounted. The meaning of the word here is difficult, but we should retain the fundamental sense of 'primacy'. The angels who fell were both among the first creations of God in time and, according to 1 En. 6: 8, among the chief angels.[6] The example is chosen to demonstrate God's punishment of disobedience, which is evidenced by lust. This understanding of disobedience to God issuing in moral failure runs through the epistle.

In verse 8 the errorists are described as those who σαρκὰ μὲν μιαίνουσιν, κυριότητα δὲ ἀθετοῦσιν, δόξας δὲ βλασφημοῦσιν. This use of κυριότης (singular) is unique in the NT, apart from the derivative 2 Pet. 2: 10.[7] The plural use almost certainly represents angelic beings in Col. 1: 16, but the singular here is more problematical. It seems to stand for the Lordship of Christ, which the blasphemers set at nought.[8] This view is strengthened by the following words. For the plural δόξαι is also unparalleled in the NT, except again in the derivative 2 Pet. 2: 10. An original example of the idea may be found in Ex. 15: 11 (LXX), where a parallelism between ἅγιοι and δόξαι suggests an angelic sense for the latter.[9] δόξα is a characteristic of God himself and the move from the singular, which is used of God, to the plural, which is used of his angelic manifestations, is exactly that which we have demonstrated for δυνάμεις and hypothesised for ἀρχαί. The whole phrase would then refer to the denial of Christ's Lordship and blasphemy in the matter of angels. This blasphemy is later described in verse 10: ὅσα οὐκ οἴδασιν, βλασφημοῦσιν. The construction in verse 8 with μέν . . .δέ . . . δέ does not necessarily imply a phrase with three equal members. In the light of the rest of the epistle it seems likely that this is a two-membered contrast between, on the one hand, the moral failure of the errorists and, on the other hand, their doctrinal error in denying Christ's Lordship and the blasphemy of the good angels of God. Both of these they do while ἐνυπνιαζόμενοι. In the LXX this word is used of the waywardness of the false prophet, for whom the confusion of belief and morals is a standard failing.[10] Is. 56: 10 (LXX) provides a perfect background to Jude at this point. The main thrust of the book is not against false morality as such but against error in belief, which itself issues in the denial of salvation. The allusions from the OT reinforce this. Although the enemies of God are described as depraved, they are primarily instanced as examples of those who denied the truth. The use of μιαίνω in verse 8 strengthens this view, for the word, rare in the NT, in the LXX refers to that spiritual defilement which is apostasy. This sense continues in the NT, where in Heb. 12: 15 it is contrasted with holiness, the means by which man sees God, and more clearly still in Tit. 1: 15, where the defiled are also the faithless.[11]

In spite of its brevity, the Epistle of Jude is important for an investigation of early Christian understandings of the spiritual world, and its clear relationship with 2 Peter is highly instructive. It is therefore necessary to attempt to find a background for this writing. The problem, however, is considerable and any such endeavour has to be carried out with a minimum of evidence. It is clear from the text that a group of Christians is addressed, whose thought derived from or was at least familiar with the OT and later Jewish ideas; and that this group would respect the name of Jude, who is described not only as 'servant of Jesus Christ' but also as 'brother of James'. Dix sees the epistle as evidence for a continued connection between the Nazarenes and the Gentile Church, regarding it as a circular letter to warn Gentile Christians of the moral dangers attaching to gnostic doctrines. The writer, he hazards, might have been a Jewish Christian leader, perhaps Judas-Justus, nephew of James.[12] This interpretation, however, does not allow for the comparative absence of direct emphasis upon the moral failure of the errorists: the main thrust is against the doctrinal errors that issue in depravity. In addition, while the Gentile Christians did become increasingly familiar with the extra-canonical Jewish literature, the allusiveness of the epistle suggests that the recipients were steeped in a Jewish background.

The Gospel of Thomas is attributed to Didymus Judas Thomas. The canonical tradition about Thomas lacks the name 'Judas', but Jn. 11: 16

may preserve a hint that the original text contained a reference to a disciple 'called twin' (i.e. Thomas or Didymus). The idea that Thomas was Jesus' twin is a distinctive mark of the Christianity that is associated with Edessa.[13] In the superscription of Jude it is notable that the author is described not as the brother of the Lord but as the servant of the Lord and brother of James. James himself was a brother of Jesus.[14] There are many evidences of Thomas legends attached to earliest Christianity in eastern Syria, especially in Osrhoëne, and also several hints that this apostle was named Judas, the title 'Thomas' being taken to describe his relationship to the Lord. The Gospel of Thomas almost certainly is connected with Edessa, either with some genuine tradition of the apostle's work in Syria or with a local belief that derives originally from Osrhoëne.[15] This is, of course, to assume that the tradition is primitive. We may alternatively take it that the name of one of the brothers of the Lord, Judas Thomas, was at an early stage appropriated by a Christian group, whose tradition took root in Edessa. In fact there seems good reason to compare the importance of the tradition about Thomas in Syria with that of Paul in Asia and that of Peter in Western Syria.

The Christianity of Edessa seems to have had little in common with the Ebionite Christianity of western Syria, not least in their differing estimates of Paul.[16] Yet there is an aspect of that Christianity which is significant for our purposes in the form as described by Epiphanius. He lists (*Pan.* 30.16) four main characteristics: the Christology was psilanthropic; it was joined to an angelology, which listed Jesus among the archangels; the practices of the group included circumcision and ritual washing; there was a strong tendency towards a dualistic opposition between a good and an evil principle. These are the very characteristics that Jude attributes to the errorists. Their chief error was Christological in setting aside the Lordship and blaspheming angels. This phrase, which has been considered above, is best explained by Epiphanius on the Ebionites:

οὐ φασκοῦσιν δὲ ἐκ θεοῦ πατρὸς αὐτὸν γεγεννῆσθαι, ἀλλὰ ἐκτίσθαι ὡς ἐνὰ τῶν ἀρχαγγέλων μείζονα δὲ αὐτῶν ὄντα

κυριότητα δε ἀθετοῦσιν.

δόξας δὲ βλασφημοῦσιν.

This interpretation takes the last phrase in verse 8 to mean 'blaspheming in respect of angelic powers', i.e. as epexegetic on the denial of Christ's Lordship. The first clause, 'defiling the flesh', may also be less a reference to lustful behaviour than a satirical characterising of the errorists' custom of circumcision or an ironic description of their ritual washings.

The letter is too short for any certainty on this, and the early history of Syrian and Ebionite Christianity is too scanty for any firm conclusions to be drawn. Clearly the letter is not addressed simply to a form of Ebionite Christianity, since the suggestion of ἀσελγεία in verse 4 would then be irrelevant. The association of the name of Jude with Thomas, however, and the probable early date for the Thomas traditions in Edessa, together with the affinities of the error that the epistle combats with the type of Christianity that is known as Ebionite, suggest Syria as both the place of origin and the destination of the letter.[17]

For the present investigation it is interesting that the book preserves the same Jewish angelology as that which is basic for Paul. The writer, however, has more interest in the esoteric, but even he remains uninterested in angels for their own sake. They are introduced for illustration only. Some commentators have suggested the intrusion of Babylonian influence in the mention of ἀστέρες πλανῆται in verse 13. This might be astrological, but more probably, like the rest of the book, it derives from 1 Enoch. In 1 En. 18: 13ff and 21: 1ff the fallen angels are treated as fallen stars and are shut up for ever in the fiery depths. The change from the fires of 1 Enoch to the darkness of Jude is due to the fact that in verse 6*b* Jude makes use of the story of the fall of Azazel and his punishment. According to 1 En. 10: 5f Azazel was bound and thrown into darkness for ever. Evil in Jude is rampant in the one being, the Devil, and the angels are always seen as servants or extensions of God. The horror of the fall of the angels, according to Jude, resides less in their moral degradation than in the fact that it was those closest to God who fell.

Jude has been given this somewhat disproportionate space for two reasons. In the first place, there is clearly nothing in common between the Christian tradition of this book and that of Paul.[18] In addition, unlike Revelation, Jude seems also to have nothing to do with Asia Minor. Yet, in this independent form of Christianity, the angelology, derived from Jewish sources, is wholly in line with that which we have noted for Paul: the angels are good and the forces of evil are concentrated in one being only; and there are no hostile forces of the universe. The second reason for the book's importance lies in the use that is made of it in 2 Peter and the development of thought that occurs between them.

3 The Second Epistle of Peter

The weight of evidence suggests that this book makes use of Jude rather than *vice versa*, and this will be assumed here.[19] The references to angels in each book are in many ways similar in appearance, but a careful study shows that the intentions of the authors are surprisingly different. This is of great interest, for we have here two documents that make use of the

Judaeo-Christian traditions about angels, one of which depends directly upon the other as source. The question is therefore to determine whether we may discern signs of development in the transition.

A key passage is 2: 4. The writer, employing Jude, argues from the severity of God's judgement in the past to a present warning for Christians. He uses the myth of Gen. 6: 1ff as transmitted through 1 Enoch, but the punishment of these fallen angels is expressed most unusually with the word ταρταρώσας. This is rare in any form of Greek and unique in the NT.[20] The relation between the argument of this section and that in Jude is clear. The author of 2 Peter is expanding the teaching of Jude and putting it into chronological order. He also, however, in verses 5, 7 and 9, introduces the theme of the salvation of the righteous, thus changing the impact of the examples from the OT. This appears not only to be deliberate reinterpretation but also to be due to the very different tradition that he employs as compared with that of Jude. In the stories of Noah and of Sodom he uses Jewish ideas that were not part of the Judaean Jewish tradition.[21] Even more noticeable is his use of the story of Lot, which treats him as a model of virtue.[22] In his reference to Tartarus he displays evidence of Greek influence that displaces Jewish ideas of the several heavens by the notion of the underworld as the abode of the sinful. There is, therefore, in 2 Peter a move away from the pristine Jewish form of exemplary myths towards a non-Judaean and certainly in one case hellenised tradition.

When the writer of 2 Peter denounces the wickedness of the errorists he employs an invective that is unparalleled in the NT. His adaptation of Jude 8 in 2: 10b is instructive. In spite of linguistic similarities there is a different intention behind the words. The connection between κυριότης and δόξα is lost. The author's obsession with moral pollution dominates, so much so that there is every indication that he has lost the meaning of κυριότης in Jude.[23] Indeed the sense that is as yet unparalleled, that of 'authority' *simpliciter*, might be considered here. There is also a moralising expansion of the phrase σαρκὰ μὲν μιαίνουσιν, and κυριότης itself is now explicitly connected with ἐπιθυμία μιασμοῦ. The change from ἀθετέω to καταφρονέω might also be evidence, the former being more concerned with action, while the latter refers to attitude. In verse 10b, which is difficult, the primary emphasis is on the arrogance of the errorists. This is demonstrated in that they δόξας οὐ τρέμουσιν βλασφημοῦντες, a phrase that is expounded in verse 11. The whole sentence may be paraphrased thus: 'Brazen and self-willed,[24] the errorists are not afraid to blaspheme the δόξας, whereas (ὅπου)[25] even the angels, although superior to these men in power and might, do not dare to bring a blasphemous judgement against the δόξας before the Lord.' The power and importance of the errorists and that of the angels is first compared, to the detriment of the men, and the position of the δόξαι is set over against both.[26] It thus becomes clear that the role of the δόξαι has changed decisively between their original appearance in Jude and their present context in 2 Peter. For whereas in Jude they were clearly the angels or archangels, with whom Jesus was associated, in 2 Peter they have become the fallen angelic leaders, who are described in 1 En. 6 as the chiefs of tens who led the descent to earth.[27] The call for their judgement is also found in 1 Enoch. The errorists thus seem to have been using the account of the fall of the angels to claim their own superiority over all God's creation, a claim that led to arrogant licentiousness. Two points in this story as recounted in 2 Peter are notable. First, the author, when compared with Jude, shows some hesitancy about using Jewish apocryphal literature. The deliberate omission of the account of Michael and the body of Moses is the most obvious instance. The second point is that the story of the fall of the δόξαι, as used here, might be another example of hellenising by the author, and the myth employed may depend primarily upon Greek myths with only reminiscences of the story from 1 Enoch.[28]

The problem of 2 Peter is considerable because there is so little evidence. Although the book displays some remarkable phraseology and many hellenisms, it may also be shown to contain distinctive semitisms.[29] The arguments that associate its rather violent approach to eschatology with Greek ideas may also be turned to demonstrate apparently direct connections with the teaching of Jesus.[30] The fact, however, of the use of Jude together with the evidence of the Petrine traditions of Western Syria might suggest some such provenance.[31] For the purposes of our present study, having admitted the paucity of the evidence, we may note two straws in the wind. In the first place, as has been noted, the two books, Jude and 2 Peter, stand together, and the author of the latter depends upon the former explicitly at the point where the role of the angelic powers is described. Secondly, it seems certain that between the books the δόξαι change from being holy archangels into evil angels. This type of confusion is endemic to the apocryphal Jewish literature, but the fact that the author of 2 Peter appears to work with hellenistic–Jewish and Christian traditions rather than in the Judaeo–Jewish field makes this change of more than usual interest. For it may point to the direction in which the Christian understanding of the spirit-world moved. Lacking complete familiarity with the confusions and detail of Jewish apocalyptic, the Christians in the Greek world tended to think in terms of mighty beings confined by God for failure rather than in terms of holy archangels. For the Greek world knew of the former, but lacked any parallel to the latter. The δόξαι, then, in 2 Peter have become evil apparently under the influence of hellenistic–Jewish and Christian thinking. Yet even here they have become only fallen angels and not hostile beings who confront man. Nor is there any hint of experience of such oppressive beings on the part of the Christians.

The three books that have been considered in this section come from very different backgrounds, which are in each case obscure. Nevertheless on the question of the spirit-world they all conform so clearly to what we have seen to be the case with Paul that we may confidently speak of a general view of the angelic world. This briefly is that there is no interest in the angelic world for its own sake; that the angels of God in the Christian tradition at this time are rarely fallen, but are mentioned mainly as evidence of God's supremacy and that of Christ; and that evil angels are not considered, for all that is personalisable as evil is attributed to Satan or to the Devil. Only in Jude and in 2 Peter, which is probably to be dated the latest of the canonical books, do the fallen angels become accepted. This is an indication of a development that occurred in the second century, to which we shall give attention. One further important point remains: there is no evidence in any of these books, even in the apocalyptic visions of Revelation, that the authors or recipients of the letters lived in a terror of some mighty, inhuman, angelic or stellar powers from which they had been released by Christ. The silence is impressive.

7

IGNATIUS OF ANTIOCH

In a recent survey on early Anatolian Christianity, S. E. Johnson concludes with these remarks:

'But there is one baffling question, though it pertains to Syria rather than to Asia Minor: the origin of Ignatius of Antioch, and *how he developed his point of view*. Like so many creative persons, like his hero St. Paul, he is a mystery. He appears almost like Melchisedek, without father or mother or genealogy or beginnings, though we think we do know his end. Certainly he is another example of an oriental alienated from the prevailing culture.'[1]

This is a useful reminder that we know virtually nothing of the development of Christianity at Antioch until Ignatius appears and that we know almost as little after his departure until late in the second century. We may, however, be certain of this: Ignatius' understanding of the gospel is fundamentally Pauline.[2] He does not pedantically recount Paul's views, but thinks for himself, although Johnson's epithet 'creative' may be generous. Now that we may be reasonably sure that we are dealing with authentic texts from the early second century, we have in these letters writings that, while coming from western Syria, are addressed to Christian communities in Asia Minor on the certain assumption that they will be understood.[3] These writings also have points of contact with certain forms of expression and ideas that are found among later gnostic writers, and at the same time they stand within the Pauline and Judaeo-Christian traditions. The debate on Ignatius, therefore, has been mainly concerned with whether we are to see a developing gnosticism behind his words or whether this involves a certain amount of anachronistic reading of the texts.[4] Clearly the place, if any, of the powers in the thought of Ignatius is important both as an aspect of this debate and, from our point of view in this present study, for the development, if any, of Paul's ideas and language. The views of so determined a Paulinist as Ignatius are of great interest.

The language that he uses of the powers is instructive. The Devil is usually described as 'the ruler of this age', but 'Satan' appears once (*Eph.* 13) and 'The Devil' four times (*Eph.* 10. 3; *Trall.* 8.1; *Rom.* 5. 3; *Smyrn.* 9.1). The plural ἄρχοντες occurs once (*Smyrn.* 6.1), although there is also the phrase τὰς συστάσεις τὰς ἀρχοντικάς in *Trall.* 5.2. The words ἀρχαί and ἐξουσίαι do not appear and there is no comparable phrase in Ignatius to the Pauline couplet. δυνάμεις appear in *Eph.* 13.1, where they are associated with Satan. In addition the cosmological descriptions ἐπιγεῖα and ἐπουράνια are a familiar aspect of his writing.[5] ἄγγελοι, however, are mentioned only once (*Smyrn.* 6.1), and the τοποθεσίας ἀγγελικάς occur in *Trall.* 5.2. Although therefore Ignatius does not employ the same terminology as Paul, there are sufficient similarities to make a comparative study valuable. A list such as this may give the impression that there are frequent references to the angels and powers in his writings. This is not the case, for, apart from the references to the Devil in various forms, the angelic language is on the whole confined to *Smyrn.* 6 and *Trall.* 5.

Ignatius' language concerning the Devil conforms to that of Paul and the other NT writers. At first sight, however, the phrase δυνάμεις τοῦ Σατανᾶ in *Eph.* 13 stands out. They appear to be the demonic forces of Satan, which are conceived in parallel to the powers of God as an extension of Satan's personal power. The context, however, suggests that this is improbable, and that the reference is simply to the power that Satan himself possesses. Ignatius is exhorting the Ephesians to more frequent attendance at worship, in particular at the eucharist. Although connections may be traced between Ignatius' language on the eucharist and the terminology of the mysteries, it is noteworthy that he understands the service only as the act of worship that expresses and contributes to the unity of the Christian assembly.[6] Any notion that it is apotropaic of demonic forces or an expression of triumph over them is not found. This suggests that Ignatius is not thinking in terms of a world of personal demonic forces. In this context δυνάμεις τοῦ Σατανᾶ are coupled with ὄλεθρος αὐτοῦ. This should not be hypostatised but is to be understood in the light of the thought that Paul expresses in 1 Cor. 5: 5, where the offender against the congregation is handed over to Satan εἰς ὄλεθρον τῆς σαρκός. If ὄλεθρος is so understood, the indications are that the δυνάμεις are not personal spirit powers of evil, but they are the mighty wiles of Satan himself.[7]

This is confirmed by some further considerations. The unusual use of Σατανᾶς, unique in Ignatius, points to his having in mind some particular sense that is probably derived from Paul, particularly since the previous section (12) certainly has Pauline overtones. In Paul, although his use of 'Satan' is wider than the sense of 'The Tempter', it is noticeable that something of this emphasis is present whenever this title is used. The only exception to this in Paul is in 2 Corinthians. Ignatius in *Eph.* 13 appears to follow this nuance in using 'Satan' instead of his usual language. This emphasises the agency of the Devil in testing Christians, a test that may only be survived through the unity of the assembly as it shares 'the medicine of immortality'. The war in question is not one between heaven and earth, but rather is the opposite of that peace which is exemplified in the unity of the Christian body, through which universal peace is produced. The phrase ἐπουρανίων καὶ ἐπιγείων may be a stereotype for 'the whole universe', and thus too much may not be read out of it. Alternatively it may refer to the cosmic dimension of worship, by which, when the people of God are one in the eucharist, there is peace in both heaven and earth.[8] The suggestion that this refers to a twofold attack on Christians by heavenly and earthly beings cannot be substantiated, for this is not what the text says. Lightfoot attempted to link δυνάμεις and ἐπουρανίων καὶ ἐπιγείων, referring them to spiritual and carnal enemies of the Christian. In the light of the meaning of δυνάμεις, however, this is incorrect.[9]

The mention of his own insights into heavenly things in *Trall.* 5.1 is unimportant, except for the introduction of the word ἀρχοντικάς. The passage is confessional and consciously modelled upon Paul (e.g. 1 Cor. 12–14 on spiritual experience, and 2 Cor. 12). We may not infer any angelological heresy at Antioch or Tralles. The citation of 1 Cor. 3: 1ff puts the passage in context. It is a call to the simple life of the gospel, a simplicity that contrasts favourably with any desire for extraordinary experience or knowledge, such as that which the writer possesses, which is about to be ratified by his martyrdom. His vision was a heavenly one and is possibly to be compared with that in 2 Cor. 12. This would account for the unusual word τοποθεσίας, the basic sense of which is geographical. The phrase τὰς συστάσεις τὰς ἀρχοντικάς is more difficult, but συστάσεις probably here means 'assemblies' rather than 'conflicts'.[10] The chief problem is whether the noun ἄρχοντες stands behind ἀρχοντικάς and, if so, in what sense it should be taken. Ignatius himself uses the noun in *Smyrn.* 6.1, where the reference is clearly to the angels of heaven. For he argues that 'both things heavenly and the angels, notwithstanding their glory (ἡ δόξα τῶν ἀγγέλων) and the archons, seen and unseen, even these will come under judgement unless they believe in the sacrifice of Christ'. There are strong similarities between this and *Trall.* 5.1. If taken literally the phrase 'seen and unseen' is strange, and therefore Lightfoot's explanation of it as a stereotype that depends upon some such passage as Col. 1: 16 must be adopted. It includes the whole range of human cognisance and the detailed reference is immaterial.

The references in *Smyrn.* 6 and *Trall.* 5 are significant for two main reasons. First, the word ἄρχοντες, previously almost unknown of angelic powers, makes its appearance in early Christian writings. Indeed, it is the first undeniably angelic use since that in Daniel. Subsequently the word becomes frequent and important. The second point is that in Ignatius the word is clearly used with reference to the holy angels of heaven, perhaps even the archangels. If some other beings, such as either fallen angels or even gnostic archons were understood by the recipients of the letters, then the argument of Ignatius, especially that in *Smyrn.* 6, becomes pointless. The amazing point, according to him, is that even the angels of heaven need to believe if they are to avoid judgement – an extension of that hyperbolic use of angels which we have noted in Galatians and, most obviously, in 1 Cor. 6: 1ff. Slight as these two references in Ignatius are, the appearance of the word 'archons' in a Christian writing in an angelic sense at the beginning of the second century is of immense significance. It is a step from Paul, who does not so employ the word, towards the gnostic texts, which employ it very freely.

No passage is of more significance in Ignatius for our purposes than *Eph.* 19, even though it contains no explicitly angelic terminology. Here, as the culminating argument of his letter, Ignatius refers to three mysteries that were hidden from the archon of this age: the virginity of Mary, the birth of Christ, and the death of Christ. How then was Christ manifested to the world? A new and remarkable star shone and all magic, wickedness and ignorance were removed. 'Hence all things were disturbed, because the abolition of death was being planned.' There is unfortunately no further exposition, and the epistle ends soon after this chapter.

The chapter, which has been subject to intensive study, is unparalleled in Ignatius both for its language and its thought. Moreover, the author himself seems to have realised its problematic nature, for he promises in 20.1 that he will write a second letter in which he will clarify what he has just begun to expound.[11] Most attempts to link Ignatius with gnostic thought have naturally fastened onto this chapter. Schlier discovered in it the myth of the gnostic redeemer, which incidentally involves a reorganisation of the material: the hidden descent of the redeemer, though lost in the passage, is hinted at in the ignorance of the ruler of this age; the redeemer is manifested to men and the powers are defeated when magic is abolished and the defeat of death is promised (19.3); and the public ascent to glory is found in the story of the star in 19.2*a*, a view that involves the excision of 2*b* as an intrusion into the myth.[12]

Corwin has offered a full refutation of this imposition on the text.[13] The ignorance of the archons has nothing to do with the myth of the redeemer, but follows from Ignatius' world view. We might also add that immediately prior to this passage in 18.1 Ignatius has cited 1 Cor. 1: 20, in which is discussed the question of wisdom and foolishness. The present reference may therefore hint at the first stage of a development whereby 'the rulers of this age' in Paul change from human rulers into demonic powers. Certainly Marcion knew of this interpretation of 1 Cor. 2: 6 and Tertullian (*adv. Marc.* 5.6.7) went to some lengths to disprove it. It has already been noted that the plural ἄρχοντες only occurs in Ignatius in the sense of 'archangels'. However, the fact of that use together with the description of the Devil as ἄρχων could well be the beginning of a mixture of plural and singular uses that could have contributed to the development of the idea of hostile forces. This is not the whole story, for Ps. 24: 7ff, e.g., probably played a part, but it is another indication. The use of the plural αἰῶνες has already been discussed. *Eph.* 19 conforms to the NT usage and there remains still no evidence prior to the end of the second century for the personalising of αἰῶνες. Schlier's treatment of the text is unwarranted, and the seeking for evidence of gnostic thought in *Eph.* 19 seems desperate.

When the text is read without the presuppositions of later gnostic thought, two points stand out. The first is the story of the star, which occupies the heart of the chapter; the second, which is briefer, is the reference to the three mysteries. These are the virginity of Mary, the birth of Christ, and the death of Christ. The theme of the silence of God is also fundamental for Ignatius and is usually expressed in two words that share the same meaning - ἡσυχία and σιγή.[14] Ignatius regards it as the very being of God himself, a God who is conceived within the Judaeo-Christian tradition. Indeed, σιγή is almost the equivalent of οὐσία, which Ignatius does not use, a word that stands for the reality of God and for his awesome remoteness. For this reason too he couples the silence of the bishop with the silence of God. 'When we find Ignatius speaking of God as silence, we conclude that he is not using a conception of only peripheral importance. If in human silence the real meaning of the person lies, to a greater degree it must be so with God.'[15] In the light of this the sense of 19.1 becomes clear; the 'cry' is the kerygma, but it is viewed in a violent way. God, who has hitherto dwelt in silence, has now shattered it with the proclamation of the gospel of Jesus.[16]

The story of the star, which here comes into prominence, is significant for early Christian thinking on the incarnation. It is based upon a messianic interpretation of Num. 24: 17, with obvious connections through the Matthaean story of the Magi.[17] Justin, *Dial.* 106.4 refers to the story, and adds Zech. 6: 12 through the connection of ἀνατολή. The general significance of this verse in some Jewish thought has been confirmed in the DSS. In CD 7.19 the star will be the interpreter of the Law and in IQM 11.6 he is the mighty warrior.[18] Ignatius, however, offers a distinctive interpretation of the verse. He pictures the sun and moon and stars doing obeisance around the central star. This is so different from other Christian ideas associated with the star that some have associated it with hellenistic astrology, but in view of the usually strong Jewish background to Christian exegesis of this concept, we should first consider a possible Jewish background.

In the story of Joseph and his dream there is a significant reference to sun, moon and stars at worship (Gen. 37: 9). The sun and moon are mentioned here as distinct from the stars. Secondly, the homage that the stars offer is to a particular person, Joseph. In the light of the messianic use of Num. 24: 17, the move from homage to a man to homage to a star is simple.[19] Yet this will not completely account for Ignatius' statement.[20] We note further that in Matthew the star leads the Magi to Christ and that for Ignatius the star is a new thing by which all magic is destroyed. This association too is significant. That the incarnation was the occasion for the overthrow of magic is a thought that is found elsewhere in early Christian thought.[21] Ignatius, however, links the star with magic in a distinctive fashion. He makes four clear points: the star is associated with the Messiah, but is not merely identified with Jesus; the myth is developed in terms of the obeisance of the other stars; the star is connected with magic rather than, as in Matthew, with the Magi;[22] and the destruction of magical powers by the incarnation is affirmed. It is possible that this would have constituted part of the elaboration promised in the second letter.

Ignatius' contribution to Christian thought is here genuinely creative. By developing the idea of the relation of the other stars to the messianic star and by amplifying the story of the Magi in terms of magic and spells, he brought the two into a correlation that later bore fruit.[23] This distinctiveness can be illustrated by a comparison with Theodotus, as reported by Clement of Alexandria. According to Theodotus the astral powers are firmly to be regarded as the objects of Christ's work. They function according to Destiny, which through them rules the world of men. The domination of the stars over the lives of men is a matter of report rather than of conjecture. When the Lord comes, he is identified with a new star that destroys the magic of the old stars. In turn the Magi become not so much magicians as profound thinkers, who perceive the truth that a king is born (Clement of Alexandria, *Exc. ex Theod.* 69–72). This appears to have a gnostic colouring, but Ignatius has interestingly not moved so far.

For all his focusing on the cross of Christ, he does not assert the defeat of the powers, nor does he use any images that point in such a direction. Magic for him dies out at the incarnation, and the magic is not related to superhuman forces or demonic powers, but to the human Magi of Matthew's Gospel.[24] He includes the death of Christ in his summary of the three mysteries, but its significance is outweighted by the two references to the incarnation. Christ's death has prepared for one thing only, which is the coming destruction of death itself (*Eph.* 19.3). Thus Ignatius stands at a point of growth. By bringing together the messianic star and the Magi with the picture of the obeisance of all the stars, he has created a climate in which the developing importance of astrology in the second century, already prominent in his native Syria, would be brought into contact with the Christian understanding of life and person of Christ.

In Ignatius' writing we observe the fading of concern with the historical that was compensated for by a shift towards myth.[25] This is partly encouraged by his explicit concern with the incarnation of Christ, which, whilst it is for Ignatius something that happened in history, in the nature of the case as mystery was more amenable to mythic development than the more blatant fact of the cross. Yet although Ignatius provides a fascinating example of the way in which the association of Pauline language with other terms can make the way clear for a development in Christian thinking, Ignatius himself does not in fact advance very much upon the thought of Paul. He is faithful to his exemplar, even in the careful use of language. It is, in the light of this, inconceivable that he would have not used Paul's teaching of the principalities and powers had he believed in a world of hostile forces and had he so understood the phrase. It seems clear, however, that he did not so understand it, and the nearest he approaches the angelic ideas in that Pauline phrase is in his remarks on angels in *Smyrn.* 6 and *Trall.* 5. The gap between Paul and Ignatius is small by comparison with that between Ignatius and later Christian gnostic thinkers. Nevertheless, the shift, slight though it be, is sufficient to point to the direction in which Christian thinking on the powers and the spirit world in the second century was likely to go.

8

THE ANGELOMORPHIC CHRISTOLOGY OF EARLY JEWISH CHRISTIANITY[1]

There is sufficient evidence among early Jewish Christian writings of the association of Christ with the notions that are in the OT connected with angels for us to postulate an 'angelomorphic' Christology.[2] This word is chosen in preference to the more usual 'angel-Christology' (*Engelchristologie*) in order to accommodate the criticisms of Martin Werner's thesis that there was a late Jewish angel-messianology, which the early Jewish Christians converted into an angel Christology.[3] Some early Christians, however, certainly took up some references to the angel of the Lord in the OT and applied them to Christ. A classic statement of this approach, which clearly demonstrates both the method that was adopted and the possible conclusion that might be reached, may be found in Justin, *Dial.* 126.1f, in which a list of OT references, including one to 'the Angel of Great Counsel', is applied to Christ.[4] The fluctuation in certain OT texts between the person of God himself and the angels was a point of growth for the angelomorphic Christological ideas of early Jewish Christianity. This was a means both of interpreting the OT in the light of the Christian revelation and of according to Christ a more than merely human status. The major exception to this tendency is found in Ebionite Christianity, which seems to have used a strictly angelic conception of Christ in order to establish a psilanthropic Christology.[5]

1 The Shepherd of Hermas

Among the most significant texts in this area of thought is the Shepherd of Hermas.[6] The angels, and especially 'the angel', are frequently mentioned. Without pursuing a detailed study of the work, we may observe several important points in the angelology. The Shepherd, an *angelus interpres*, is sent by one called ὁ σεμνότατος ἄγγελος (*Vis.* 5.2), who is also the one who justifies (*Mand.* 5.1.7). In many ways he shows that he is the Lord (e.g. *Sim.* 5.4.4). The work, however, is the product of an interim stage in the development of this idea, for in *Sim.* 8.3.3 the angel is Michael and in the next chapter (*Sim.* 9.12.7) he becomes the Son of

God. Michael's significance as the angel of Israel in the late Jewish apocalyptic was an obvious source of influence for angelomorphic thinking on Christ.[7] It is here, perhaps more than in the general Jewish traditional belief in angels, that the source for an angelomorphic understanding of Christ is to be found. A second point of interest is that while there is no full discussion of the archangels, the Shepherd of Hermas seems to move away from the assumption of a simple count of seven (or four) to a count of six plus one. In *Vis.* 3.4.2 mention is made of the six senior angels who build a tower (cf. *Vis.* 3.1.6), and in *Sim.* 9.2.7f the mighty and glorious angel is accompanied by six men. The writer, then, seems to be developing a distinctive line of thought from Ezek. 9: 2, which became increasingly prominent later.[8]

It is noticeable that on the demonic side Hermas tends towards a dualism, especially in the *Mandates*, where the division between God and the Devil results in a consequential dualism of two spirits, two angels, and a double tongue. Although similar in thought to The Testaments of the Twelve Patriarchs and the DSS, Hermas shows no advance upon their ideas here.[9]

Among the lesser points, it is worth noting that the suggestion that the just become angels at death begins to appear (*Vis.* 2.2.7 and *Sim.* 9.25). Also the word δυνάμεις seems to be used to mean 'virtues' rather than 'powers'. In *Vis.* 1.3.4 God is described as ὁ θεὸς τῶν δυνάμεων, but the phrase clearly has a moral sense that is far removed from the LXX and ὁ κύριος τῶν δυνάμεων. This is confirmed when in *Sim.* 9.13.2 and 9.15.2 the maidens are described as δυνάμεις τοῦ Υἱοῦ θεοῦ. What is most striking, however, is the complete absence of the Pauline language of the powers from these writings. In language, and to a large degree in thought, the world reflected is that of the OT and late Jewish literature. For example, the Devil is the tempter (*Mand.* 4.3.6) and an otherwise unknown angel, Thegri, shuts up the beast of persecution (*Vis.* 4.2.4). This is typical of most early Jewish Christian writing, in which there are varieties of interpretation of the angels, whether of Michael and Christ, or of Gabriel as the Spirit or as the Word.[10] But the angels themselves continue to function in a wholly Jewish way: they worship God in heaven and administer the world for God.[11] This latter task is also elaborated in terms of angelic guardianship of the ascending soul.

2 The Ascension of Isaiah

There is little development of the concept of the Devil in early Jewish Christianity. Increasingly he is described as 'the ruler of this world' and the discussion about the fall of the angels is also developed. Several streams of thought coalesce to create this view. The greater stress upon the fall of the angels is coupled with a heightened appreciation of the power of Satan in order to create a strong doctrine of Satan's rebellion and fall. The two are mixed in Justin, *Dial.* 124.3. Another theme, that of the jealousy of Satan at Adam, begins to appear (e.g. *Vit. Adam.* 12: 17 and 2 Bar. 61: 10), and is much developed by the gnostics. The way in which passages of the OT were open to such elaboration may be seen in the early exegesis of Gen. 1: 26. The rabbis allowed a reference to angels only alongside a firm monotheism. The gnostic approach, however, with its assumption of a large number of supramundane beings, also latched onto this text.[12] Only in one work is there comprehensive mention of demonic principalities, and this is The Ascension of Isaiah.

This work is composite, and therefore we have to take careful note of which sections contain these references. There are two basic works – The Martyrdom (1–5) and the Ascension (6–9). The latter is certainly Christian, including the additional material in 9: 2–22. The Martyrdom, however, is more complex. Flemming and Duensing regard only 1: 1–2*a*, 5*b*–12; 2: 1–5, 16 as original and the rest as Christian interpolations. Charles, however, allows that 1: 1–2*a*, 6*b*–13*a*; 2: 1–8; 2: 10 – 3: 12; and 5: 1*c*–14 are original.[13] The Christian passages in the Martyrdom and the Ascension may date from the second century, although Charles is inclined to put them earlier. Certainly Heb. 9: 37 would seem to suggest that the Martyrdom was known to Christian groups, probably before A.D. 70. It is especially noteworthy that the prince of this world, who has his own ranks of angels, authorities and powers, is only mentioned in the Christian sections of the work, with the possible exception of 2: 2, where interpolation seems probable. These references are among the earliest in which Satan is not merely a powerful figure who is opposed to God, but one at whose command there are mighty powers greater than the demons. His authority is magnified so that he is portrayed as the mirror image of God: both are surrounded by their angelic hosts, who give them their status. To this extent we may agree with Daniélou's distinction between the higher and lower demons, but at the same time note that this particular distinction is only found in the Ascension of Isaiah and is not widespread in this area of Judaeo-Christian thought.[14]

In the Ascension there is an account of the hidden descent of Christ, who, when he reaches the lowest of the seven heavens, comes to 'the angels of the air' who were 'plundering and doing violence to one another'. This is a mixture of ideas. In general the book follows the lines of Jewish apocalyptic and thinks of seven heavens, below which is the firmament, the lower part of which is the air. In the firmament are the prince of the world (Sammael in 7: 9 and Satan in the same verse) and his hosts, while immediately below are the angels of the air.[15] In behaviour and function there is little difference between them. The idea that the air was full of demons had gained wide acceptance by the second century A.D. and the fact that the word 'angels' is used here is not surprising in the light of Philo's remark (*de gig.* 6) that what the Greeks call demons, the Jews call angels. The main stream of Jewish apocalyptic, such as that in 1 Enoch, understood the demons as the souls of the giants, who were the illicit offspring of the union of the angels with the daughters of men. On this point, however, Ascension shows a new confusion, which is similar to that in Athenagoras (*Leg.* 25). According to this the air is full not only of demons but also of the fallen angels themselves. It may remind us of the haunting of the firmament by Sammael (2 En. 29: 4), and the use of this idea in Eph. 2: 2. This constitutes a distinctively Judaeo-Christian imprint on the notion of the air being full of demons. Pagan thought on the subject developed in the second century and onwards, being attributed by Porphyry to 'some Platonists'.[16] Plato had described the demons as intermediaries between God and men, and the daemonising of the world was a basic aspect of the substratum of Greek religion.[17] The idea, however, of the lower air being peopled with hostile forces is a characteristic of Jewish Christian thinking that rapidly gained ground and is itself unparalleled in Jewish or pagan thought at this time.[18] The evil spirits or demons were in Jewish apocalyptic and later in rabbinic thought mainly concerned with the world of men. They were thus agents e.g. of sickness and disease, and as such called for exorcism or apotropaic magic. Sometimes that took on a moral connotation, and then required resistance or repudiation. Both ideas are also found in Christian thought, but the distinctive idea that the demons as evil spirits inhabit the air created within Christianity a climate for the concept of the conquest of these demonic forces, who, as here in the Ascension, began to be associated with the mighty powers that were being ranged alongside Satan. Once the demons are understood as wholly evil and the Greek term has lost its basic neutrality, it is no great step to the associating of the language of the powers with them so that they too become evil. In addition these ἀρχαί are clearly mightier than mere demons, since they are the hosts of Satan himself. In time a distortion of the Pauline texts and revaluation of his teachings becomes inevitable.

The contribution of the angelomorphic Christologies of early Jewish Christianity to the development of Christian thinking on demonic forces was not very significant. It was in the first place fairly localised. So long as it represented a development of the angelology of the OT it produced nothing startling. But as soon as the angels are associated with unconsciously revalued demons, then the way is open to a whole new range of interpretations. It is interesting that Syria is an important location for this development. It was open to Greek influence through Antioch and to Persian ideas from the East. If, as seems likely, Cumont is right that the evil demons of neo-Platonism were in part developed under Zoroastrian influence, then such influences were also in all probability part of the environment in which Jewish Christians of Syria lived.[19] The linking of these ideas with the apocalyptic emphasis on the fall of the angels would make way for the notion of a kingdom of evil that was ruled over by God's almost equal adversary, Satan.

Nor should the implications of the anti-Pauline stance of some Jewish Christianity, notably Ebionism, be overlooked. Naturally all Jewish Christianity in Western Syria was not Ebionite, but it is interesting that the Petrine tradition, which possibly derives from that area, is directed against Paul both as a man and as a teacher.[20] This is clearly expressed in the Clementine Homily 17: 13–20 and in the strange comment in 2 Pet. 3: 15f. The latter reference is usually interpreted as referring to early gnostic exegesis of Pauline texts.[21] But it is also a sign of the spread of an anti-Pauline stance in some Syrian Churches, against which the writer of 2 Peter, albeit with a rather double-edged remark, places himself. In the light of this, two points become clear with regard to the interpretation of the Pauline texts on the powers. They are, first, not cited in this Jewish Christian literature because their authority is not accepted. Thus the position of Jewish Christianity on the place of the powers will offer nothing positive for the interpretation of Paul. Secondly, however, although the actual Pauline texts were not considered, the association of the fall of the angels with the mighty figure of Satan, together with the development of the concept of demons under the influence of the East, all contributed to the creation of a doctrine of evil powers. When this belief later was received by other Christian writers, who themselves were well separated from the original Jewish Christian environment and were exposed to the spiritual ideas of the Graeco-Roman world, it naturally attached itself to and was interpreted in terms of the Pauline texts, which themselves were returning into vogue. These were unconsciously reinterpreted and Paul's thought took on a new meaning. This process will be outlined in detail below.

9

THE GREEK APOLOGISTS

Concerning the powers as such there is little in the Greek apologists, although some passages in Justin require attention.[1] On the demons, however, there is abundant material. Consciously writing for the pagan world, these apologists had to give careful thought to the religious assumptions of that world in order to present their own faith. They focused this difference primarily in the idolatry of the pagan, and it is this that makes the apologists fundamentally different from their Christian predecessors.[2] They show every sign of being aware of the Judaeo-Christian explanation of idols in terms of demons. However, their apology is primarily aimed at the pagan world of which δεισιδαιμονία was a general characteristic. In order to encounter this word, they take the Greek sense of δαίμων to themselves. This is part of their positive approach to the Greek world as a basis upon which they can develop their Christian argument. Justin's evaluation of Socrates (*1 Apol.* 5.3) is another example of this approach. They then, however, have to deal with idolatry and demons, and they are thus led to a position similar to that which they found in the Judaeo-Christian tradition. The fact that they reach the same end point, however, should not obscure the other fact that they reach it by arguing *de novo* about genuine Greek assumptions about demons. They do not simply impose a Judaeo-Christian solution. We observe them taking the term δαίμονες in its normal Greek sense and revaluing it in their own context in order to denounce idolatry and to prepare for the proclamation of the gospel. A similar process may be observed in Justin's use of ἄγγελος, which at times reverts to its basic Greek meaning of 'messenger' (*Dial.* 56.4). He calls the Word an angel, not on the basis of any Jewish Christian angelomorphic Christology, but simply because the Word for him is God's messenger to men. There is here a coalescing of the OT concept of the angel of God with the pagan belief in Hermes as the messenger of the Gods and of the doctrine of the Logos (*1 Apol.* 22.2; cf. *Dial.* 24.2; 76.3; 126.1). To reinforce this theoretical basis the apologists made frequent use of Jesus' teaching on the attitude towards demons as recorded in the gospels.

In the case of Justin this contrasts with his ignorance of the Pauline literature, which interestingly contains only one reference to demons.[3] The two
apparent quotations from Paul in Justin are very doubtful.[4] There is, however, one further reason why Justin shows little concern with the powers
as such. His longest work, *The Dialogue with Trypho*, is addressed to a Jew
and therefore is based upon the common ground between Jew and
Christian. Questions concerning the interpretation of the OT abound and,
in the light of the lack of concern in the OT with hostile powers, it is not
surprising that they play so small a role in Justin's thought. Tatian, like
Justin, begins with the Judaeo-Christian concept of demons. By contrast
Athenagoras adopts a more Greek approach, arguing from the givenness of
idolatry but saying nothing about hostile powers since, as we have seen,
they play no part in Greek thought at that time.[5]

1 Justin Martyr

Justin's *Apologies* are explicitly addressed to the pagan world and therefore contain a critique of contemporary religion and its practice (especially
see *2 Apol.* 15.2ff). He knows and employs the myth of the fallen angels
(*Dial.* 79.1), but avoids speculation about hierarchies of angels or of
demons. A major point of interest, particularly in view of his ignorance of
Paul, lies in his use of the couplet ἀρχαὶ καὶ ἐξουσίαι. It occurs twice in the
Dialogue (49.8 and 41.1) and there is a similar phrase – ἀρχαὶ καὶ
βασιλεῖαι – in *Dial.* 131. In *Dial.* 49.8 Justin mixes certain texts from the
OT and argues that the concealed power of God was present in Christ
crucified. The demons are mentioned along with the powers, but there are
indications that the latter are not viewed as demonic forces. For they are
localised by the addition of τῆς γῆς, and in the parallel (*Dial.* 131) the
reference is certainly to the nations of the world. In that passage Justin
compares the faith of converted Gentiles with that of Jews, employing in
the course of his argument Deut. 32: 7ff. He seems to be expressing the
hope that Christ will become Lord of all the kingdoms of the world. The
demons in Justin function in a distinctive way; there is an amalgam of the
Greek daemonising of the world with the Judeao-Christian belief in maleficent demons. Their chief importance for the Christian is as the object of
exorcisms, the demonstrable efficacy of which in the name of Christ is
proof of the truth of the gospel.

This viewpoint also explains his confusion over the defeat of the
demons. According to *1 Apol.* 2.60 this is achieved through the incarnation, while in *Dial.* 49.8 it is associated with the cross, as is the defeat of
the Serpent (*Dial.* 91 and 94). The answer to the Greek daemonising of the
world lies in the revelation of the incarnation, while the connection of the

demons with the Devil and the Serpent points typologically towards the cross. Generally Justin understands the demons to be the old gods (*1 Apol.* 5), who are involved in magic, with the Magi (*1 Apol.* 56), and with idols (*1 Apol.* 41). However, he personalises the idols more than is usual in the OT. An example of this tendency may be seen in *2 Apol.* 5, in which he makes a rare allusion to the demons as the offspring of the union of angels and women, but then confuses this offspring with the fallen angels themselves.[6] He also combines the angelic custodians of the world with the fallen angels. The way is thus left open for the development of the concept of a kingdom of mighty powers who are under Satan's control and are opposed to God.[7] The same notion is found in the other mention of the powers in *Dial.* 41.1, where they are explicitly evil. It is notable that he can use the Pauline couplet to refer to evil powers without explanation. More interesting, however, is the fact that logically there is no place in Justin's theology of redemption for the cross, but that it nevertheless plays a significant part in his thought.[8] In this passage the connection of the cross with the overthrow of the powers is explicit, but no consequences are drawn from it. Indeed, the phrase may even be a quotation.

In facing the problem of continuing evil after Christ Justin offers the concept of the economy of God, but he defies systematisation. For he retains some of the language that he is beginning to apply to evil forces in its traditional reference to good angels. Thus e.g. οἱ ἄρχοντες (*Dial.* 24) are good, as are on occasions (e.g. *Dial.* 85) δυνάμεις. This latter word, however, is as ambivalent in Justin as elsewhere: in *Dial.* 85 they are good angels of God, but they are certainly malevolent as the forces of magic (*Dial.* 77.9f) and of witchcraft (*Dial.* 105.4f). As always with this word, it is difficult to determine to what extent it is being hypostatised. In the singular Justin often uses it to refer to the indwelling power of God in the Word, which is demonstrated by the power of exorcisms in his name.

One further point that deserves notice is Justin's use of Ps. 110: 1. In *Dial.* 32f there is no Christological importance whatever, but in *1 Apol.* 45 the 'enemies' are identified as demons. Yet Justin's exegesis is exact: there is no mention of a battle between Christ and the demons, but, as according to the psalm itself, a reference only to the heavenly session of the Son until God has defeated the demons and accomplished his aims. The third occurrence, *Dial.* 54, is exactly like the uses in the NT, where, without interest in the enemies, the text is proof of the relationship between the Father and the Son.

That Justin does not come to a theology of the cross as the place of mighty conflict between Christ and the demonic forces is primarily due to his historical context. The problem of the inevitability of Fate rapidly increased in the second part of the second century and we therefore find it faced squarely by Justin's pupil, Tatian. The Christological questions that faced Justin were less soteriological than cosmological. He therefore adopted cosmological language for his discussions of the person and work of Christ.[9] This cosmology includes the question of demons, but they are still conceived as part of the created universe and external to men. According to Justin, men are subject to the attacks and deceits of the demons, especially through idols, with their demand for bloody sacrifice, and through magic. Rescue is achieved through the divine revaluation of the cosmos at the incarnation. Ultimately there is no place for demons, and the Christian need have no regard for them. The hostility of the world to the believer is based upon the work of the Devil, and he is fitted into an overriding concept of the economy of God. Such a position could be held only for a short time in the light of experience, for the world, when interpreted radically in terms of Fate, demanded something more coherent and more effectively soteriological. There was a need for a theology of the experience of salvation, and we may discern the beginnings of this in Tatian, particularly in his counter to the claims of astrology.[10]

2 Tatian

By comparison with his teacher, Tatian seems to stand slightly aloof from Jewish thought. His conviction, however, is that even the, to him, barbarian culture of Judaeo-Christianity is superior to the wisdom of the Greeks, inspired as it is by demons. He emphasises the demonic aspects of paganism and derives his understanding of demons from the Judaeo-Christian myth of the rebellion of Satan. This effectively puts the fall of the demons, who are associated with idolatry, prior to the fall of man. The deceit that the demons practise on all men is exactly that which they formerly practised on the first man, Adam (*Orat.* 7 and 14). There is, however, a subtle change in Tatian from Justin's view of demons. Tatian constantly stresses the desire of the demons to enslave men: they are more than beings that cause evil and have become beings in their own right who wish to bring men into servitude. Thus the way is open for demons in their hostility to men to be interpreted in terms of wider cosmic forces (*Orat.* 16ff). Historical circumstances explain this change. Tatian lived later than Justin, just at the time when magic was being influenced in the West by oriental ideas, such as those of Hostanes.[11] He can view the whole range of pagan belief – idolatry, magic, and astrology – as being directly under demonic control. Most significant here is the mention of astrology, which appears for the first time in this connection in Christian apology. Tatian accepts a sympathy between the stars and earthly events (*Orat.* 8), but he is also aware of the developed astrology of Graeco-Roman thought, by which the planets were linked with acknowledged deities, and therefore for Tatian also with the demons. The enslavement of the world to the vagaries of Fate in the stars is for him just one example of the activity of demons, from whom the Christian may be released by baptism.[12]

3 Conclusion

Justin and Tatian, and to a lesser degree Athenagoras, represent an import-ant stage in the growth of belief in the malevolence of the powers. Holding to the Jewish Christian emphasis on the incarnation, Justin now brings the fact of the cross into parallel with it. He also publicly fuses the Judaeo-Christian position on demons with the underlying Greek understanding of δαίμονες. In so doing he probably reflects tendencies in the world as he found it rather than consciously attempts a synthesis. However, from this time on in the Christian tradition it is reckoned that the religions of the world are demonically inspired and that the demons are to be interpreted as evil. Nor should we overlook the occurrence of the couplet ἀρχαὶ καὶ ἐξουσίαι. Justin does not develop it, but the fact that he could use the phrase in such a sense is interesting and a clear pointer to future trends. His identification of Satan with the Serpent and his treatment of the defeat of that Serpent on the cross are also signs for the future. For the way is now open for the agglomeration of kindred ideas around the mighty figure of a rebellious angelic leader, who establishes his own kingdom of powers, which are hostile both to man and to God. In Justin we may discern the beginnings of that mixture which became a presupposition of the Christian message to the world and led to the eventual reinterpretation of Paul's references to ἀρχαὶ καὶ ἐξουσίαι.

Tatian, like Justin, appears to be unaware of these Pauline texts. Never-theless, in his work too we may see significant developments. For once the rebellion of Satan and the host of demons prior to the creation of man becomes a dogma, then the deception of men by the demons through magic and idolatry, which the apologists saw around them, was given theological validity and was used to explain that domination of men by the forces of destiny, which became in the second half of the second cen-tury a preoccupation of the Graeco-Roman world. The apologists by their commitment to the changing thought of their day witness to the setting of the stage for a revaluation of Paul's words because of the new meanings that were being given to the terminology that he had employed.

10

CLEMENT OF ALEXANDRIA

On two counts a place in this survey must be found for Clement of
Alexandria. As a thinker in his own right he demonstrates many of the
important trends in Christian thought in the second half of the second
century. Although he worked mainly in Alexandria with its Graeco-
Egyptian culture, he had also travelled and his writings and thought are
thoroughly Greek. In the second place, he is important as the immediate
predecessor of Origen, the man who above all contributed to the theology
of cosmic forces.

Clement's philosophy is fundamentally Platonic. In *Strom.* 5.92.5f,
in a discussion of Greek borrowings from Hebrew literature, Clement
speaks of the Devil, 'the Prince of Demons', with reference to Plato,
Leg. 10.896DE, *Phaedr.* 240AB, and *Leg.* 10.906A. In his exposition of
the Platonic world soul, he simply mentions the texts and does not
attempt to come to grips with the problem of evil in the world. This is for
him, as it was for Plato, one of the given facts of life, and Clement shows
himself to be at some remove from the problem of the experience of a
force of evil to which the Christian message might attempt the offer of
salvation.[1] On the other hand, he also shows that he is fully conversant
with the Judaeo-Christian tradition, by which the demons are identified
with the fallen angels and are wholly evil. They are greedy for bloody
sacrifices and are worshipped in the guise of idols. These demons, however,
play a significantly less important part in Clement's thought than they do
in Origen's. In his discussion of the spiritual world Clement is directly in
debt to Philo and to Jewish–Alexandrian philosophy. He has much to say
about the δυνάμεις, 'powers of the Spirit', who coalesce in the Logos, and
in the context of his Platonism they function very much as the forms do
for Plato himself.[2]

As an exegete Clement uses almost the whole NT corpus. This means
that we can observe how he handles the Pauline texts on the powers. Of
the relevant passages he cites only 1 Cor. 2: 6ff; possibly 1 Cor. 15: 24,
with Phil. 2: 10; Rom. 8: 38f; Eph. 6: 12; and Col. 1: 16. In the citation

of 1 Cor. 2: 6ff he attached no importance to the ἄρχοντες (*Strom.* 5.25.2; 6.68.1; 5.65.5). The text is mainly used in connection with wisdom and the one occasion when it is cited in full (*Strom.* 5.25.2) the ἄρχοντες are probably identified with philosophers. The use of Eph. 6: 12 is similarly oblique. In the *Stromateis* there are two passing references in which the struggle is interpreted in psychological terms and the powers are internalised (*Strom.* 3.101.3 and 5.93.2). In *Exc. ex Theod.* 48.2 he reports on the work of the Demiurge, who is said to have made the πνευματικὰ πονηρίας, with whom we struggle, out of matter and Λυπή. The most important text, however, is *Ecl. Proph.* 20.1, in which there is a blatant psychologising of the evil spirits, which achieve their ends through the sins that were man's masters.

Apart from the use of Col. 1: 16 (*Exc. ex Theod.* 43.3), in which the forces are not regarded as evil but as evidence of the importance of the angel of counsel as head of all things after the Father, there only remains *Strom.* 4.96.1 in which a discussion of martyrdom involves a citation of Rom. 8: 38f. Having refuted the views of Basilides and Valentinus, Clement offers thoughts on the theme 'Love your enemies'. Beginning with Matt. 5: 44f, he adds Matt. 5: 24, in which the adversary is interpreted not as the body but as the Devil. He then continues with a citation and exposition of Rom. 8: 38f, which is significant. The text that he uses, or recalls from memory, is distinctive. The word δυνάμεις, which floats in the MSS tradition, is completely missing, and τὰ μέλλοντα is also absent, so that the series of couplets in the verse is destroyed. The reason for this, probably, is that Clement is arguing about the immediate experience of the Christian and any reference to the future would undermine his case by enabling the whole argument theoretically to be transferred away from the present. The omission of δυνάμεις is a general textual problem, but in this instance it may be that in the light of Clement's philosophy of δυνάμεις there is no exegetical point that he can develop. There is the additional fact that, although in his exposition he uses the couplet ἀρχαὶ καὶ ἐξουσίαι, he seems not to have the text that incorporated the word ἐξουσίαι.[3] When Origen later cites the passage, however, he does include the word and he also certainly interprets these ἐξουσίαι as hostile forces against which the Christian has to fight (*de princ.* 3.2).

Apart from the significance of the text, there are three areas of interest in Clement's exegesis. There is, in the first place, a strongly human understanding of the Devil. Clement is trying to explain the suffering that Christians endure in this world, as opposed to that suffered by the gnostics. He accepts the existence of the Devil, but avoids transferring the problems of Christian experience to some metaphysical explanation. Rather we have here a combination of two aspects of his thought: the Devil, conceived in terms of a maleficent world soul and thus to some extent depersonalised, is joined with the demons, who have also been depersonalised by being internalised and the struggle with them put into psychological terms. Thus the conception of the Devil is focused in the acts of men, in which the evil force in the world is specified in the particular situation of persecution. Secondly, we may discern how the word ἀρχαί becomes evil when Greek thinking is applied to a text the background of which lay primarily in the Jewish world. The ἀρχαί are first made singular (ἀρχή), and this term is then referred to Satan, probably by association with ἄρχων. The title 'Satan' is unusual in Clement, who prefers 'The Devil'. He also seems aware of the double sense of ἀρχή as both 'beginning' and 'rule'. The beginning of the life of Satan as opposer occurred when he wilfully rebelled against God – ὁ βίος ὃν εἵλετο – and in the same way his demonic Lordship also derives from that rebellion. The word εἵλετο refers to an act of deliberate intent. After the neutral term ἀρχή has been brought in to explain ἀρχαί, it is then given evil overtones by explicit reference to the rebellion of Satan. The complete explanation is finally introduced by Clement with τοιαῦται γάρ: the evil ἀρχαί depend for their existence (κατ᾽ αὐτόν) upon the rebellious Satan. This is a perfect example of a trend that reaches its climax with Origen. The words of Paul are reinterpreted in the light of the changed presuppositions of the time, in this case that of the rebellion of Satan. Clement does not develop this thought, but his argument here is a sign of what was to come. The third point of interest is that which explains why Clement does not develop a theology of evil powers. Christian gnosis is the key. The gnostic Christian will be able to endure his martyrdom, for he will with philosophic calm evaluate the concerns of life and, recognising in the creation activity rather than being, he will avoid being dragged down. The explanation of τὰ ἐνεστῶτα in terms of the merchant and the soldier echoes the accommodation of the gospel to life in Alexandria, which is most clear in *Quis div. salv.* 11ff, where the right use of wealth as an aid to righteousness is discussed. The difference in the valuation of the world between Clement and Origen also to some extent explains why the one has no fear of evil forces, while the other sees them all around.

Clement's understanding of salvation is in terms of knowledge.[4] Theologically he has a spatial theory: just as the world is viewed in three tiers (*Strom.* 4.1.57), the lowest of which is where Christ and the apostles preached, so salvation is regarded as an ascent (*Strom.* 6.44f). In *Strom.* 6.105 he arranged the degrees of glory. The goal of faith is to become like the angels, who themselves move up and down the ladder of hierarchy, the highest rank of which allows contemplation of the divine (*Ecl. Proph.* 57). This hierarchical arrangement persists even to the consummation of all things (*Ecl. Proph.* 56). The end product of the work of God is that men are divided into three classes: the unbelievers, who are dead; the Christian gnostics, who contemplate God; and ordinary believers, who have not attained this blessedness.[5]

It is clear even from so brief a survey that any concept of salvation in terms of the defeat of the powers is not likely to figure prominently in Clement's work.[6] This is confirmed by the absence of reference in the existing writings to Col. 2: 15 and his avoidance of the demonic interpretation of the rulers in 1 Cor. 2: 6ff. The importance for Clement of Eph. 6: 12 is itself significant in the way in which it is wholly understood in moral and psychological terms. If salvation is to be by invitation of Christ into union with himself (e.g. *Strom.* 4.1.57), then he is bound to be regarded primarily as a teacher and instructor (*Paed.* 1.2). Upon Platonic suppositions about the One and the Many, Christ is bound to be viewed in static terms, and the Platonic conception of God in terms of the highest good means that evil is not given independent and personalised existence. With such a Christ and such a view of evil, Clement, in spite of his knowledge of the Christian tradition, has no room for any defeat of the powers of evil.

Finally, we may note his distinctive view of the protoctist angels.[7] These are the chief angels, who rank with the archangels and usually number seven (*Strom.* 6.16). The number seven binds the archangels, the seven-branched candlestick, the planets, the seven eyes of God, and the seven days of the week together. Of particular interest is Clement's connection of the seven first-born angels with the seven days of creation. In *Ecl. Proph.* 56 a double association is made: on the one hand they are connected with the stars, in particular the ἀρχοντικὸς ἄγγελος and the sun. This is the place of supreme contemplation of God, where at the parousia the just will stand with the apostles. On the other hand, they are also connected with the days: ἡμέραι δ' ἄγγελοι ἐκλήθησαν.[8] Elsewhere the Logos himself is described as the day of all days.[9] This awareness of the number seven and the connection of angels with the days becomes increasingly significant in Christian thinking.

Three main points may be made on Clement's angelology. In the first place, although the significance of the number seven is noted, he does not give a very important place to the astronomical (and therefore to the astrological) significance of the number. Even in Alexandrian Christianity at the end of the second century there seems little connection between angels and planets. This is a concrete reminder that astrology was not the all-pervading terror for men of that period that it is sometimes made out to be. Secondly we see in Clement further alignment of the seven-day week with the significant number seven of the Judaeo-Christian tradition. Thirdly, and most important, in the amalgam of ideas that Clement presents, one may see how easily a powerful doctrine of evil, angelic forces could begin to exist. But such a doctrine is not yet prominent, and Clement's angelology, in spite of the number mysticism, still remains close to the Judaeo-Christian tradition of angels and to Philo's understanding of the δυνάμεις.

Clement's major impact for our purpose lies in his use of the Pauline texts. He there shows not the slightest awareness of any tradition that sees in those texts a world of mighty demonic forces. His exegesis of Rom. 8: 38f, however, is of fundamental importance to this study, for in it we have the clearest example of the way in which the Pauline texts, when interpreted outside the context of the mid-first century, were capable of yielding new meaning. At the same time, however, the fact that he does not interpret the ἀρχαί here or elsewhere as mighty demonic powers is also a timely reminder that any particular understanding of salvation requires a particular world of experience to which to relate. Clement had no experience or philosophy of mighty evil forces, and his theology consequently shows little interest in them. The situation of others, especially some gnostics and Origen, was quite different and their experience demanded a new doctrine of salvation. To meet that, Paul was reinterpreted yet again. Clement, however, provides a sure link in the chain of evidence that such new understandings of Paul were developing, and in his exegesis of Rom. 8: 38f provides a paradigm of the method by which the powers were read into Pauline theology.

11

THE INFLUENCE OF GNOSTICISM

No area of early Christian thought contains more references to intermediaries than gnosticism. All gnosis, using the definition for this suggested by the Messina Colloquium, has this tendency, but our concern is
limited to 'gnosticism', a specific phenomenon of the second century.[1]
Because the writings of Irenaeus and, on this particular question, of
Tertullian are closely connected with gnosticism, they are also discussed
in this chapter. This is a limited study, which aims not at surveying the
various understandings of intermediaries that appear in the gnostic texts,
but only at continuing work at establishing the interpretations of the
powers that were current in the second century and determining the use
made of the Pauline texts on the subject.

1 Irenaeus

The powers played an important part in all the various systems that
Irenaeus combats in *adversus haereses*. Simon Magus was considered the
source of all gnostic error. He employed the myth of the fallen angels and
of the powers, which were generated to create the world. Redemption was
thus both from the Law, as given by angels, and from the world, as created
by them.[2] A similar distancing of God from the world by means of intermediaries is discernible in Saturnilus, who, following Menander, argued
that the Unknown Father created ἀγγέλους, ἀρχαγγέλους, δυνάμεις καὶ
ἐξουσίας, and that by the seven chief angels was the world made (*adv.
haer.* 1.17f). Clearly Simon, Menander and Saturnilus relied upon Jewish
or Judaeo-Christian material in their arguments, particularly in their use
of Gen. 1: 26.[3] When, however, we come to the account of Basilides, we
notice a more developed view of the powers.[4] The Father produced Logos
and Phronesis, whence came Sophia and Dynamis, who in turn produced
'virtutes, principes et angelos, quos et primos vocat' (*adv. haer.* 1.19).
These form the heaven from which other heavens emanate, and man seeks
to escape from the lordly creators of the world. There is in addition some
astrological influence on this system, which becomes clear in the

calculations of the 365 heavens and the use of the name Abraxas.[5] Ophite thought is similarly concerned with the world rulers and the control of the planets over men. But there are further complications, notably the problem of the relation of Ialdabaoth to the Hebdomad and the place of the Mother.[6] There is a second Hebdomad too, which consists of seven demons, who are conceived in a wholly Jewish way. The specifically astrological conceptions of the Ophites are confirmed by the account in Origen (*contra Cels.* 5.24ff).

Amid this variety of views of the supramundane world it is important to note that both Simon and Saturnilus use the Jewish myth of the fallen angels in order to stress the corruption of these powers, whilst Basilides and the Ophites simply assume the hostility of these forces towards men. There is common ground in the understanding of the powers as malevolent and hostile, wherever the idea is originally conceived. They are always concerned with the creation of the material world and by their nature and function they emphasise the dualism that is fundamental to all gnostic thought.[7] This appears very clearly in the second book of *adversus haereses*, in which Irenaeus begins his full refutation of the errors. His anti-gnostic arguments are always based upon the doctrine of creation and are designed, through use of scripture, notably John 1: 3, to undermine the speculative nature of gnostic cosmogony. For Irenaeus the angels and powers, whatever language is used, always remain part of God's heavenly court and are not allowed to become intermediaries in the process of creation, and certainly not to be beings that act in their own right against the will of God. The demons and apostate spirits, who are at the Devil's command, tend in accord with the Judaeo-Christian tradition to be connected with magic and with idols. Irenaeus' own view of any other beings is most clearly expressed in *adv. haer.* 2.46.3, where he denies the concept of the Demiurge: 'quid autem illa quae sunt super coelum, et quae non praetereunt, quanta sunt, Angeli, Archangeli, Throni, Dominationes, Potestates innumerabiles?'[8] His answer is that they are all made by God as spiritual and holy beings. There is no room for fallen powers, as is clear in the similar argument in 3.8.3. It is the very simplicity of this theology of powers that commends itself. Three points are regularly made: all things, visible and invisible, were created by the Father through the Word; the angelic forces are God's powers; the demons and devils are focused in the person of the Devil, who is the fount of all evil, and they function in magic and idolatry. Irenaeus, then, stands firmly in the Judaeo-Christian tradition.

The question of the work of Christ and the demons is more complex.[9] In *adv. haer.* 3.36 the victory of Christ is understood in terms of sin and the antichrist, together with the destruction of death. In this passage, which includes a citation of 1 Cor. 15: 24f and 55, Irenaeus shows familiarity with Pauline language and interprets it. The nexus of sin, death and Adam (for which also see *adv. haer.* 5.27.2) is derived from Rom. 5: 6ff. The Irenaean addition is the Devil and Antichrist. But this, we may surmise, was only due to the development of the association of death with the Devil, which increases in post-biblical Christian and rabbinic thought.[10] Unlike the gnostics, Irenaeus does not see the world as dominated by powers and Fate, but regards man's bondage in terms of sin (the radical disjunction of man and God), death (the consequence of sin), and the Devil, who is sin and death incarnate (*adv. haer.* 5.27.2). The incarnation and the cross are both part of the total process of man's redemption from these forces. Like Paul, Irenaeus needs no proliferation of the powers of evil. The inevitable result of such a proliferation is a tendency to cosmological dualism, which was for the Christian fundamentally impossible.[11] Thus against the gnostics Irenaeus opposes the totality of creation as the work of God through the Word, so that salvation essentially becomes reconciliation.

Irenaeus is fully conversant with Paul's theology and uses many of the Pauline texts regularly. In his appreciation of the work of Christ, however, and of its ability to meet man's need, it is very noticeable that he never employs any text that can be interpreted in terms of a defeat of the cosmic powers. Thus e.g. he cites Colossians nineteen times and specifically uses 2: 14 and 2: 16, but the crucial verse 2: 15 is not found.[12] Again, the list of powers from Col. 1: 16, although found, is not used of evil powers.[13] And although considerable use is made of texts from Romans, Rom. 8: 38f is not employed. Yet, if Irenaeus himself was familiar with Paul's thought, it is clear from his accounts of the heresies that spiritual and malevolent powers were becoming prominent within the Christian Church. In particular the term ἄρχοντες, which appears frequently in the literature, requires investigation. As the texts stand at present, they appear without any given background. We have already noted the use of the term in Daniel and that in Paul it conforms to standard contemporary Greek usage. In the light, however, of the methods and possibilities inherent in gnostic exegesis, the actual Pauline meaning would count for little in the interpretation of such texts as 1 Cor. 2: 6ff.

2 The archons of gnosticism

Among the documents from Nag Hammadi is one entitled *The Hypostasis of the Archons*. The manuscript may be dated to *c.* 350 A.D., but the original, which must have been written in Greek, was probably much earlier.

Continuing studies on the text and particularly on the parallels, which are collected in Layton's edition, suggest that this text may be crucial evidence for second-century gnostic thinking on the archons.[14]

The meaning of *Hypostasis* in the title is disputed, but the work purports to give an account of the origin of the archons. Bullard has detected three possible sources: a gnostic writing on the Genesis account of creation; some apocalyptic material; and a framework that was composed by a Christian gnostic writer who was fond of the writings of John and the Letter to the Ephesians.[15] In accordance with this Christian tradition there is both a Chief Archon and a group of lesser archons, who all lack individuality. And, as we have noted from Irenaeus' account, they are chiefly important for cosmogonic reasons. The term $\dot{\alpha}\rho\chi\alpha\dot{\iota}$ does not occur, but there is a question over the use of $\dot{\epsilon}\xi o \upsilon \sigma \dot{\iota} \alpha \iota$, which is not easily resolved.[16] The term is clearly used in a personification for the spiritual forces of evil. Sometimes these appear as powers that are subservient to the Great Archon, i.e. the lesser archons. At other times, however, the seven powers themselves are $\dot{\epsilon}\xi o \upsilon \sigma \dot{\iota} \alpha \iota$ and include in their number the Chief Archon. This confusion should not occasion surprise. Bullard suggests concerning a later confusion in the book between the numbers twelve and seven that this is due to a common gnostic vocabulary from differing linguistic traditions.[17] Certainly gnostic writers borrow from any convenient source without regard for consistency. *HA* exhibits this characteristic at many points, but in particular the concept of the archons in this work exhibits an independence and confusion that show they are neither a Christian concept nor clearly derived from anywhere else. They are, therefore, a distinctively gnostic creation.[18] The significance, however, of the association of the numbers seven and twelve should not be overlooked. These numbers are similarly confused in *The Apocryphon of John*, where they appear to have astrological connections.[19] In *HA*, however, the twelve do not appear and the seven archons are the offspring of the Chief Archon. This probably does not relate to the seven planets and seven heavens, but to the angels of creation.[20] The Jewish myth of the angels of creation was taken over in the Jewish Christian tradition, but the seven are connected not with the planets but with the days of the week.[21] These seven days are those of the seven-day week, which itself is enshrined in Genesis, and not those of the planetary week.[22] Indeed some writers interpret the plural in Gen. 1: 26 in terms of the angels of creation.[23] Irenaeus only mentions the planets in connection with the Ophites, and Saturnilus is reported as referring to the seven angels without attaching them to planets. This suggests that the concept of the archons was developed in the Judaeo-Christian tradition of the angels of creation and that this tradition was originally prominent in gnostic thought. It is, therefore, of interest that the discussion of these archons in *HA* at the end of the fourth century is devoid of astrological interest. It might also be evidence for the persistence of this Judaeo-Christian view, even in the face of the undoubted pressures of astrology throughout this period.[24] This in itself is a definite development upon the thought of Paul and of John, who show no signs of awareness of such a connection between the angels and creation. But this approach certainly provides a background to the notion of archons as emanations (the δυνάμεις as angelic angels of God), and as creative powers (Gen. 1: 26) and, most importantly, as evil (the fallen angels). This collocation of ideas in its completeness is first found in the gnostic writers of the second century and the use of the term ἄρχοντες to refer to the beings produced by this amalgam is their special contribution.[25]

3 Tertullian

Among the writings of Tertullian are treatises against the Valentians and against Hermogenes. He is of additional value, however, as providing a different thought world from that with which we have so far dealt. He was not a great speculative theologian, but both before and during his Montanist phase showed himself an acute and spirited polemicist. In a discussion of the development in understanding of Pauline thought, however, Tertullian is of considerable importance. He had read Paul and devoted much time to expounding his thought. The sheer volume of material available also means that we have an opportunity to examine more questions in Tertullian than in any other writer prior to Origen. We may, therefore, discern tendencies and discover what appear to have been for him and for his opponents the fundamental points of Christian faith.[26] Because his writings are neither speculative nor, on the whole, historical, but immediate and combative, what is essential alone is used and peripheral matters are left aside.

It might, however, be objected that in dealing with Carthaginian Christianity we have moved from the Judaeo-hellenistic East into a Latin environment, and that Tertullian should be regarded less as a builder upon the Christian tradition than as one who relates that tradition to a new conceptual world. Of the origins of Christianity in North Africa little is known.[27] Yet clearly a large part of the populace was Greek-speaking and many inhabitants were immigrants from the East. Indeed, in many aspects, both Christian and pagan, the city exhibits a direct relationship with the Greek East. The evidence, for example, of Montanism at Carthage suggests that it was imported directly from Asia Minor. We are not then dealing with a Latin Church as opposed to the Greek and Jewish Churches at which we have hitherto looked.[28] The distinctiveness of African tradition lay not in its doctrines but in its ethos, with its uncompromising rejection of the world, eagerness for persecution, and schismatic tendencies. Tertullian is therefore a very valuable source of evidence for the ordinarily accepted beliefs of Christians in the second and early third centuries.

His treatment of the world of angels, demons, and the Devil is similar to that which we have noted in the developing Christian tradition. The demons are related to idols (*de spect.* 9; *de test. an.* 2; *ad Scap.* 2; *de idol.* 4), and he takes magic and exorcisms as facts of everyday life.[29] A similar conventionality is found in his treatment of angels. Myriads of them surround the throne of God and do his bidding (e.g. *adv. Prax.* 3), and his discussion of the flesh of Christ allows him to expatiate on the nature of angels (*de carn. Chr.* 6). Without doubt for him, however, the plurals of the OT prefigure the Trinity and Tertullian's writing is therefore devoid of that type of speculation which is found in the Judaeo-Christian tradition and gnosticism.[30] Three points are worth note in his treatment of angels. First, the term 'angelus' may now take on evil associations without any need for qualification. For this Tertullian depends on the phrase 'the Devil and his angels', because of which the whole concept of angels has become ambiguous (e.g. *de carn. Chr.* 14). Secondly, there is only one reference to ecstatic sharing in the worship of angels, in which a Montanist sister shares when she goes into ecstasy (*de an.* 9). Thirdly, the story of the fall of the angels retreats into the background. In some of the remarks on women it appears, but little use is made of it. Thus in *de cultu feminarum* the origin of female ornamentation is traced back to the attraction of women for the lustful angels. Yet for Tertullian this has little significance in itself, for the fall of man is dependent upon the prior fall of the Devil, who gains mastery over man through Eve ('ianua Diaboli'), who is realised in every woman.[31]

The question of theodicy was for Tertullian crucial, but his approach was through a dualism between God and the Devil. The classic statement is found in *adv. Marc.* 2.10, and in *de test. an.* 6 he remarks blatantly: 'Deus ubique et bonitas dei ubique; daemonium et maledictio daemonii ubique'. Satan as 'interpolator' and 'aemulator' (*de spect.* 2) fell from heaven, and for the moment is all powerful, ruling a kingdom of evil (*de spect.* 4). The conquest of evil, then, is transferred to the future and the final consummation (*Apol.* 23). There is no room in Tertullian's faith for a world ruled by a host of forces. Evil is concentrated in the Devil, who rules by the permissive will of God. When expounding God as Creator, it is instructive to note that the emphasis is wholly on the visible and experienced world, with little or no reference to a spiritual world of powers. In *Apol.* 17, for example, God is one 'qui totam molem istam cum omni instrumento elementorum, corporum spirituum Verbo quo iussit . . . de nihilo expressit'.[32] Similarly the person of Jesus and the incarnation are revelatory. A creed with a Montanist slant occurs in *de praesc. haer.* 13, which, when compared with earlier Christian writings and those of the gnostics, contains a notable lack of sense of achievement by the incarnation and death of Christ. This is partly explained by Tertullian's severely non-mythological approach to religion, but also because the concept of triumph is taken by Tertullian to apply to the struggle of the Christian in martyrdom rather than to a mythical war between Christ and the demons: 'et illos [*sc.* daemonas] numquam magis detriumphamus quam cum pro fidei obstinatione damnamur' (*Apol.* 27).

The psychologising of traditional concepts is especially obvious in his use of Eph. 6: 12.[33] In *ad mart.* 3 the language of Christian warfare is used, but without any obvious reference to Eph. 6. The passage is instructive, however, since it reminds us that Tertullian's understanding of the Christian life is always immediate and human rather than spiritual. It is rooted in physical asceticism and the ever-present hope of martyrdom. Thus Eph. 6: 12 is reapplied so that, for example, in *de praesc. haer.* 39f the πνευματικὰ πονηρίας ('spiritalibus nequitiae') are not demons but gnostics. A similar humanising or psychologising of the spirits is clear in two further passages of note. In *de ieiun.* 17 the hearty eating of the non-Christian athlete is contrasted with the asceticism of the Christian preparing for martyrdom. The hostile forces are those who would throw the Christian to the beasts. The translation of κοσμοκράτορες as 'mundi potestates' effectively removes any sense of otherworldly dynasties and allows a fully human interpretation.[34] Tertullian was aware of the technical Valentinian use of this word, but notably uses the more usual translation 'munditenens' (*adv. Val.* 22). The psychologising of the text is clear in *adv. Marc.* 3.14.3, where the genitive of quality in the original phrase, πονηρίας, has become a genitive of content, which is expanded by the addition of 'concupiscentia', and the whole thought again placed in the context of martyrdom.

The Christian tradition that Tertullian received seems to have lacked any strong ideas of salvation as release from the domination of mighty hostile forces and any concept of their defeat by Christ on the cross. The reality of the present Lord was experienced as much as was the reality of the Devil. In such a situation the demands upon religion are that it must give assurance in the present, when preparing for and facing the lions, and hope for the future. This is exactly what we find in Tertullian: the future hope is of the judgement and condemnation of the Devil and his angels; the present assurance is found in the identification of the earthly enemies of the Christians with the servants of Satan.[35] Certainly, as has been noted, Tertullian applied some conventional Christian texts to this experience, and in so doing he linked the present experience of the Church firmly with the tradition in which it stood. That tradition, however, seems not to have included the axiomatic assumption of a world of hostile forces that Christ had once and for all defeated.

4 Conclusion

Irenaeus meets the need for salvation in terms of that reconciliation with God which results in the restoration of all things. Tertullian demands more immediacy, thus interpreting sin less as that radical disjunction between God and man than as the culpable actions of man, which require juridical satisfaction. The gnostics offered release from the oppression of existence, which was interpreted in terms of a cosmogony. This approach could and did lead to a denial of monotheism and a consequent increase in the number of intermediate beings. By contrast the orthodox offered an interpretation of life not simply in terms of cosmogony but also in terms of psychology. Thus one of the chief reasons for orthodox hostility towards the gnostics was the gnostic dualism, which, when expressed theologically in terms of the Father Unknown and the Demiurge, could not relate to experience. The Christian message, however it adapted to its environment, always emphasised the experience of God as part of the fact of salvation. Since knowledge alone was insufficient, this experience was expressed often in terms of the moral life, by contrast with the gnostic tendencies to libertinism or asceticism. But we should note that neither the Christians nor the gnostic approach specifically offered release from experienced hostile powers, because there appears to have been at this time no demand for such release.

Throughout this study we have noted the rise in interest in astrology during the second century. In some parts of society men were clearly in thrall to such powers, but in many other parts there is little evidence for their authority, and it is dangerous from the absence of such evidence to infer their preponderance.[36] The archons, for example, in various gnostic systems were on occasions related to the planets. But they are not the main obstacles to salvation or the controllers of men's lives. They are primarily the agents by which the world is created and, in some systems, the guardians of the barriers to the heavenly ascent of the soul.[37] But there is no indication that men are now to live in fear of the archons. Salvation is from the world that is their work, not from the archons themselves. It is also worth recalling that the stars are part of the creation and, although they may be worshipped, they do not require placating.[38] Nor are they parties to the creation of the world and therefore they have not the same status as the creators. Thus they may dominate life but are not a hostile first cause of all existence.[39] The ethical issue of gnosticism, whether libertinism or asceticism, itself reminds us that the question to which it proposes its answer was not one concerning Fate and hostile powers so much as one of the nature and destiny of man.[40]

There is one frequently cited piece of evidence that has led to confusion at this point and therefore is worth brief consideration. There are certain epitaphs that contain the hour, day, month and year of the man's death. These are interpreted as evidence for a terror of cosmic forces, but fatalism in fact does not necessarily involve fear of such forces.[41] We cannot hypothesise a belief in mighty powers in a personal sense from an expression of a feeling of alienation from a man's environment. For example, Frend takes the Lambiridi inscription as evidence for such terror in Africa; he then explains the offer of immortality from gnosticism, Hermes Trismegistos, and Christianity, although recognising that the inscription is practically unique and that the teaching of Hermes Trismegistos must have reached only very few; finally he instances Cyprian's conversion as an example of the mental processes involved.[42] Cyprian's conversion, however, is most interestingly based upon a sense of personal self-estrangement and an attraction to the moral impact of the Christian faith. The only oppression that may be discerned is an internal pressure on his soul and mind, and there is no hint of a man beset by unseen powers.[43] Tertullian too has nothing in his writings on the oppression of powers. It would appear that even in Africa the belief in such forces exercised little influence on society.

The general silence of Irenaeus, Tertullian, and the gnostics about the defeat of hostile powers, together with a lack of use of the Pauline texts that might have been so interpreted, is due precisely to this: that the experience of life was interpreted in these terms only in certain limited places to which the gospel went and it was not part of a widespread framework of belief in the ancient world. Answering the vital question of existence the gnostics offered cosmological and cosmogonic explanation and the Christians answered in terms of a temporal, eschatological and moral view of the world. Both viewpoints tended to dualisms, the one between God and matter and the other between God and the Devil. Both views also therefore tended towards the multiplication of intermediaries, but at this point it is essential to distinguish between the explanation of human experience and hypotheses that are designed to complete theories. The major questions were those of human experience, but in order to sustain their answers both Christians and gnostics were obliged by their Jewish background to accommodate the notions of lesser intermediaries, which, however, did not on the whole correspond to anything in man's experience. For this development we need to look later in history and consider finally the writings of Origen.

12

ORIGEN

Origen, the final writer to be considered in this survey, represents a major turning point in the history of Christian thinking, not least on the question of angels, demons and powers. On the one hand, he stood firmly in the tradition of his predecessors. He succeeded Clement at Alexandria and he shows familiarity with the Judaeo-Christian tradition. He was also a careful interpreter of Paul. On the other hand, it may also be claimed that much Christian thought after him was dependent upon his interpretations and innovations.[1]

There are many references to angels and demons in his work, and everywhere we find a systematic presentation of their status and functions. Along with questions of Christ and the Holy Spirit, they are among the 'magna et maxima' of the faith. Important as they are for the believer, their significance too for the unbeliever is emphasised by their prominence in Celsus' attack on Christianity. Angels are ministers of God, both towards men and from men to God (*de princ.* 1.8.1; *contra Cels.* 5.4f). The list in Col. 1: 16 is taken to refer to angelic beings. Fundamental is the concept of 'naturae rationabiles' (*de princ.* 1.5), which is Origen's means of systematising all beings, angelic, demonic and human, to create a synthesis that is most important in his interpretation of Col. 2: 15. When he expounds Col. 1: 16 all terms refer to holy angels. It is here too that he deals with the stars as rational beings that are angelic and not malevolent.[2]

Opposed to these angels are the demons and evil powers. In essence they too are rational beings (*contra Cels.* 4.29). They are involved in magic (*contra Cels.* 1.60ff), although Origen is sceptical about this (1.67), and in divination (7.5ff). They manifest themselves in two ways: sometimes they possess a man, who then requires exorcism; sometimes they blind a man's heart and lead him into error, as they did Judas (*de princ.* 3.3.4). This latter approach associates the demons with Jewish ideas on the evil inclination by which men are led to sin.[3] When evil is so interpreted by Origen, he approximates to the doctrine of the two spirits in man, although he does not allow two classes of demons: the internal and external experience

168

of demons are one (*de princ.* 3.2.4). The leader of demons is the Devil, and while the question of his origins is a matter of debate, it is clear that Origen only employs the Christian tradition of Satan's rebellion with his angels and their expulsion from heaven (*de princ. praef.* 6; *contra Cels.* 4.65). His knowledge of the OT also leads him to realise that, in spite of its generally neutral sense, δαίμων is never used in the LXX in any sense other than the maleficent (*contra Cels.* 5.5).

Origen makes interesting use of some Pauline texts, by which he expresses his understanding of the world. Rom. 8: 38 is cited in *de princ.* 3.2.5, a section within a discussion of the Christian struggle with opposing powers. The key however is found in Eph. 6: 12, which is interpreted on two levels. For the 'simpliciores' he speaks of the internal origin of temptation, upon which weakness the Devil capitalises.[4] The battle can only be won if the Christian has the power of God with him as he struggles with the Devil and against all that is hostile to God.[5] Those, however, who know more than this, realise that the true struggle is a matter of discipline within the spiritual life and that it depends wholly upon the relationship with God.[6] The powers are thus not disregarded, but they are also not given the prominence that they appear to have in the verse in Ephesians. This verse is frequently used by Origen, both in exact citation and allusively, but almost always it is interpreted exactly in this way.

Col. 2: 15 is cited twice in *contra Celsum*. The first occasion (1.55) is in the context of a discussion of the atonement in terms of Is. 53. There are several points of note. First, Christ is assumed to be the subject of the verb and not God, as always when Origen uses the text. Consequently, ἐν αὐτῷ is altered to refer explicitly to the cross (ἐν τῷ ξύλῳ). ἀπεκδυσάμενος is not taken absolutely in a middle sense but as an active participle with the powers as the object. This is reinforced by the addition of αὐτάς. The main problem, however, is the addition of ἐν ἡμῖν to the phrase ἀρχὰς καὶ ἐξουσίας. The second citation (*contra Cels.* 2.64) is even more strange. Following a discussion of the ἐπίνοιαι of the Son, the text is cited with, again, ἀπεκδυσάμενος as active and τὰς ἀρχάς as its object.[7] The really distinctive feature of these quotations, however, is that Origen does not make use of the motif of the triumph. The suggestion in each passage is that the powers are a garment that Christ wore and finally discarded. This is to be understood in the context of Origen's treatment of the ἐπίνοιαι of Christ: he was only visible to the world of men, controlled as this is by demons, while he himself was part of that world and was therefore himself 'demonised'. This interpretation of Col. 2: 15 appears to originate with Origen, whose view then becomes normative for the Greek Fathers.

In these two passages Origen's use of Col. 2: 15 is inhibited by the context. Elsewhere in his exegetical writings he uses the whole verse in a different way. This is most clearly seen in *Comm. in Matt.* 12.40, according to which the period between the incarnation, when the powers began to be weakened, and the cross, when they were finally exposed to ridicule, was a period of major demonic activity. The cross for Origen is mainly understood in terms of Col. 2: 15, the powers being clearly evil. It was the place where they were despoiled (*Hom. in Jos.* 8.3), where the way to paradise was opened for men (*Hom. in Lev.* 9.5), and where the Devil was hoodwinked (*Comm. in Matt.* 13.9). Whichever of these aspects Origen is stressing, he continually bases his doctrine on Col. 2: 15, interpreting it in terms of the defeat of hostile powers. For him the image of the conquering hero in battle is so dominant that he often substitutes an explicit word of battle or devastation for the original θριαμβεύσας (*Hom. in Lev.* 17.6; 18.4). How this happens is easily observable in his collocation of texts. For example, in *Hom. in Lev.* 9.5 he links Col. 2: 15 with Luke 23: 43, for the idea of paradise into which the saved go, and Luke 11: 26f, for Christ leading the evil spirits into the wilderness, i.e. the underworld, where they belong. This mixing of a verse of the Gospels relating to demons and the Pauline texts concerning the powers is due to Origen's understanding of scripture and to his concept of the hierarchy of being. Once the demons and powers are identified, the Pauline position is lost. This defeat of the powers and demons is extended into the life of every Christian. Just as Christ's triumph was in part an example, so too the lives of Christians should be lives of triumph over these demons (*Comm. in Matt.* 12.25). As ever, such a triumph is all the greater for a martyr.[8]

With this interpretation of Col. 2: 15 new ground is broken. The reason does not lie in a deeper insight into Paul, although Origen's knowledge of the Bible was immense. It lies rather in his systematising of the world of evil, so that all facets of evil fitted into one realm of evil. The particular problem of why a Christian has still to struggle after Christ's victory on the cross is answered in terms of the hierarchy of being. In addition, his belief in the *apokatastasis* of all things removes from the image of triumph the associated and implied image of total defeat and destruction. It is vital to Origen that the demons, although active, cannot act without the permission of God and no initiative is allowed to them. In the second place Origen inherits a, by now, long Christian tradition of the demons in terms of idols, magic and divination. This he synthesises with the concept of man's internal evil propensities. In such a way the theology of a demonic world is separated neither from the internal nor from the external experience of a Christian. He has also inherited the Christian identification of the Devil with death, which enables him to relate the Pauline texts on the destruction of death to the destruction of the Devil. And since Origen belongs to the Church of the martyrs, he sees the hostility of Satan not only in temptations to sin but also in the demands of the world for apostasy.

By creating the hierarchy of being, Origen ties the experience of life to the theology of the Church's tradition in such a way as to produce for the first time a unified view of daily experience and of evil. This evil is wholly opposed to God in Christ, containing all manifestations of evil – evil tendencies, evil demons, evil angels, and evil powers. There is no longer any need for a distinction between the various beings, since within the hierarchy of being what may be predicated of one may be predicated of all. Having created this synthesis, Origen finds in Col. 2: 15 the perfect expression of the struggle with evil, both for day-to-day triumphant living and for the once-for-all triumph of Christ. He thus sets the text upon a new and definitive path of interpretation, which has dominated the Church from that day onwards.

CONCLUSION TO PART 3

It has not been my aim in this section to study intensively the material of Christian history between the time of Paul and the writings of Origen. Rather, by selection of some of the most important and representative authors, I have attempted to show the trends of thought on demonic forces and upon Christ's relationship to them. In reading much of the ancillary material, which is not here discussed, I have found nothing that contradicts what is here presented.

The Judaeo-Christian tradition provides the basic material from which all later ideas develop. Thus the angels are generally understood as the servants and messengers of God. The understanding of demons and of evil is tied usually to two points. The first is that of exorcism, which, being still an experience of the Church, naturally fostered an understanding of demons that the Church found in its Gospels. The second is that of the fall of Satan, which at an early stage began to take precedence over the fall of man and the lust of the angels, with the consequence that a position of leadership and importance was attributed to Satan or the Devil, which he could not have held even in the extremes of Jewish apocalyptic. The image of the struggle was important both for the moral life of the Christians and later in understanding persecution and martyrdom. In these circumstances it lent itself to the twofold tendency either towards internalising the struggle in the individual or towards humanising the adversaries in terms of the actual persecutors of the Church. In this context Eph. 6: 12 came into prominence, whatever its source, but the notion of Christ's victory, however understood, was not easily accommodated and the implicit triumphalism of Col. 2: 15 was not found. Gnosticism was of little significance in this matter. The gnostic view of the world of spirits was a peculiar creation, which the orthodox writers, especially Irenaeus, countered in two ways. One was, using Paul to some degree, to offer a more coherent world view; the second was to make sense not only of theory but of human experience.

The crucial writer for this study is undoubtedly Origen. His knowledge and exposition of biblical texts, including those of Paul, exceeds that of his predecessors. In a remarkable way he was able to use the whole of the Bible in his exegetical thinking. His own Christian experience, as witnessed by his youthful excesses, seems to have forced him always to come to terms with experience. He thus stood in the classic line of thinkers from Irenaeus, Tertullian and the Apologists, but less in direct relation to his immediate precursor, Clement of Alexandria. His conception of a hierarchy of all being and his application of this to Christian theology enabled him in a new way to relate the disparate aspects of human experience and the inherited Judaeo-Christian tradition on evil, demons and the Devil, and the spiritual world in general.[1] In the course of this solution he dealt with Christ's relationship with such forces and found a biblical key in his reading of Col. 2: 15. The thought world of Origen, however, was far removed from that of Paul, and the demands for coherence in his theology made it inevitable that at this point Paul would be reinterpreted. It should also be noted that on this verse, as compared with Rom. 8: 38f and Eph. 6: 12, Origen seems not to have had any previous tradition of exegesis that he could appropriate. Thus a new situation provided a new interpretation for a hitherto neglected and unused text.

The argument of this chapter has not been that there was a linear progression of Christian thought between Paul in the mid-first century and Origen at the beginning of the third. It has rather been that different Christians came to terms with the world and the Christian Church at different points in its history. In turn magic, divination, idols, planets and Fate play their part. What is significant, however, is that these were not identified with some hostile forces over which Christ had triumphed. The way to overcome or to avoid their power was sought and explained in other directions. Yet a valuable idea was to hand in Col. 2: 15 and the fact of its neglect is important. It suggests that these Christians simply did not think in terms of a fear of mighty cosmic forces, whether in the planets or elsewhere, and that this was not the framework of their daily experience of life or of their religious belief.[2] Indeed, it could not be, for the moral, and sometimes physical, struggle was such that any proclamation of the defeat of powers by Christ would have been nonsense. Such an interpretation of the Pauline texts was only possible when some means of effectively tying the spiritual world and physical world of beings together had been devised. The Origenist concept of the hierarchy of being did this comprehensively, for the first time, with the consequent reinterpretation of the Pauline texts and developments in the doctrine of the atonement.

PART 4

Final remarks

The conclusions of this study have been drawn in each section as it has been completed. There is, therefore, no need now to list them in detail, and I shall content myself with a summary alone.

The first clear conclusion must be that the historical situation in which the early Christians began their mission was not that of a world overtly seeking release or salvation. This was a later mood, for which we have attempted to give an explanation for Asia Minor and the West. There was, therefore, no demand from outside the Church for a theology of cosmic, demonic powers, nor within the Church for an interpretation of Christ in terms of victory over hostile powers. Nor, as has been argued, is the letter to the Colossians directed at some local manifestation of such a belief.

The Jewish background from which Christianity grew said much about angels and showed a growing concern with demons. The language, however, clearly demonstrates that the chief emphasis was upon angels as a means both of interpreting the activity of God among men and of extolling the Lordship of Yahweh. Evil was increasingly focused in the figure of Satan, with whom the demons were gradually associated. The whole area of evil, however, was one of remarkable confusion and obscurity, especially when compared with the increasing confidence about names, ranks, and duties of the angels. Nowhere, either in Jewish thought or in Paul, is Satan so clearly delineated as he was in post-apostolic Jewish thought. The terms that Paul uses of the powers are employed in Jewish material to refer to those angelic powers whose activity and presence confirm the status of Yahweh.

Similarly the pagan world to which Paul went lacked any sense of mighty, hostile forces that stood over against man as he struggled for survival. This conclusion is the product of carefully chronological assessment of the evidence from the socio-political history of Asia Minor in the mid-first century A.D. and of the discernible trajectories of belief that traverse the period. Only by reading back from the second century is it

possible to adduce evidence for a significant belief in such powers. The
Acts of the Apostles incidentally appears reliable on this point. There has
been a tendency among some scholars to associate the powers with astrological belief, especially in Rom. 8: 38 and in the phrase 'the elements of
this world'. Yet on two counts this may be faulted. In the first place, the
impact of astrology at the particular time of the Pauline mission was
minimal and Paul would appear not to have had occasion to use such
language. In the second place, it has been shown that although such
terminology is found in later periods in astrological contexts, in the first
century it has no such explicit reference. We may therefore also discount
the notion that the powers are in some way connected with the mighty
forces of the stars, from which burden men sought relief.

We conclude, therefore, that there was at the time of Paul on the one
hand no demand from the world for release from powers or for a doctrine
of a cosmic battle in which Christ rescued men from the domination of
such forces. On the other hand, there was no material to hand in the
Jewish background of Christianity from which such a myth could be con-
structed at that time.

When we turn to Paul we find that his use of the language of αἱ ἀρχαὶ
καὶ αἱ ἐξουσίαι and associated terms exactly conforms to Jewish assumptions, and that such language would also have been accessible to non-Jews.
The crucial passage in his epistles is Col. 2: 15, for which in the present
work an exegesis has been offered that takes seriously the historical context. It must be noted that the concept of exaltation and of triumph, of
which celebration is a key-note, does not necessarily require the con-
comitant notions of battle and victory in order to be meaningful. The
exaltation of the Son, according to Ps. 110: 1, is not the result of his
victory in battle. Similarly in Col. 2: 15 Paul does not speak of a war but
of a celebration. The powers do not need to be defeated, since they are
the angels of God. Just as in Jewish thought these enhance the glory of
Yahweh, so in Paul's thought they exalt the Lord Christ.

The letter to the Ephesians presents particular problems. It was the
thought contained especially in Eph. 6: 12 that became prominent in the
Church and affected all other interpretations. We have attempted to show,
however, that this verse is unlikely to have been part of the original text,
and that if it was, it represents a considerable move away from the Pauline
notion of the Christian life and of the nature of the world. Apart from this
verse the letter is not too distinct from the genuine Pauline thought on
the powers and the spirit-world.

As for the connection between demonic powers, angels and the state,
sufficient evidence has been adduced to show that the curious notion that

behind the rulers stand angelic beings is misguided. Paul's ethical position is notable for its interpretation of reality as it was experienced by the Christian Church and for its acceptance of the facts of social life. He did not have recourse to an obscure mythology at a central point of his social thinking. It has been beyond the scope of this present work to offer a detailed examination of Pauline thought on the state and the magistrates, but such a work must begin without the theory of the angels of the nations.

Finally it has been demonstrated to how small an extent the notion of demonic and hostile powers generally featured in the thought of the earliest Christians. Angels, as in Judaism, were prominent, but there is no evidence for a belief in demonic forces of any stature, apart from Satan, until towards the end of the second century. The reasons for such a development have been explained and it has been shown that once Paul's writings are again absorbed into the mainstream of Christian thinking, the humanising and psychologising of the powers, as evidenced in Eph. 6: 12, has become the predominant concept. Col. 2: 15 is of little significance until Origen finds in it the peg for his particular understanding of the nature of being and the activity and work of Christ. This, however, is the product of a world of thought and a tradition of religion that is by now far removed from that of Paul himself, and the inevitable reinterpretation of Paul's references to the powers, which has continued since, begins at this point in Christian history. Mighty demonic forces are now part of the fabric of belief and the answer to them is found in the new notion of Christ's cosmic battle. It is also not without significance that the development of the concept of the harrowing of hell, itself a concept of battle and victory, also became prominent around this time. The earlier thinking about Hades, which is found in Justin, Irenaeus and Tertullian, is of a place of the departed souls, whence Christ between his death and resurrection brings out prophets and patriarchs. The first official mention of the descent to hell occurs in the Fourth Formula of Sirmium (A.D. 359), by which time hell has become the abode of evil powers, demons and Satan.[1] Christ's descent is no longer to proclaim but to harrow, and the image is significantly first found in Origen (e.g. in *Gen. Hom.* 17.5).[2]

We must conclude that far from being a fundamental part of the background and proclamation of the Christian message, the notion of the mighty forces of evil ranged against man was not part of the earliest Christian understanding of the world and the gospel. There is nothing in the Pauline writings that refers to a battle between Christ and hostile forces. Indeed, it is also noticeable that there is no conflict directly between Christ and Satan. Such categories for the life and work of Christ, whilst hinted at in parts of the tradition, form no part of the Pauline preaching of Christ. The consequences of this perception will be of significance in dogmatics and ethics. For the so-called 'classic' theory of the atonement will require re-examination, as will the widely accepted biblical basis for the concept of the cosmic Christ; and Christian social ethics, which in recent years have developed and enlarged the potential scope of Christ's victory over hostile forces, will require a firmer foundation.

NOTES

General Introduction

1 A convenient summary of earlier views may be found in K. L. Schmidt, 'Die Natur- und Geistkräfte im paulinischen Erkennen und Glauben', *Eranos Jahrbuch* 14 (1947), 87ff.

2 J. S. Stewart, 'On a Neglected Emphasis in New Testament Theology', *SJT* 4 (1951), 292ff; G. H. C. Macgregor, 'Principalities and Powers: The Cosmic Background of Saint Paul's Thought', *NTS* 1 (1954), 17ff.

Introduction

1 G. Delling, *TDNT*, I, 481. See too J. Héring, *The First Epistle of St. Paul to the Corinthians* (ET London, 1962), on 1 Cor. 2: 6ff, who connects ἄρχοντες in that context with ἀρχαί in Rom. 8: 38 without any argument.

2 See W. Dittenberger, *SIG* and *OGIS*. Also J. Juster, *Les juifs dans l'empire romain* (Paris, 1914), I, 443ff.

3 W. Foerster, *TDNT*, II, 573.

4 Eschatology provides a clear and specific example. See T. F. Glasson, *Greek Influence in Jewish Eschatology* (London, 1961).

5 δεισιδαίμων means 'excessively religious' rather than 'superstitious'. See P. J. Koets, *Deisidaemonia: A Contribution to the Knowledge of Religious Terminology in Greek* (Purmerend, 1929).

6 Josephus, *AJ* 12.268ff.

7 I. Lévy, *La légende de Pythagore de Grèce en Palestine* (Paris, 1927). See too A. Dupont-Sommer, *The Jewish Sect of Qumran and the Essenes* (New York, 1955). R. N. Frye makes an important observation in 'Reitzenstein and Qumran Revisited by an Iranian', *HTR* 55 (1962), 261ff: 'I suspect that if we had sources from Babylonia and Iran they would show a similar mixed syncretistic hellenism such as we find in the western hellenistic world.'

8 A.-J. Festugière, *Personal Religion among the Greeks* (Berkeley, 1954), has demonstrated the experiential importance of religion in Greece in every period. On the *lares compitales* see below.

1 The environment in which Paul worked

1 Tacitus, *Ann.* 3.55.

2 In general see D. Magie, *Roman Rule in Asia Minor* (Princeton, 1950), I, 566. Tacitus (*Hist.* 2.8.1ff) lists three false Neros prior to A.D. 96, the first occurring as early as A.D. 69. In the second century Dio Chrysostom (*Orat.*

21.10) records that many believed Nero still to be alive in Asia. See too
Augustine, *de civ. dei* 20.19. The movement of Mucianus is recorded in
Josephus, *BJ* 4.632 and Tacitus, *Hist.* 2.8.3. He had previously been legate
in Pamphylia and knew the area well. See Magie, *Roman Rule*, II, 1386,
n. 48.

3   Of the many studies see e.g. G. W. Bowersock, *Augustus and the Greek
World* (Oxford, 1965); Magie, *Roman Rule*; N. H. Baynes, *The Hellenistic
Civilisation and East Rome* (London, 1946); A. N. Sherwin-White, *Roman
Society and Roman Law in the New Testament* (Oxford, 1963); V. Chapot,
La province romaine proconsulaire d'Asie (Paris, 1904).

4   Juvenal, *Sat.* 3.60ff. Both Juvenal and Tacitus are guilty of hyperbole on
this matter (cf. *Ann.* 10.44). For a more balanced Roman view see Seneca,
Cons. ad Helv. 6ff.

5   Dio Cassius, 54.30.3 and Suetonius, *Aug.* 47. The devotion of Asia was
more than mere fawning upon a victor, for the inhabitants usually continued to display genuine devotion to their heroes, even in defeat. See Dio
Cassius, 42.2.1 for the case of Pompey. See too the inscription from
various sources in Asia in *OGIS*, 458, with another version from
Halicarnassus (*Insc. BM*, 894). See W. H. Buckler, 'An Epigraphic Contribution to Letters', *CR* 41 (1927), 119ff. On mainland Greece there was no
parallel recovery, except most interestingly in Athens, where the personal
involvement of Augustus may again be detected. See J. Day, *An Economic
History of Athens under Roman Domination* (New York, 1942), pp. 167ff.

6   Propertius, *Carm.* 1.6.31.

7   On the constant movement of Romans in the East see J. Hatzfeld, *Les
trafiquants italiens dans l'orient hellénique* (Paris, 1919). On the aggressive
stance of the colonies see B. Levick, *Roman Colonies in Southern Asia
Minor* (Oxford, 1967) and Magie, *Roman Rule*, I, 459f, 462f and 472f.
On Roman residents, other than colonists, see Dio Cassius, 51.20.6.

8   Augustus, *Res Gestae* 20.4; Dio Cassius, 53.2.4. Whether Augustus was
genuinely religious or not it is difficult to say. See generally A. D. Nock,
'The Augustan Restoration', *CR* 39 (1925), 60ff. It seems that Augustus
harnessed the sense of loss and guilt of the people to give the city a new
start. See Horace, *Od.* 3.6.1. The remarkable fusion of ideas in Vergil, *Aen.*
6 is also the product of reflection in difficult times.

9   On the *koina* see A. N. Sherwin-White, *The Roman Citizenship* (Oxford,
1939), pp. 326ff. On the absorption of Augustus into the indigenous
religion see L. R. Taylor, *The Divinity of the Roman Emperor* (Middletown, 1931), pp. 270ff. At Teos there is mention of Διωνυσίακα καισάρηα
(*CIG*, 3082), and an Augusteum was built within the Artemisium at
Ephesus (*CIL*, III, 6070//7118). An altar existed to Augustus alone (i.e.
without Roma) in Paphlagonia by 3 B.C. (*ILS*, 8781). See also Tacitus,
Ann. 4.37 and Suetonius, *Aug.* 52.

10 The last recorded example is that of C. Marcius Censorinus, who was
consul in 8 B.C. (*SEG*, II, 549). See Dio Cassius, 56.25.6.

11 A good example of a Roman import that quickly received widespread
approval is that of gladiatorial contests, which were unknown in Asia prior
to the Roman Empire. See L. Robert, *Les gladiateurs dans l'orient grec*
(Paris, 1940), especially for our period inscriptions 49ff, 86, 105, 152, 157

and 272. For general social influence see also Levick's account of Pisidian Antioch, *Roman Colonies*, pp. 190f and 130ff.

12 Roads – *CIL*, III, 6983; Seleucia-Sidera was renamed Claudio-Seleucia (*IGRR*, III, 328). For Claudius' conscious emulation of Augustus see M. P. Charlesworth, *CAH*, X, 679f.

13 'Methodology in the Study of Mystery Religions and Early Christianity', *HTR* 43 (1955), 1ff.

14 Asclepius – see E. J. and L. Edelstein, *Asclepius* (Baltimore, 1945), II, 117ff. Sabazius – see e.g. F. Cumont, 'Les mystères de Sabazius et le Judaisme', *CRAI* (1906), 63ff. For the general movement of this type of religion in the second century see C. J. Cadoux, *Ancient Smyrna* (Oxford, 1938), p. 204. On the problems of chronology see also F. Cumont, *Les religions orientales dans le paganisme romain*, 4th ed. (Paris, 1929), p. ix.

15 *CIL*, VI, 504 and 510. See R. Duthoy, *The Taurobolium* (Leiden, 1969), pp. 112ff.

16 E. R. Goodenough, *Jewish Symbols in the Greco-Roman Period* (New York, 1953–68). Goodenough created a 'normative Judaism', which was as misconceived as the 'rabbinic Judaism' against which he protested. See the assessment by D. M. Smith, 'Goodenough's Symbols in Retrospect', *JBL* 86 (1967), 53ff.

17 On the language see A. D. Nock, 'The Vocabulary of the New Testament', *JBL* 52 (1933), 132ff. An interesting contrast between avowed mythology and historical claims is found in 1 Cor. 15: 1ff and Plutarch, *de Is. et Os.* 355B and 374E.

18 Baptism – G. Wagner, *Pauline Baptism and the Pagan Mysteries* (ET Edinburgh, 1967). Eucharist – W. J. Groton, *The Christian Eucharist and the Pagan Cults* (New York, 1914). On the wider notion of resurrection see J. Beaujeu, *La religion romaine à l'apogée de l'empire* (Paris, 1955), I, 312ff.

19 See R. E. Brown, 'The Semitic Background of the New Testament *mysterion*', *Biblica* 39 (1958), 426ff and 40 (1959), 70ff.

20 On Eleusis in general see K. Kerényi, *Die Mysterien von Eleusis* (Zurich, 1962). For Augustus' initiation see Dio Cassius, 51.4.1. P. F. Foucart, 'Les empereurs romains initiés aux mystères d'Eleusis', *RP* 22 (1893), 197ff.

21 Cicero, *de leg.* 2.14.36 and *in Verrem* 2.5.72, 187.

22 Dio Cassius, 54.9.2.

23 H. W. Pleket, 'An Aspect of the Emperor Cult: Imperial Mysteries', *HTR* 53 (1965), 331ff. M. P. Nilsson remains sceptical about the existence of such mysteries (*The Dionysiac Religion of the Hellenistic and Roman Age*, Lund, 1957, pp. 138ff). This, however, may be because he appears to put too functional an interpretation upon the ruler cult. See *Geschichte der griechischen Religion* (Munich, 1955), II, 385ff. If we recognise in the imperial cult an expression of genuine religious feeling, which is as significant as any political relevance, the possibility of its association with local mysteries increases.

24 Lucian, *Deorum Conc.* 12. Cf. *Alexander* 19.

25 See Robert's articles in *Anatolian Studies* from 1950 onwards. See also A. Bouché-Leclerq, *Histoire de la divination dans l'antiquité* (Paris, 1880),

III, 249ff. Tacitus gives his account in *Ann.* 2.54. The temporary resurgence of oracles under the later Flavians is well illustrated in Plutarch, *de def. or.* and *de Pyth. or.*

26 An example is found at Panamara: A. Laumonier, *Les cultes indigènes en Carie* (Paris, 1958), pp. 257ff. See further Bouché-Leclerq, *Histoire*, III, 229ff and especially p. 255.

27 C. G. Starr, *Civilisation and the Caesars* (New York, 1954), p. 240. See also S. Gaselee, Appendix in G. Thornley, J. M. Edmonds and S. Gaselee, *Longus* (London, 1916).

28 E.g. S. Angus, *The Religious Quests of the Graeco-Roman World* (London, 1929), p. 254; W. L. Knox, *Paul and the Church of the Gentiles* (Cambridge, 1939), p. 106; G. H. C. Macgregor, 'Principalities and Powers', *NTS* 1 (1954), 17ff.

29 See generally F. Cumont, *Astrology and Religion among the Greeks and Romans* (New York, 1912); *Les religions orientales*, ch. 7; Nilsson, *Geschichte*, II, 465ff; G. Haufe, 'Hellenistische Volksfrommigkeit' in J. Leipoldt and W. Grundmann (eds.), *Umwelt des Urchristentums* (Berlin, 1967), I, 82ff; W. Gundel, 'Astrologie', *RAC*, I, 817ff; *idem*, 'Astralreligion', *RAC*, I, 810ff.

30 Columella, 9.1.31.

31 *Astrology in Roman Law and Politics* (Philadelphia, 1954), p. 19. Persius interestingly brings the two together in *Sat.* 5.18ff and 45ff.

32 Juvenal, *Sat.* 3.42ff and 6.553ff.

33 E.g. Varro (*de re. rust.* 1.37.2) on cutting hair at the time of the full moon.

34 The Stoic Posidonius was regarded as an *astrologus*: Augustine, *de civ. dei* 5.5. On the inevitable and important connection between Stoicism and astrology see A. Bouché-Leclerq, *L'astrologie grecque* (Paris, 1899), pp. 28ff.

35 Ovid, *de arte amat.* 1.15f; Quintilian, *Inst. Or.* 10.1.55.

36 *Cena* 30ff. Cf, Propertius, 2.27.4; Nilsson, *Geschichte*, II, 467.

37 Details in Cramer, *Astrology*, pp. 234ff.

38 Suetonius, *Vit.* 14.4 and Dio Cassius, *Epit.* 64.1.4.

39 See E. R. Dodds, *The Greeks and the Irrational* (Berkeley, 1951), pp. 245ff.

40 Dio Cassius, 56.25.4. This is considered at length by Cramer (*Astrology*, pp. 248ff), but there is not really enough evidence concerning the edict to allow its use as the *legal* foundation for imperial acts against the astrologers in the first century. See R. J. Getty in a review in *CP* 51 (1956), 104. It may, however, be used as an expression of Augustus' attitude.

41 For texts and discussion see P. Wuilleumier, 'Cirque et astrologie', *MélArch* 44 (1927), 184ff.

42 The evidence for the restoration is obscure. See Ovid, *Fasti* 5.145. Three reasons, however, suggest that Augustus did this: (1) as evidence of his new control over Rome it would have been significant. The rites had been suppressed because of rioting and political disturbance. (2) It would have been in line with his revitalising of the old religion (*compitalia*) and his making of political capital out of it (*genius Augusti*). (3) It would have been a suitable bequest to the ordinary people of Rome, who otherwise would have not been directly involved in his reforms. On the whole question see

M. P. Nilsson, 'Roman and Greek Domestic Cult', *Opuscula Selecta* (Lund, 1960), III, 279ff; also A. D. Nock, *CAH*, X, 480f.

43 Astrological symbols first appear on Roman coins, apart from Egyptian influence, under Antoninus Pius. See Beaujeu, *La religion romaine*, I, 323.

44 Interestingly the writings of the rabbis also reflect their awareness of the development of the belief in Fate and in the effect of the stars in the world around them. See S. Liebermann, *Hellenism in Jewish Palestine*, 2nd ed. (New York, 1962), p. 130, n. 8.

45 *Roman Society and Roman Law in the New Testament* (Oxford, 1963). The earlier work of Sir W. M. Ramsay is also still valuable; see the restatement of it by W. W. Gasque, *Sir William M. Ramsay, Archaeologist and New Testament Scholar* (Grand Rapids, 1966). Also E. M. Blaiklock, 'The Acts of the Apostles as a Document of First Century History', in W. W. Gasque and R. P. Martin (eds.), *Apostolic History and the Gospel* (Exeter, 1970), pp. 41ff.

46 *The Acts of the Apostles* (ET Oxford, 1971), p. 403.

47 Pagan parallels to the episode are collected by B. Gärtner, 'Paulus und Barnabas in Lystra', *SEÅ* 27 (1962), 63ff. See also W. M. Calder, 'Acts 14.12', *ExT* 37 (1926), 528 and, for the names, *idem*, 'The Cult of the Homonades', *CR* 24 (1910), 77ff. On the story in Ovid, *Metam.* 8.626ff, see A. S. Hollis, *Ovid Metamorphoses Book VIII* (Oxford, 1970), pp. 106ff.

48 H. J. Cadbury, *The Book of Acts in History* (London, 1955), p. 23.

49 On the status of these people in antiquity see E. R. Dodds, 'Supernormal Phenomena in Classical Antiquity', *The Ancient Concept of Progress and Other Essays on Greek Literature and Belief* (Oxford, 1973), pp. 199ff.

50 R. E. Wycherley, 'St. Paul at Athens', *JTS* n.s. 19 (1968), 619ff.

51 See the important remarks of T. D. Barnes, 'An Apostle on Trial', *JTS* n.s. 20 (1969), 405ff.

52 Sherwin-White, *Roman Society*, p. 84.

53 *CIL*, III, 6070/7118.

54 Discussed by F. Sokolowski, 'A New Testimony on the Cult of Artemis of Ephesus', *HTR* 58 (1965), 427ff.

55 Philostratus, *Vit. soph.* 1.7.2.

56 E. A. Judge, *The Social Pattern of Christian Groups in the First Century* (London, 1960), p. 20.

57 See C. C. Vermeule, *Roman Imperial Art in Greece and Asia Minor* (Cambridge, Mass., 1968), p. 228, who emphasises the strong Roman influence on Greek portraiture during the period 30 B.C. to A.D. 70.

58 Starr, *Civilisation and the Caesars*, p. 270; Sherwin-White, *Roman Society*, pp. 83ff.

59 Starr, *Civilisation and the Caesars*, p. 264.

60 See F. Cumont, *Lux Perpetua* (Paris, 1949), especially ch. 5.

61 Epictetus, *Diss.* 3.13.9f. Cf. the well-known *Laudatio Turiae* (*ILS*, 8393, col. II, lines 35f).

62 '[Orationes] mediis divi Augusti temporibus habitae, postquam longa temporum quies et continuum populi otium et adsidua senatus tranquillitas et maxima principis disciplina ipsam quoque eloquentiam sicut omnia alia pacaverat' (*Dial.* 38.7). Amongst the 'alia' was religious innovation.

2 The powers in Jewish and pagan thought

1 H. Wheeler Robinson, *Inspiration and Revelation in the Old Testament* (Oxford, 1946), pp. 167ff, and F. M. Cross Jnr, 'The Council of Yahweh in Second Isaiah', *JNES* 12 (1953), 274ff.

2 G. Cooke, 'The sons of (the) God(s)', *ZAW* 76 (1964), 22ff. For a history of interpretation, together with his own reassertion of a reference to heroes, see F. Dexinger, *Sturz der Gottessöhne oder Engel vor der Sintflut* (Vienna, 1966).

3 E.g. Jer. 8: 2; Zeph. 1: 5; Deut. 4: 19.

4 D. S. Russell, *The Method and Message of Jewish Apocalyptic* (London, 1964), pp. 237ff.

5 See generally L. Jung, *Fallen Angels in Jewish, Christian and Mohammedan Thought* (Philadelphia, 1926).

6 The unusual word ἐἰρ (Theodotion), but more usual ἄγγελος appears in LXX. The term seems to mean 'watcher'.

7 M. Noth, 'Die Heiligen des Höchsten', *Gesammelte Studien zum AT*, 2nd ed. (Munich, 1960), pp. 274ff, argues for the angelic reference. N. W. Porteous, *Daniel, A Commentary* (London, 1965), p. 116, seems to advocate a double reference. There is always some confusion over this word in later Jewish and Christian writing. See O. Proksch, *TDNT*, I, 88ff, especially p. 109.

8 The argument is not conclusive. Thucydides (5.47 and 6.54) appears to suggest that ἀρχαί may be bearers of authority, but the papyrus from the third century B.C., cited by BAG and LSJ (*PHal.* 1.226) as evidence that ἀρχή may refer to a specific magistrate, has been misunderstood. Here ἀρχή is parallel to ἄρχων and means, as elsewhere, 'the locus of authority'. In this use it is parallel to the English use of 'the court', by which persons are deliberately de-personalised in order to emphasise the office and authority that they bear.

9 J. C. Hindley, 'Towards a Date for the Similitudes of Enoch. An Historical Approach', *NTS* 14 (1968), 551ff; J. T. Milik, with the collaboration of M. Black, *The Book of Enoch. Aramaic Fragments of Qumran Cave 4* (Oxford, 1976), pp. 89ff.

10 R. H. Charles lists as the Noachic Fragment 6–9; 54: 7 – 55: 2; 60; 65 – 69: 25, and 106–7. If Semjaza stands for Samia Azza, then the astrological connections of the name make it probable that Semjaza entered the story when the fall as one of rebellion against God became prominent. Azazel originally led in the version based on the lust of the angels, and Semjaza is inserted into ch. 6 because of his position in the later story. On the whole question see C. Kaplan, 'Angels in the Book of Enoch', *ATR* 12 (1930), 425.

11 The link between the seven and the four may be provided in 87: 2. The two traditions may survive together in the four beasts and seven spirits of Rev. 4: 5ff. The identity of the chief angels is always confused. See e.g. for Qumran the table in Y. Yadin, *The Scroll of the War of the Sons of Light against the Sons of Darkness* (ET Oxford, 1962), pp. 237ff. A different origin for the seven may be found in Ezek. 9: 2. For a full discussion see G. Dix, 'The Seven Archangels and the Seven Spirits', *JTS* 28 (1927),

233ff. The approximation by Dix of Istrael to Ishtar is probably mistaken. See J. Z. Smith, 'The Prayer of Joseph' in J. Neusner (ed.), *Religion in Antiquity. Essays in Memory of Erwin Ramsdell Goodenough* (Leiden, 1968), pp. 262ff, especially p. 263, n. 1.

12 On the various strata of this work and their significance see G. L. Davenport, *The Eschatology of the Book of Jubilees* (Leiden, 1971). On the angelology see M. Testuz, *Les idées religieuses du livre des Jubilés* (Paris and Geneva, 1960), pp. 82ff.

13 The only references outside ch. 10 are (i) to Mastema who tests Abraham (17: 16; cf. 43: 1ff and 49: 2); (ii) to evil spirits as idols (11: 5) and as rulers over men's minds (12: 20); (iii) to an angel appearing in place of God to Hagar (17: 11).

14 Dibelius, *Die Geisterwelt*, pp. 88ff.

15 O. Cullmann, *Christ and Time* (ET London, 1962), pp. 192, italics mine.

16 The problem of the text is now probably resolved by the discovery of a fragment in Cave 4 at Qumran, which suggests that the LXX reflects an original Hebrew. See P. W. Skehan, 'A Fragment of "The Song of Moses" (Deut 32) from Qumran', *BASOR* 136 (1954), 12ff. Jewish tradition widely understands there to have been seventy nations, a number that was obtained by adding the nations that derive from the sons of Noah in Gen. 10. See L. Ginzberg, *The Legends of the Jews* (Philadelphia, 1938–47), V, 194ff, and *Encyclopaedia Judaica*, XII, 882ff. The emphasis is generally upon the uniqueness of God's relationship with his people and this was picked up by the early Christian use of the text, e.g. Irenaeus, *adv. haer.* 3.12.9. Later astrological influence may be detected as the number becomes seventy-two. See H. Odeberg, *III Enoch* (Cambridge, 1928), p. 105. See also G. E. Wright, 'The Lawsuit of God: A Form-Critical Study of Deuteronomy 32', in B. W. Anderson and W. Harrelson (eds.), *Israel's Prophetic Heritage* (London, 1962), pp. 26ff, and G. von Rad, *Deuteronomy* (ET London, 1966), p. 200.

17 So Glasson, *Greek influence*, p. 72.

18 See M. Delcor, *Le livre de Daniel* (Paris, 1971), p. 46.

19 So D. S. Russell, *The Method and Message of Jewish Apocalyptic* (London, 1964), p. 246; Odeberg, *III Enoch*, p. 105.

20 Delcor, *Livre de Daniel*, p. 209, suggests Deut. 4: 19 also refers to angels of the nations. It seems rather to be about the dangers of worshipping the stars. These are not the special property of Israel, and are used in verse 20 as evidence for the community of nations out of which God chose Israel.

21 R. H. Charles, *I Enoch* (Oxford, 1912), p. 200.

22 *Method and Message*, p. 247.

23 Y. Kaufman, *The Religion of Israel* (ET London, 1961), p. 384. See too E. J. Kissane, *Isaiah* (Dublin, 1941), *ad loc.*

24 The researches of M. de Jonge have argued convincingly for a Christian provenance for the Testaments. See *The Testaments of the Twelve Patriarchs* (Assen, 1953) and 'The Testaments of the Twelve Patriarchs', *NovT* 2 (1960), 181ff. They clearly, however, rely upon a Jewish background.

25 The evidence is listed in H. Bietenhard, *Die himmlische Welt im Urchristentum und Spätjudentum* (Tübingen, 1951), pp. 110ff, although he assumes

the usual view regarding the angels of the nations. The uniqueness of Israel, however, is the constant theme. See S-B, II, 359f and III, 50.

26 On gnostic influence on rabbinic material see e.g. A. Altmann, 'The Gnostic Background of the Rabbinic Adam Legends', *JQR* 35 (1944), 371ff. For Philo's hierarchy see e.g. *de spec. leg.* 1.13.

27 *Christ and Time*, p. 192.

28 Glasson, *Greek Influence*, pp. 69ff; E. Peterson, 'Le problème du nationalisme' in J. Daniélou, *Les anges et leur mission d'après les pères de l'église* (Paris, 1953), p. 161.

29 W. W. Tarn, *CAH*, V, 436.

30 Origen, who worked with rabbis, provides useful evidence. See J. Daniélou, 'Les sources juives de la doctrine des anges des nations chez Origène', *RechSR* 38 (1951), 132ff.

31 Gen R 18. 1. See also S-B, II, 90.

32 See G. F. Moore, *Judaism in the First Centuries of the Christian Era* (Cambridge, Mass. 1946–8), I, 40f. This was true even amid the extravagances of the non-canonical apocalypses. See H. B. Kuhn, 'The Angelology of the Non-Canonical Jewish Apocalypses', *JBL* 67 (1948), 228.

33 H. H. Rowley, *The Relevance of Apocalyptic*, 3rd ed. (London, 1963), p. 57. The evidence of the rabbinic writings also suggests that this was popular religion, although it was later refined into mysticism. See e.g. JT, Berakoth 13*a*; Mekilta 10 on Ex. 20: 23; BT, Abodah Zarah 42*b*. For the non-literary manifestations see generally Goodenough, *Jewish Symbols*, but even here it is noticeable that angels feature infrequently.

34 See G. A. Barton, 'The Origin of the Names of Angels and Demons in the Extra-canonical Apocalyptic Literature to 100 A.D.', *JBL* 31 (1912), 156ff, and his earlier article 'Demons and Spirits (Hebrew)', *ERE*, IV, 594ff.

35 Jung, *Fallen Angels, passim*.

36 Y. Yadin, *Scroll of the War*, pp. 229ff; J. Strugnell, *The Angelic Liturgy at Qumran* (Leiden, 1960). On Belial see P. von der Osten-Sacken, *Gott und Belial. Traditionsgeschichtliche Untersuchungen zum Dualismus in der Texten aus Qumran* (Göttingen, 1969), pp. 239ff.

37 It is a word of God's self-manifestation, an idea reflected in the early Christian use. See J. Daniélou, *The Theology of Jewish Christianity* (ET London, 1964), pp. 147ff.

38 Moore, *Judaism*, II, 336f. The theme of co-judges with Yahweh increases in prominence in apocalyptic and Christian writings. See Delcor, *Livre de Daniel*, pp. 149ff. For rabbinic views see BT, San. 38*b* and Hag. 14*a*. Matt. 19: 28 might be a Christian contribution to this Jewish debate. See C. H. Dodd, *According to the Scriptures* (London, 1952), p. 68.

39 The numerous references to demons are not paralleled in Paul, who refers to δαιμόνια once only (1 Cor. 10: 20f) and to πνεύματα not at all. E. E. Ellis has tried to give an unusual sense to the term in 1 Cor. 12–14. See 'Christ and the Spirit in I Corinthians' in B. Lindars and S. S. Smalley (eds.), *Christ and the Spirit in the New Testament* (Cambridge, 1973), pp. 269ff and 'Spiritual Gifts in the Pauline Community', *NTS* 20 (1974), 128ff. The arguments are dealt with below; they seem not to stand against the usual view that πνεῦμα in Paul is confined to references to the Holy Spirit and to the spirit of man.

40 *The Bible and the Greeks* (London, 1935), pp. 16ff.

41 J. Daniélou, *Philon d'Alexandrie* (Paris, 1958), p. 153.

42 Daniélou, *Philon d'Alexandrie*, pp. 160ff. See also E. Bréhier, *Les idées philosophiques et religieuses de Philon d'Alexandrie*, 3rd ed. (Paris, 1950), pp. 128ff.

43 W. Grundmann, *TDNT*, II, 284ff, especially pp. 290f. In particular note should be made of the occurrence of reference to divine power in the doxological ascriptions of the OT (*ibid.*, 294).

44 E.g. 3 Bar. 1: 8, and the curious phrase in 1 En. 61: 10: 'all the angels of power and all the angels of principalities'. Possibly the same idea lies behind 2 Thess. 1: 7. Philo also makes his angels the ministers of the powers in *de conf. ling.* 175.

45 G. Delling, *TDNT*, I, 482ff. His information is derived from Everling through Dibelius.

46 On A.D. 66 see Juster, *Les juifs*, II, 184; Josephus, *BJ* 2.19. According to Josephus, *BJ* 2.388 direct help only came from Adiabene. On the war of A.D. 132 see S. W. Baron, *A Social and Religious History of the Jews in Palestine*, 2nd ed. (New York, 1957), II, 106ff and 374, n. 22, and Juster, *Les juifs*, II, 191ff. Without adducing evidence Michael Grant denies the interest of the Diaspora. See *The Jews in the Roman World* (London, (1973), pp. 205ff.

47 Delling, *TDNT*, I, 480 cites Zeno, 2. 3.

48 *Strom.* 4.96.1. This is discussed later.

49 C. F. Burney, 'Christ the 'APXH of Creation', *JTS* 27 (1925), 160ff. The objections made by A. Feuillet depend rather upon its application to Colossians than to the basic notion of this concept in Jewish thought. See *Le Christ, Sagesse de Dieu d'après les épîtres pauliniennes* (Paris, 1966), p. 189.

50 W. Foerster, *TDNT*, II, 562ff. On the meaning of εἱμαρμένη see H. Ringgren, 'The Problem of Fatalism', *Fatalistic Beliefs in Religion, Folklore and Literature* (Stockholm, 1967), pp. 7ff.

51 In Test. Lev. 3.8 ἐξουσίαι are joined with θρόνοι, but this is probably from the Christian era.

52 See generally F. Cumont, 'Les anges du paganisme', *RHR* 72 (1915), 159ff. Dibelius provides the evidence, sometimes inaccurately, in *Die Geisterwelt*, pp. 209ff. There is a brief discussion of this aspect of pagan religion in J. Barbel, *Christos Angelos* (Bonn, 1941).

53 F. Sokolowski, 'Sur le culte d'Angelos dans le paganisme grec et romain', *HTR* 53 (1960), 225ff; A. T. Kraabel, 'Hypsistos and the Synagogue at Sardis', *Greek, Roman and Byzantine Studies* 10 (1969), 81ff. See also A. D. Nock in *HTR* 29 (1936), 63.

54 So Cumont, 'Les anges', p. 180 and Sokolowski, 'Sur le culte', p. 225. Nilsson, *Geschichte*, II, 518, n. 3, regards the question as still open.

55 The texts are collected by R. Wunsch, 'Neue Flüchtafeln', *RhMP* n. f. 55 (1900), 62ff, and *Antike Flüchtafeln* (Bonn, 1907). On the mixing of Greek, Jewish and Christian ideas in this field see F. Cumont, 'Les mystères de Sabazius et le Judaisme', *CRAI* (1906), 63f and S. E. Johnson, A Sabazius Inscription from Sardis', in J. Neusner (ed.), *Religion in Antiquity* (Leiden, 1968), p. 549.

56 Published in A. Deissmann, *Light from the Ancient East* (ET London, 1910), pp. 423ff.

57 F. Cumont, 'Le mysticisme astral dans l'antiquité', *BCLARB* (1909), 256ff.

58 There is a very attractive poem on this astral mysticism attributed to the philosopher Ptolemy (first century A.D.) in *Anth. Pal.* 9.577. See also F. Cumont, *Astrology and Religion*, p. 96.

59 Delling, *TDNT*, I, 488, attributes too much importance to this one obscure page.

3 The powers and Christ triumphant

1 Against Pauline authorship are Lohse and Conzelmann, but for it stand Prat, Abbott, Moule, Bruce, Dibelius-Greeven, Percy, Lightfoot, Hugédé and Kümmel.

2 See S. E. Johnson, 'Laodicea and its Neighbours', *BA* 13 (1950), 1ff.

3 A convenient, recent summary of the arguments may be found in J. T. Sanders, *The New Testament Christological Hymns* (Cambridge, 1971), especially pp. 12f and 75ff.

4 For details see E. P. Sanders, 'Literary Dependence in Colossians', *JBL* 85 (1966), 28ff. I, however, do not accept his theory of composition.

5 'Versuch zu Kol. 1, 15-20', *ZNW* 52 (1961), 88ff.

6 On certain assumptions about the Colossian error, J. M. Robinson suggests that the whole text from τὰ ὁρατά to ἐξουσίαι is an interpolation. This, as will be seen, depends on a mistaken view about the supposed error. See 'A Formal Analysis of Col. 1: 15-20', *JBL* 76 (1957), 270ff.

7 There are no examples in secular Greek of the personalising of θρόνος. See LSJ and O. Schmitz, *TDNT*, III, 160ff.

8 ἀρχή in Acts 10: 11; 11: 5 in the meaning 'corner', and Rom. 8: 38. ἐξουσίαι in Rom. 13: 1 and 1 Pet. 3: 22.

9 The reading ἀρχαῖς ἐξουσίαις in Tit. 3: 1 should probably stand, although the asyndeton is harsh. See BDF 460.1.

10 Delling argues for a Stoic interpretation in Colossians (see *TDNT*, I, 484) as does H. Hegermann, *Die Vorstellung vom Schöpfungsmittler im hellenistischen Judentum und Urchristentum* (Berlin, 1961), pp. 88ff. This is fully and rightly criticised by F. B. Craddock, 'All things in Him – A Critical Note on Col. I 15-20', *NTS* (1965), 78ff.

11 Foerster, *TDNT*, II, 562ff.

12 See E. G. Selwyn, *The First Epistle of Saint Peter*, 2nd ed. (London, 1947), pp. 207f.

13 C. Bigg, *The Epistles of St. Peter and St. Jude* (Edinburgh, 1901), *ad loc.*

14 See W. J. Dalton, *Christ's Proclamation to the Spirits* (Rome, 1965), pp. 163ff.

15 Dalton, *Christ's Proclamation*, pp. 87ff. The hypothesis is considerably elaborated by M. E. Boismard, *Quatre hymnes baptismales dans la première épître de Pierre* (Paris, 1961), pp. 57ff. The connection of 1 Peter with baptism is rightly questioned by David Hill, 'On Suffering and Baptism in 1 Peter', *NovT* 18 (1977), 182ff.

16 Both Dalton and Selwyn take the spirits as fallen angels. For the alternative see E. Schweizer, *TDNT*, VI, 446ff and C. Spicq, *Les épîtres de Saint Pierre* (Paris, 1966), pp. 136ff. If the reference is to the spirits of the departed,

ἐκήρυξεν may easily be taken in its usual sense. This interpretation is impossible if we attach a consistent meaning to πορευθείς, which must be taken to refer to the ascension of Christ. See J. N. D. Kelly, *A Commentary on the Epistles of Peter and of Jude* (London, 1969), pp. 155f.

17 Only Rev. 5: 2 and, notably, Lk. 12: 3. Sanders parallels 1 Tim. 3: 16f and tentatively suggests κηρυχθείς. See *NT Christological Hymns*, p. 18, and for the same idea Boismard, *Quatre hymnes*, p. 66.

18 See Dalton, *Christ's Proclamation*, p. 159 and F. Hauck and S. Schulz, *TDNT*, VI, 166ff. When the aorist participle is used with an aorist main verb the notion of the past is removed. See BDF, 339.1.

19 'Sometimes the idea of obedience is clearly dominant (e.g. Rom. 8: 7), but in the majority of cases, while it may be included, it is not clear that it predominates' (C. E. B. Cranfield, *A Commentary on Romans 12 and 13* (Edinburgh, 1965), p. 69).

20 Note πότε in verse 20 contrasted with νῦν in verse 21.

21 C. F. D. Moule, *The Epistle of Paul the Apostle to the Colossians and to Philemon* (Cambridge, 1962), p. 66.

22 The thought in 2: 10 is to be connected with that of 1: 15f and is discussed with the whole complex of references to ἀρχαί καὶ ἐξουσίαι below.

23 E. Lohse, *Die Briefe an die Kolosser und an Philemon* (Göttingen, 1968), p. 160, citing G. Schille, *Frühchristliche Hymnen* (Berlin, 1962), pp. 31ff, who regards it as a baptismal hymn. Lohse has developed his own thought further in 'Ein hymnisches Bekenntnis in Kol. 2, 13c-15' in A. Descamps et A. de Halleux (eds.), *Mélanges bibliques en hommage au R. P. Béda Rigaux* (Gembloux, 1970), pp. 427ff.

24 This expands my article, 'Two Notes on Colossians', *JTS* n.s. 24 (1973), 492ff. References are all to commentaries *ad loc.*, except in the case of F. Prat, *The Theology of St. Paul* (ET London, 1957), II, 228f, and B. N. Wambacq, 'Per Eum reconciliare . . . quae in caelis sunt. Col. i. 20', *RB* 55 (1948), 35ff.

25 The church at Colossae was evangelised by a Gentile, Epaphras (1: 6), and there are few signs of Jewishness in the epistle. In addition every indication is that the Jews in that area were neither familiar with nor concerned about the Law. See I. Lévy, 'Notes d'histoire et d'épigraphie', *REJ* 41 (1900), 174. A. S. Peake in *The Expositor's Greek Testament* (New York, 1903) assumes too conscious a Jewishness for the locality.

26 G. Megas, 'Das χειρόγραφον Adams', *ZNW* 27 (1928), 305ff.

27 J. A. T. Robinson, *The Body* (London, 1952), p. 43, n. 1.

28 J. Daniélou, *The Theology of Jewish Christianity* (ET London, 1964), pp. 192ff. O. Blanchette, 'Does the cheirographon of Col. 2.14 represent Christ himself?', *CBQ* 23 (1961), 304ff. See also W. C. van Unnik, 'The Gospel of Truth and the NT', in F. L. Cross (ed.), *The Jung Codex* (London, 1955), p. 108.

29 So A. J. Bandstra, *The Law and the Elements of this World* (Kampen, 1964), pp. 157ff.

30 The suggestion of M. Dibelius-H. Greeven, *An die Kolosser, Epheser, an Philemon* (Tübingen, 1953), *ad loc.*, that the reference is to the nailing of the *titulus* to the cross, seems even weaker.

31 This point is rightly emphasised by O. Roller, 'Das Buch mit sieben Siegeln', *ZNW* 36 (1937), 98ff.

32 See R. Pettazzoni, 'Confessions of Sin and the Classics', *HTR* 30 (1937), 1ff. The section in F. Steinleitner, *Die Beicht im Zusammenhange mit der sakralen Rechtspflege in der Antike* (Leipzig, 1913), pp. 70ff, is inadequate.

33 Mainly collected and surveyed by Steinleitner. See also K. Latte, 'Schuld und Sühne in der griechischen Religion', *ARW* 20 (1921), 292ff; D. G. Hogarth and W. M. Ramsay, 'Apollo Lermenus', *JHS* 8 (1887), 376ff; W. M. Ramsay, 'Artemis-Leto and Apollo Lairbenos', *JHS* 10 (1889), 216ff; W. H. Buckler, 'Some Lydian Propitiatory Inscriptions', *BSA* 21 (1914), 169ff; W. M. Ramsay, *The Cities and Bishoprics of Phrygia* (Oxford, 1897), I, 134ff; Cumont, *Les religions orientales*, p. 36; A. D. Nock, 'Early Gentile Christianity and its Hellenistic Background', reprinted in *Essays on Religion and the Ancient World* (Oxford, 1972), I, 66; Nilsson, *Geschichte*, II, 552ff.

34 Steinleitner, *Die Beicht*, no. 20.

35 *JHS* 10 (1889), 227.

36 Lightfoot, Abbot and Prat.

37 Lightfoot, *Colossians*, p. 188, for a list of commentators. Blanchette, 'Cheirographon', and G. Kittel, *TDNT*, II, 230ff.

38 Robinson, *The Body*, p. 43, n. 1.

39 Both LSJ and BAG regard the verb as passive. It is not a common word, usually being found in an active form meaning 'to promulgate a decree'. There are only two possible references in Colossians to someone perverting the gospel (2: 8 and 16); the rest of the letter implies an accommodation of the whole Church to its surroundings. This could well fit a middle sense to the verb: 'Do not bind yourselves with decrees.' See, too, Abbott.

40 So Abbott, Dibelius–Greeven, Lohse, Masson, Lohmeyer and Hugédé. A change of subject is accepted by Lightfoot, Moule, Bruce and Robinson.

41 *Colossians*, p. 185.

42 *Colossians*, p. 101.

43 J. H. Moulton and W. F. Howard, *A Grammar of New Testament Greek* (Edinburgh, 1929), II, 310. And BDF, 316.1.

44 See Lightfoot, *ad loc.* The attempt by Masson (*Colossiens, ad loc.*) to retain the middle force by *sibi exspolians* is no better.

45 See P. W. van der Horst, 'Observations on a Pauline Expression', *NTS* 19 (1973), 181ff. He has shown that the phrase τὸν ἄνθρωπον ἐκδῦναι was used in the third century B.C. in a sense very close to that employed by Paul in Col. 3: 9.

46 *Colossians*, pp. 190f: 'This interpretation is grammatical; it accords with St. Paul's teaching; and it is commended by the parallel uses of the substantive in ver. 11 and of the verb in iii. 9.'

47 *Colossians*, p. 259.

48 *The Body*, p. 41, n. 3. He acknowledges a debt to C. A. A. Scott, who suggested that the flesh was the locus of the authority of the powers. Many commentators hardly consider the issue, since, on the assumption of God as subject, it does not arise.

49 See L. Williamson, 'Led in Triumph: Paul's use of THRIAMBEUO', *Interp* 22 (1968), 316ff.

50 E. Lohmeyer, *Die Briefe an die Philipper, an die Kolosser, und an Philemon* (Göttingen, 1964), pp. 119f.

51 See the very full inquiry, which provides most of the evidence, by H. S. Versnel, *Triumphus: An Inquiry into the Origin, Development and Meaning of the Roman Triumph* (Leiden, 1970). A complete description is found in Plutarch, *Aem. Paul.* 32ff. See also W. Ehlers, 'Triumphus', *RE*, vii.2, 493ff. On the significance of the insignia see Th. Mommsen, *Römisches Staatsrecht*, 3rd ed. (Leipzig, 1887), I, 126ff.

52 The point is made explicitly by Varro, *de ling. lat.* 6.68: 'triumphare appellatum, quod cum imperatore milites redeuntes clamitant per urbem in Capitolium eunti "Io triumphe"; id a θριάμβῳ Graeco Liberi cognomento potest dictum'.

53 R. B. Egan, 'Lexical Evidence on Two Pauline Passages', *NovT* 19 (1977), 34ff.

54 On the root δειγμ– see F. Prat, 'Le triomphe du Christ sur les principautés et les puissances', *RechSR* 3 (1912), 218.

55 H. B. Swete, *The Apocalypse of St. John* (London, 1906), p. 250. R. H. Charles and G. B. Caird in their later commentaries take the reference to be martyrs because of the colour of the robes, but the context seems to demand angels. On the notion of the angel train of the Son of Man see J. Jeremias, *Jesus' Promise to the Nations* (ET London, 1958), pp. 69f, and on the background of this idea in Jewish exegesis see J. W. Doeve, *Jewish Hermeneutics in the Synoptic Gospels and Acts* (Assen, 1954), pp. 149ff especially p. 151.

56 E.G. IQM vii.6. Interestingly, the angels at Qumran are good or bad according to the context in which they occur. See J. A. Fitzmyer, 'A Feature of Qumran Angelology and the Angels of I Cor. xi.10', *NTS* 4 (1958), 48ff.

57 *Theology of Jewish Christianity*, pp. 234ff. He provides very little evidence.

58 'The Conquest of the Powers', *Studies in Paul's Technique and Theology* (London, 1974), pp. 1ff.

59 J. D. M. Derrett in an extended review of Hanson's book (*Heythrop Journal* 16 (1975), 421ff) commends this emphasis on the rabbinic tradition as background. But for a general assessment of the importance of Greek background for Paul see E. A. Judge, 'Saint Paul and Classical Society', *JAC* 15 (1972), 19ff.

60 See Moule, *Colossians*, p. 30, where his list allows a separation of βρῶσις ('part of pure Judaism') from πόσις ('predominantly Hellenic'). He also allows the separation of sabbaths from festival and new moon.

61 'Taking delight in' receives support from Lohse and others (details in *Kolosser*, p. 174), but is improbable: see Moule, *Idiom Book*, p. 173 and Percy, *Probleme*, pp. 145ff. For the meaning 'deliberately' or 'of his own will', see A. Fridrischen, 'THELŌN. Col 2, 18', *ZNW* 21 (1922), 135ff. This assumes that θέλων ἐν is taken with καταβραβευέτω. F. O. Francis, 'Humility and Angel Worship in Col. 2.18', *ST* 16 (1962), 109ff, suggests 'bent on'.

62 Phil. 2: 8. Cf. 1 En. 6: 7ff; 69: 15 etc. In general see J. A. Sanders, 'Dissenting Deities and Philippians 2. 1–11', *JBL* 88 (1969), 279ff, especially p. 287.

63   The importance of this aspect of Jewish mysticism is well attested. See e.g.
      4 Esd. 5: 13; 6: 31 etc; Asc. Is. 2: 7ff; Philo, *Somn.* 1.33f; and, among the
      rabbis, BT, Hag. 13*b*. See in general G. Scholem, *Jewish Gnosticism,
      Merkabah Mysticism and the Talmudic Tradition* (New York, 1960), pp.
      34ff.

64   See J. W. Bowker, '"Merkabah" Visions and Paul's Visions', *JSS* 16 (1971),
      157ff.

65   The evidence is collected by Francis, 'Humility and Angel Worship'.

66   This section expands my article, 'Two Notes on Colossians – II', *JTS* n.s.
      24 (1973), 496ff.

67   W. M. Ramsay, 'Religious Antiquities in Asia Minor', *BSA* 18 (1911), 44ff.
      There is a full discussion in M. Dibelius, 'Die Isisweihe bei Apuleius und
      verwändte Initiations-Riten', reprinted in *Botschaft und Geschichte.
      Gesammelte Aufsätze* (Tübingen, 1956), pp. 30ff, especially pp. 56ff.
      Lohse tried to avoid the main criticisms of this view by making ἐμβατεύων
      a catch-word of the errorists. *Kolosser*, pp. 176f.

68   A. D. Nock, 'The Vocabulary of the NT', *JBL* 52 (1933), 132ff. See also
      H. Preisker, *TDNT*, II, 535.

69   So *OGIS*, 530.15. See also C. Picard, 'Un oracle d'Apollon Clarios à
      Pergame', *BCH* 46 (1922), 190ff.

70   Percy, *Probleme*, pp. 170f.

71   S. Lyonnet, 'L'épître aux Colossiens (Col. 2.18) et les mystères d'Apollon
      Clarien', *Biblica* 43 (1962), 93ff. S. Eitrem considers that Paul has reversed
      the order of events through ignorance of the mysteries. See 'ΕΜΒΑΤΕΥΩ
      – Note sur Col. 2.18', *ST* 2 (1949), 90ff. A similar position is developed by
      L. Cerfaux, 'L'influence des "mystères" sur les épîtres de Saint Paul aux
      Colossiens et aux Ephésiens' in J. Coppens, A. Descamps and E. Massaux
      (eds.), *Sacra Pagina. Miscellanea Biblica Congressus Internationalis
      Catholici de Re Biblica* (Brussels, 1959), II, 373ff.

72   F. O. Francis, 'The Background of EMBATEUEIN (Col. 2: 18) in Legal
      Papyri and Oracle Inscriptions', in F. O. Francis and W. A. Meeks (eds.),
      Conflict at Colossae (Missoula, Montana, 1975), pp. 197ff. The book con-
      tains English translations for the first time of some of the essays that are
      quoted above.

73   E. R. Dodds, *Euripides' Bacchae* (Oxford, 1960), pp. xxff. See also *The
      Greeks and the Irrational* (Berkeley, 1951), Appendix 1. For the continu-
      ation of these rites into Roman times see Nilsson, *Dionysiac Religion*,
      pp. 45ff.

74   Has τὰ ἄνω in 3: 1 some such allusion in it? Climbing the mountain to be
      near the god was integral to Dionysiac religion.

75   See K. L. Schmidt, *TDNT*, III, 155ff.

76   On this whole question see A. L. Williams, 'The Cult of Angels at Colossae',
      JTS 10 (1909), 413ff. The relevant texts are collected in this article. For
      rabbinic evidence see e.g. JT Berakoth 13*a* and BT Abodah Zarah 42*b*.

77   Goodenough, *Jewish Symbols*, II, 45 and 145.

78   Confusion between a recognised local god and the unknown God of the
      Jews was not uncommon. See e.g. the identification of Yahweh with
      Bacchus, the evidence for which is presented by E. Babelon, 'Bacchius
      Judaeus', *RBN* 47 (1891), 5ff.

79 Williams, 'The Cult of Angels at Colossae', p. 433. See also the full survey by G. Delling, *TDNT*, II, 1ff. The careful distinctions drawn by Plato (*Symp.* 202D) repay careful study.

80 Cited by Lightfoot, *Colossians*, pp. 66ff.

81 See Theodoret, *Ep. Col. ii. 16 Interpretatio*.

82 Dibelius–Greeven, *Kolosser, ad loc.* relate the angels to the physical elements that control the lives of men. Percy, who soundly rejects this (*Probleme*, pp. 160f), himself suggests that the reference is to the angels behind the Law. Both views depend on an untenable interpretation of τὰ στοιχεῖα, which is refuted below.

83 See Francis, 'Humility', pp. 109ff. He lists among those who have taken the genitive subjectively Ephraem, Luther, Melanchthon, Wolf, Dalmer, Hofman, Zahn and Ewald. There remains a small problem in the absence of the article before the noun θρησκεία, but in so syntactically difficult a passage as this the objection is not very strong.

84 The objection is made by Lohse, *Kolosser, ad loc.*

85 See E. de W. Burton, *A Critical and Exegetical Commentary on the Epistle to the Galatians* (Edinburgh, 1921), *ad loc.* A. J. Bandstra, *The Law and the Elements of this World* (Kampen, 1964), pp. 54ff, emphasises the word τοῦ κόσμου in the phrase, which leads him to some improbable exegesis.

86 G. Delling, *TDNT*, VII, 670ff; Burton, *Galatians*, pp. 510ff. There is also a useful study by J. Blinzler, 'Lexikalisches zu dem Terminus τὰ στοιχεῖα τοῦ κόσμου bei Paulus', *Studiorum Paulinorum Congressus Internationalis Catholicus 1961* (Rome, 1963), II, 429ff, with a table of use on p. 440.

87 *TDNT*, VII, 677. There is additional evidence in the Mazdaean literature, in which a cult of the physical world is certainly present. See F. Cumont, *Textes et monuments figurés relatifs aux mystères de Mithra* (Brussels, 1894–9), I, 107ff, and J. Bidez and F. Cumont *Les mages hellénisés* (Paris, 1938), II, 102. In this the στοιχεῖα are certainly divinised physical elements. See also W. H. P. Hatch 'τὰ στοιχεῖα in Paul and Bardaisan', *JTS* 28 (1927), 181ff, although his connection of Paul and this eastern usage is highly speculative.

88 This is done e.g. by Dibelius–Greeven, *Kolosser*, pp. 28f.

89 See Delling, *TDNT*, VII, 681.

90 F. H. Colson, *The Week: An Essay in the Origin and Development of the Seven Day Cycle* (Cambridge, 1926).

91 *The Law and the Elements*, p. 12.

92 R. M. Grant, 'Like 'Children'', *HTR* 39 (1946), 71ff.

93 *TDNT*, VII, 685.

94 *Probleme*, pp. 160f. See also B. Reicke, 'The Law and this World according to Paul. Some Thoughts concerning Gal. 4. 1–11', *JBL* 70 (1951), 261ff. H. Weiss, 'The Law in the Epistle to the Colossians', *CBQ* 34 (1972), 303, considers that the στοιχεῖα cannot be impersonal: 'I find it difficult to see Paul ... working conceptually with impersonal forces in an abstract cosmos.' If, however, the word means 'elementary teaching', there is little problem. We may compare the phrase τύπος διδαχῆς in Rom. 6: 17. The personification of the Law in the LXX, which Weiss uses as a parallel, did not lead to its worship, and there is a difference between personification and hypostatisation.

95 So Dibelius–Greeven (1953), Masson (1950), Abbott (1897), Lohmeyer (1930), Bruce (1957), Hugédé (1968) and Lohse (1968). Also G. Bornkamm, 'Die Häresie des Kolosserbriefes', in *Das Ende des Gesetzes - Paulusstudien, Gesammelte Aufsätze* (Munich, 1966), I, 139ff. Lohse makes the worship of στοιχεῖα as star spirits central to the Colossian error.

96 2 Peter and Jude are considered further below.

97 Delling argues that the phrase is a Pauline creation, but Blinzler ('Lexikalisches', pp. 440f) has shown that it is found in Philo, the Sibylline oracles and several later writers.

98 *Theology*, p. 284.

99 So Percy, *Probleme*, p. 158.

100 Moule, *Colossians*, p. 93.

101 M. D. Hooker, 'Were there false teachers in Colossae?', in B. Lindars and S. S. Smalley (eds.), *Christ and Spirit in the New Testament. Studies in honour of C. F. D. Moule* (Cambridge, 1973), pp. 315ff.

102 See Lightfoot, *Colossians*, pp. 257ff; J. A. Robinson, 'On the Meaning of πλήρωμα', *St. Paul's Epistle to the Ephesians* (London, 1904), pp. 255ff; Moule, *Colossians*, pp. 164ff. Against this view see G. Delling, *TDNT*, VI, 298ff.

103 R. McL. Wilson, *Gnosis and the New Testament* (Oxford, 1968), pp. 56f, accepts the view of E. Best, *One Body in Christ* (London, 1955), p. 148, that 'the Hellenistic philosophical conception of the universe as filled by God was at this time passing into the Gnostic conception of the divine *pleroma*, at once the abode of the aeons and the aggregate of them'. But it seems likely that this process should be placed nearer the end of the century. See S. Lyonnet, 'Saint Paul et le Gnosticisme' in U. Bianchi (ed.), *Le Origini dello Gnosticismo* (Leiden, 1967), p. 539, n. 2.

104 H. Langkammer, 'Die Einwohnung der "absoluten Seinsfülle" in Christus. Bemerkungen zu Kol 1, 19', *BZ* 12 (1968), 258ff, has argued for a cosmic dimension to the term in its LXX use. This may be the case, but we may not conclude from this that Paul was here implying a cosmic salvation on the basis of Christ's habitation of πᾶν τὸ πλήρωμα. This would reverse Paul's stress that the *pleroma* is in Christ.

105 See M. L. Peel, *The Epistle to Rheginos* (London, 1969), pp. 106f, who points out that the gnostic emphasis is upon the incompleteness of the *pleroma*, while Paul stresses completeness.

106 *Probleme*, pp. 76f.

107 See O. Cullmann, 'The Tradition: The Exegetical, Historical and Theological Problem', *The Early Church* (ET London, 1956), p. 64. The nearest parallel to this description of Christ, that in 1 Cor. 4: 5, lacks the articles and is therefore easier. The dependence of the imperative on the indicative is wholly Pauline.

108 κεφαλή is used in a basically Jewish sense, rather than any Stoic or gnostic way. See S. F. B. Bedale, 'κεφαλή in the Pauline Letters', *JTS* n.s. 5 (1954), 211ff.

109 The importance of banqueting in Asiatic religion is well attested. See M. Perdrizet, 'Reliefs mysiens', *BCH* 23 (1899), 529ff.

110 The commentary by L. B. Radford (1931), is the only one that attempts this.

111 On Paul's accommodation to the Colossian situation in ch. 3 see E. Grässer, 'Kol 3, 1–4 als Beispiel', *ZThK* 64 (1967), 139ff.

112 So W. Schmithals, *Die Gnosis in Korinth: eine Untersuchung zu den Korintherbriefen*, 2nd ed. (Göttingen, 1965).

113 G. Bornkamm, 'Die Hoffnung im Kolosserbrief', *Geschichte und Glaube II, Gesammelte Aufsätze IV* (Munich, 1971), pp. 206ff.

114 See M. Peel, 'Gnostic Eschatology and the NT', *NovT* 12 (1970), 141ff.

115 See C. F. D. Moule, 'The Influence of Circumstances on the Use of Eschatological Terms', *JTS* n.s. 15 (1964), 1ff; *idem*, 'The Individualism of the Fourth Gospel', *NovT* 5 (1962), 17ff.

116 E. Käsemann, 'A Primitive Christian Baptismal Liturgy', ET in *Essays on New Testament Themes* (London, 1964), pp. 149ff.

117 The collection of motifs in this verse is notable but not impossibly Pauline. It may be based upon Paul's experience on the Damascus road. See Moule, *Colossians*, p. 56.

118 R. P. Martin, *Carmen Christi: Philippians ii. 5–11 in Recent Interpretation and in the Setting of Early Christian Worship* (Cambridge, 1967).

119 So J. B. Lightfoot, *St. Paul's Epistle to the Philippians* (London, 1891), p. 115.

120 *Die Geisterwelt*, p. 231.

121 *Christ and Time*, pp. 192ff.

122 *Carmen Christi*, p. 260, n. 2.

123 The argument from J. Jeremias, *Die Briefe an Timotheus und Titus* (Göttingen, 1963), p. 21, is totally refuted by Moule, *Birth of the New Testament*, p. 24.

124 E.g. Heb. 12: 1; IQH 3.21; BT, Hullin 91*b*.

125 *Christ and Time*, p. 193.

126 That the whole of the psalm was not necessarily of importance seems clear from the omission of verse 3 in Christian apologetic, although it would presumably have been useful regarding the birth of Jesus. See Moule, *Birth of the New Testament*, p. 64.

127 *Glory at the Right Hand. Psalm 110 in Early Christianity* (Nashville, 1973), p. 155.

128 *Ibid.* p. 122, notes the rarity of any notion of subjection in connection with the use of Ps. 110: 1, and remarks that 'the subjection of powers or persons to Christ is at most a secondary concern'. He appears not to notice the moderating effect of Ps. 8.

129 This is to take τὸν ὑποτάξαντα to refer to God.

130 See generally J. G. Gibbs, 'The Cosmic Scope of Redemption according to Paul', *Biblica* 56 (1975), 13ff.

131 See H. Conzelmann, *I Corinthians* (ET Philadelphia, 1975), p. 274; also R. Bultmann, *TDNT*, III, 11ff.

4 The powers and the spiritual world

1 BAG, *s.v.* τοποθεσία, wrongly suggests that '*either* the ranks of the angels *or* the place where they live' are alternatives.

2 H. Odeberg, *The View of the Universe in the Epistle to the Ephesians* (Lund, 1934). See also F. Mussner, *Christus das All und die Kirche* (Trier, 1955), pp. 9ff, and J. B. Lightfoot, *Notes on the Epistles of St. Paul*

(London, 1895), p. 312. None of these adequately accounts for the problem of 6: 12.

3 *Probleme*, pp. 182f. A similar explanation is attempted by R. M. Pope, 'Studies in Pauline Vocabulary: Of the Heavenly Places', *ExT* 23 (1912), 365f.

4 H. Schlier, *Der Brief an die Epheser* (Düsseldorf, 1957), pp. 86ff. He is very much influenced by M. Dibelius and H. Greeven, *An die Kolosser, Epheser, an Philemon* (Tübingen, 1953), p. 58.

5 See K. G. Kuhn, 'Ephesians in the Light of the Qumran Texts', and F. Mussner, 'Contributions made by Qumran to the Understanding of the Epistle to the Ephesians', ET of both in J. Murphy-O'Connor (ed.), *Paul and Qumran* (London, 1968). The Jewishness of Ephesians was recognised apart from the Qumran discoveries. See J. C. Kirby, *Baptism and Pentecost* (London, 1968), and for an uncritical list of parallels, ·D. Flusser, 'The Dead Sea Sect and Pauline Christianity', in C. Rabin and Y. Yadin (eds.), *Aspects of the Dead Sea Scrolls*, Scripta Hierosolymitana 4 (Jerusalem, 1958), 215ff, especially p. 263nn.

6 See R. J. McKelvey, *The New Temple* (Oxford, 1969), pp. 108ff; B. Gärtner, *The Temple and the Community in Qumran and the New Testament* (Cambridge, 1965), especially pp. 60ff; also Mussner, 'Contributions', pp. 164ff.

7 E.g. IQS 11: 7; IQH 3: 21.

8 Mussner, 'Contributions', p. 167.

9 This is overlooked both by E. Käsemann, 'Ephesians and Acts', in L. E. Keck and J. L. Martyn (eds.), *Studies in Luke–Acts* (New York, 1966), pp. 288ff and by R. P. Martin, 'An Epistle in Search of a Life Setting' *ExT* 79 (1968), 296ff. The apparent similarity in the eschatology of the two books and in particular the possible separation of Easter from the Ascension/Pentecost motif is interesting, but it cannot distract from the difference in the function of the Spirit in each book.

10 See H. Traub, *TDNT*, V, 540; J. A. Allan, 'The "In Christ" Formula in Ephesians', *NTS* 5 (1958), 54ff.

11 IQS 11: 7; IQSa 2. For the joint action of the hosts of heaven and the earthbound people see also IQM 12.

12 If this is the case, the 'sons of disobedience' in verse 6 are not the godless world but apostates or morally corrupt members of the community. See Kuhn, 'Ephesians in the Light of Qumran', pp. 121ff.

13 *The View of the Universe*, pp. 4ff.

14 The phrase comes from J. G. Gibbs, *Creation and Redemption. A Study in Pauline Theology* (Leiden, 1971), pp. 130f.

15 G. B. Caird, 'The Descent of Christ in Eph. 4, 7–11', in F. L. Cross (ed.), *Studia Evangelica*, 11 = *Texte und Untersuchungen*, 102 (Berlin, 1964), 535ff.

16 The construction is not uncommon in Ephesians: e.g. 2: 14; 15; 6: 14ff; and, perhaps, 2: 20. Caird's view is held against BDF, p. 167, which follows F. Büchsel, *TDNT*, III, 641. See also F. F. Bruce, 'St. Paul in Rome. 4. The Epistle to the Ephesians', *BJRL* 49 (1966), 318ff, and especially the note on p. 320.

17 A similar argument is put forward by A. T. Lincoln, 'A Re-examination of

"The Heavenlies" in Ephesians', *NTS* 19 (1973), 468ff, who sheds light on the phrase by reading it in the context of Pauline eschatology, in particular noting the description of Christ in 1 Cor. 15: 49.

18   See Lightfoot, *Philippians*, p. 113.

19   E.g. 1 En. 16: 3 and 2 En. 24: 3 for the restricted knowledge of the hosts of heaven. In the NT an obvious example is Mk. 13: 32, as is Lk. 15: 10. For a development of the idea to include the OT saints, and perhaps the Christian departed, see Heb. 11: 13ff.

20   So Schlier, *Epheser*, p. 102, and J. L. Houlden, *Paul's Letters from Prison* (London, 1970), p. 281. Abbott, *Ephesians*, p. 40, rightly comments: 'αἰών, being a technical word of the gnostics, it was to be expected that some expositors would adopt a similar meaning here'.

21   Those who see here a personalised Aeon usually also regard Ephesians as engaged in a controversy with some form of gnostic thought: e.g. Bultmann, Dibelius, Schlier, Pokórny. Kümmel, *Introduction*, p. 257, gives a full list.

22   A. D. Nock, 'A Vision of Mandulis Aion', *HTR* 27 (1934), 84. The article summarises the Greek ideas that bear on the word.

23   See e.g. Pindar, *Isth.* 8.14; *Anth. Pal.* 9.51. Also D. Levi, 'Aion', *Hesperia* 13 (1944), 269ff and C. Bonner, 'An Obscure Inscription on a Gold Tablet', *Hesperia* 13 (1944), 134.

24   See Cumont, *Les religions orientales*, pp. 280f; Mussner, *Christus das All*, pp. 18f; Dibelius, *Die Geisterwelt*, p. 156; and for the belief in later Christianity, F. Andres, *Die Engellehre der griechischen Apologeten des zweiten Jahrhunderts und ihr Verhältnis zur griechischen-römischen Dämonologie* (Paderborn, 1914), pp. 124ff and 147.

25   As has been noted, the demonology of this book is hopelessly confused. On this passage see H. Bietenhard, *Die himmlische Welt im Urchristentum und Spätjudentum* (Tübingen, 1951), pp. 217ff.

26   Schlier, *Epheser*, p. 103, identified the firmament and the air, but Percy, *Probleme*, p. 257, n. 4, offers convincing arguments against.

27   The text is discussed by E. Peterson, 'La libération d'Adam de l'Ἀναγκή', *RB* 55 (1948), 211f. See also Bidez and Cumont, *Les mages hellénisés*, II, 159.

28   See Foerster, *TDNT*, I, 165.

29   The rabbinic notion of demons as causing sickness etc. is absent from Qumran. See H. Ringgren, *The Faith of Qumran* (ET Philadelphia, 1963), pp. 90ff.

30   See P. Wernberg-Moeller, 'A Reconsideration of the Two Spirits in the Rule of Community – IQS III.13 – IV.26', *RQ* 3 (1961), 413ff, and M. Treves, 'The Two Spirits of the Rule of the Community', *RQ* 3 (1961), 449ff. For the mixture of ideas in Qumran, Judaism and early Christian thought see O. J. F. Seitz, 'The Two Spirits in Man: an Essay in Biblical Exegesis', *NTS* 6 (1959), 82ff.

31   Abbott, *Ephesians*, p. 42, compares 1 Cor. 2: 12, making the genitive depend upon τὸν ἄρχοντα, 'the harshness of which is diminished by distance'.

32   Mentioned without details by Abbott, *Ephesians*, p. 41.

33   *De gig.* 8.

34　See G. Zuntz, *The Text of the Epistles* (London, 1953). A few Latin MSS make the same correction.

35　See too 2 Tim. 2: 3ff. V. C. Pfitzner, *Paul and the Agon Motif. Traditional Athletic Imagery in the Pauline Literature* (Leiden, 1967), p. 159.

36　J. Sevenster, *Paul and Seneca* (Leiden, 1961), p. 162.

37　See Seitz, 'Two Spirits', pp. 90ff.

38　The description would fit a Roman legionary (see Polybius, 3.62 and 4.56), but this is probably incidental. The *pilum* and *hasta*, offensive weapons, are not mentioned.

39　See A. Oepke and K. G. Kuhn, *TDNT*, V, 295ff.

40　See J. Murphy O'Connor, 'Truth: Paul and Qumran', *Paul and Qumran*, p. 205.

41　See Bietenhard, *Die himmlische Welt*, p. 116, on a similar problem in the rabbinic tradition.

42　See O. Michel, *TDNT*, III, 913. Although ὁ ἄρχων τοῦ κόσμου might seem to provide a parallel, it is the plural that particularly constitutes the problem.

43　See e.g. Irenaeus, *adv. haer.* 1.27.2 (Marcion), and 1.5.4 (Valentinus). The final use of the term for the Devil occurs in *Test. Sal.* 8.2 (*PG*, CXXII, 1328B), after which the word 'Lucifer' is used. See F. Cumont and L. Canet, 'Mithra ou Sarapis ΚΟΣΜΟΚΡΑΤΩΡ?', *CRAI* (1919), 327ff.

44　By the time of Chrysostom, when the Church was ordering the world to suit its dogmatic presuppositions, the κοσμοκράτορες were given a place under heaven and their power was restricted to this present world. See *Incomp.* 4.2 (*PG*, XLVIII, 730). Even at this date the word was being explained through its component parts.

45　J. Jeremias, 'Flesh and Blood cannot inherit the Kingdom of God. I Cor. xv.50', *NTS* 2 (1955), 151ff.

46　Cumont and Canet, 'Mithra ou Sarapis', pp. 324f, regard this use of the plural as very unusual. See also Michel *TDNT*, III, 914.

47　On the neuter plural and genitive see BDF, 263.4. The noun πνεύματα is rare in Paul, and the readings in 1 Cor. 14: 12 suggest that it may be used interchangeably with πνευματικά. On that passage see E. E. Ellis, 'Spiritual Gifts in the Pauline Community', *NTS* 20 (1974), 128ff. I, however, do not accept his theory. See too A. van Roon, *The Authenticity of Ephesians* (Leiden, 1974), p. 174.

48　See Bietenhard, *Die himmlische Welt*, p. 211, who, following Percy (*Probleme*, p. 181) associates it with 2: 2 and 2 En. 29: 4. Against this see Odeberg, *The View of the Universe*, pp. 7ff, and above.

49　So Percy, *Probleme*, p. 181. See also Traub, *TDNT*, V, 540f.

50　*Ephesians*, p. 182.

51　If this refers to the days of Belial's rule, then the explicit connection of πονηρία with the Devil in this passage is emphasised. See Flusser, 'Dead Sea Sect', p. 218.

52　Ignatius is expressing the universality of hostility towards the Christian. His understanding of heaven and earth is discussed below. See also J. B. Lightfoot, *The Apostolic Fathers* (London, 1889), II, 67. For the longer text see I, 237ff.

53　*Test. Sal.* 8.2 (*PG*, CXXII, 1328B).

54   See Flusser, 'Dead Sea Sect', p. 263, n. 163.
55   On the dramatic decline in popularity of Paul's letters in this period, see
     A. E. Barnett, *Paul Becomes a Literary Influence* (Chicago, 1941).
56   For the citations in Clement, see M. Mees, *Die Zitate aus dem Neuen
     Testament bei Clemens von Alexandrien* (Rome, 1970), p. 200. Interest-
     ingly he seems to attempt to return a normal sense to πνευματικά, rather
     than the unusual absolute use of Eph. 6: 12, by reading πνευματικὰ τῶν
     ἐν οὐρανοῖς.
57   'The Case against Pauline Authorship', p. 29, in F. L. Cross (ed.), *Studies
     in Ephesians* (London, 1956).
58   On οὔτε see BDF, 445. The sequence of pairs is intended to signify univer-
     sality. See P. van der Osten-Sacken, *Römer 8 als Beispiel paulinischer
     Soteriologie* (Göttingen, 1975), p. 317.
59   See M. Takahashi, 'An Oriental's Approach to the Problem of Angelology',
     ZAW 78 (1966), 343ff.
60   The suggestion of Sanday and Headlam (*Romans*, p. 223) that the word
     was inadvertently omitted from a text and then added in the wrong place
     overlooks the way in which its presence at any point destroys the
     parallelism.
61   So J. A. Fitzmyer, 'A Feature of Qumran Angelology and the Angels of
     I Cor. xi.10', *NTS* 4 (1958), 54, and the postscripts in *Essays on the
     Semitic Background of the NT* (London, 1971), pp. 187ff.
62   Everling, *Die paulinische Angelologie*, p. 9, regarded them simply as angels
     neither good nor bad, but Dibelius, *Die Geisterwelt*, p. 112, aligned them
     with 'the powers of this age', an identification that has met with wide-
     spread approval.
63   See Burton, *Galatians*, pp. 25f.
64   See e.g. W. L. Knox, *Paul and the Church of the Gentiles*, p. 106.
65   Plutarch, *Mor.* 149A; Vettius Valens, 241.26.
66   See H. Schlier, *TDNT*, I, 517. On 1 Cor. 2: 10 U. Wilckens has remarked
     that the phrase τὰ βάθη τοῦ θεοῦ is typically gnostic (*Weisheit und Torheit*
     (Tübingen, 1959), p. 82), but this is not necessarily so.
67   See Gundel, 'Astrologie', *RAC*, I, 825f, and G. Bertram, *TDNT*, VIII, 614.
68   See Sister S. Mary CSMV, '2 Corinthians 12, 1–4 and the Recent Dis-
     cussion on "height" and "depth"', in F. L. Cross (ed.), *Studia Evangelica*,
     IV = *Texte und Untersuchungen*, 102 (Berlin, 1968), 462ff, especially p.
     466.
69   Lagrange and Leenhardt in their commentaries defend the sense 'forces of
     nature'.
70   See C. F. D. Moule, *Man and Nature in the New Testament* (London,
     1964).
71   Grundmann, *TDNT*, 307ff.
72   This conclusion is tentatively proposed by J. Murray, *The Epistle to the
     Romans* (Michigan, 1959), I, 333.
73   See Bultmann, *Theology*, I, 258ff, and for a theological exposition, K.
     Barth, *The Epistle to the Romans* (ET Oxford 1933), p. 329. Also J. G.
     Gibbs, 'The Cosmic Scope of Redemption according to Paul', *Biblica* 56
     (1975), 13ff.

5 The powers and the political world

1 For the early history see in particular W. Affeldt, *Die weltliche Gewalt in der Paulus-Exegese: Römer 13, 1–7 in den Römerbriefkommentaren der lateinischen Kirche bis zum Ende des 13. Jahrhunderts* (Göttingen, 1969). Also W. Parsons, 'The Influence of Romans 13 in pre-Augustinian Political Thought', *TS* 1 (1940), 337ff, and R. Deniel, 'Omnis Potestas a Deo. L'Origine du pouvoir civil et sa rélation à l'Église', *RechSR* 56 (1968), 43ff.

2 The debate up to about 1956 is well summarised and annotated by C. D. Morrison, *The Powers that Be: Earthly Rulers and Demonic Powers in Romans 13. 1–7* (London, 1960). Among the more significant publications since that date we may mention E. Käsemann, 'Römer 13, 1–7 in unserer Generation', *ZThK* 56 (1959), 316ff; *idem*, 'Principles of Interpretation of Romans 13', ET in *New Testament Questions of Today* (London, 1965), pp. 205ff; F. Neugebauer, 'Zur Auslegung von Röm. 13, 1–7', *KuD* 8 (1962), 151ff; G. Delling, *Röm. 13, 1–7 innerhalb des NT* (Berlin, n.d.); Cranfield, *A Commentary on Romans 12–13*; V. Zsifkovitz, *Der Staatsgedanke nach Paulus in Röm 13, 1–7* (Vienna, 1964); E. Barnikol, 'Römer 13. Der nichtpaulinische Ursprung der absoluten Obrigkeitsbejahung von Röm. 13, 1–7', *Studien zum NT und zur Patristik, E. Klostermann zum 90. Geburtstag dargebracht* (Berlin, 1961), pp. 65ff.

3 *Die Geisterwelt*, pp. 189 and 193ff. Others who held this view include Schmidt, Dehn, Nieder, W. Schweitzer and Morgenthaler. Details may be found in Morrison, *The Powers*. Dibelius, in the light of this debate, changed his position. See 'Rom und die Christen im ersten Jahrhundert', reprinted in *Botschaft und Geschichte, Gesammelte Aufsätze* (Tübingen, 1956), II, 181.

4 The article (originally in *TZ* 10 (1954), 321ff) is translated as an *Excursus* to *The State in the New Testament* (New York, 1957). The quotation is from p. 114.

5 This is the point on which there is most agreement and that is, of course, most questioned by the present study in general.

6 *Christ and Time*, p. 104. The curious value judgement in 'legitimate', around which centre most of the problems for the Christian in relation to the state, is not explained.

7 *The State in the New Testament*, pp. 112.

8 See H. von Campenhausen, 'Zur Auslegung von Röm. 13; Die dämonistische Deutung des *exousia*-Begriffes', *Festschrift für A. Bertholet* (Tübingen, 1950), p. 99; so too A. Strobel, 'Zum Verständnis von Römer 13', *ZNW* 47 (1956), 72ff.

9 'Zur Auslegung', p. 104.

10 *Ad Autol.* 3.14 (*PG*, VI, 1142): see too 1.11 (*PG*, VI, 1140).

11 *The Powers*, p. 61.

12 *The Powers*, p. 68.

13 *The Powers*, p. 99.

14 See too the brief review of *The Powers* by S. Sandmel, *JBL* 80 (1961), 81ff, who alludes to the mystification that this conclusion creates.

15 This section is an abbreviated presentation of my article 'The Rulers of this

Age – I Corinthians II, 6–8', *NTS* 23 (1976), 20ff.

16 Origen, *de Princ.* 3.2; Marcion in Tertullian, *adv. Marc.* 5.6. Bultmann, *Theology*, I, 147ff; Lietzmann, *An die Korinther I, II* (Göttingen, 1949), *ad loc.*; Delling, *TDNT*, I, 489; Schlier, *Principalities*, pp. 45f; C. K. Barrett, 'Christianity at Corinth', *BJRL* 46 (1963), 278ff, and *I Corinthians, ad loc.*

17 J. Héring, *The First Epistle of St. Paul to the Corinthians* (ET London, 1962), pp. 26f.

18 R. Leivestad, *Christ the Conqueror* (London, 1954), p. 106; J. Wendland, *Die Briefe an die Korinther* (Göttingen, 1946), p. 19; G. Dehn, 'Engel und Obrigkeit; ein Beitrag zum Verständnis von Röm. 13. 1–7', in E. Wolf (ed.), *Theologische Aufsätze für Karl Barth* (Munich, 1936), p. 104; Caird, *Principalities and Powers*, pp. 16f.

19 J. Schniewind, 'Die Archonten dieses Äons: I Kor 2, 6–8', *Nachgelassene Reden und Aufsätze* (Berlin, 1951), pp. 104ff. The article by G. Miller, "ΟΙ ἈΡΧΟΝΤΕΣ ΤΟΤ ἈΙΩΝΟΣ ΤΟΤΤΟΤ – A New Look', *JBL* 91 (1972), 522ff, also supports this position, but overlooks all recent work, including that of Schniewind and Feuillet.

20 Schniewind, 'Die Archonten', p. 107. See also the general remarks in H. Conzelmann, *An Outline of the Theology of the NT* (ET London, 1969), p. 204.

21 'Les "chefs de ce siècle" et la sagesse divine après I Cor 2, 6–8', *Studiorum Paulinorum Congressus Internationalis Catholicus* (Rome, 1963), I, 383ff. See also W. Wuellner, 'Haggadic Homily Genre in I Corinthians 1–3', *JBL* (1970), 199ff.

22 H. St. J. Thackeray, *The Septuagint and Jewish Worship* (London, 1923), pp. 95ff. These arguments were developed by E. Peterson, 'I Korinther i.1ff und die Thematik des judischen Busstages', *Biblica* 32 (1951), 97ff, following L. Cerfaux, 'Vestiges d'un florilège dans I Cor. i.18–iii.24?', *RHE* 27 (1931), 521ff.

23 J. Munck, *Paul and the Salvation of Mankind* (ET London, 1959), pp. 145ff.

24 See L. Vischer, *Zur Auslegungsgeschichte von I Kor 6, 1–11* (Tübingen, 1955). A. Stern has attempted to show that the reference is to Christians turning to the rabbi to solve disputes, but his attempt to show that ἄδικοι means 'Jews' is strained. See A. Stern, 'Wo trügen die Korinthischen Christen ihre Rechthändel aus?', *ZNW* 59 (1968), 86ff.

25 In Philostratus, *Vit. Soph.* 1.25.3. the word is used in a legal context for 'mundane matters'.

26 Moule, *Idiom Book*, p. 164, and BDF, 427.2.

27 Moule, *Idiom Book*, p. 114.

28 See Barrett, *I Corinthians*, p. 136.

29 This is a typical attitude of close-knit groups. See B. R. Wilson, *Sects and Society* (London, 1961). The word 'conscience' in the NT may refer to observable aspects of the Christian life. For the importance of this outward directedness see D. Hill, 'On Suffering and Baptism in I Peter', *NovT* 18 (1976), 188.

6 Texts within the New Testament

1 The striking description of the angel proclaiming the gospel in 14: 6 is difficult only if the term εὐαγγέλιον is not given its usual sense of 'the good news of God'. See G. B. Caird, *The Revelation of St. John the Divine* (London, 1966), pp. 182f, which should be supplemented by G. Friedrich, *TDNT*, II, 735. On strength as a divine attribute see A. M. Farrer, *The Revelation of St. John the Divine* (Oxford, 1964), p. 93.

2 For a defence of a reference to guardian angels see Caird, *Revelation*, p. 24. John does not go as far as the writer of The Ascension of Isaiah, who sees the era of the Church in terms of the descent of 'the angel of the church which is in the heavens' (3: 15).

3 See P. S. Minear, 'The Cosmology of the Apocalypse', in W. Klassen and G. F. Snyder (eds.), *Current Issues in New Testament Interpretation* (London, 1962), pp. 23ff, especially pp. 30f.

4 Farrer, *Revelation*, p. 152.

5 The dispute between Michael and the Devil over the body of Moses may come from the lost portion of The Assumption of Moses.

6 The Christian interpretation of Jewish angelology at this point tended to adopt the story that the creation of the angels was the first act of God on the first day of creation. See e.g. 2 En. 29: 3. See also Hermas, *Vis.* 3.4.1 and *Sim.* 5.5.3, and an exposition in Clement of Alexandria, *Ecl. Proph.* 51 and 54.7.

7 In Eph. 1: 21 // Col. 1: 16 the singular is collective.

8 So, too, K. H. Schelkle, *Die Petrusbriefe, der Judasbrief* (Freiburg, 1964), p. 157. For the use of the term with respect to God see Did. 4.1 and with respect to Christ see Hermas, *Sim.* 5.6.1. In the light of Jude 4 it is probable Christ is the referent here.

9 Philo, *de spec. leg.* 1.45 is sometimes cited. The connection of δόξα with δύναμις points to the way in which the plural use develops, but it is unique in Philo. See G. Kittel and G. von Rad, *TDNT*, II, 236. A similar collocation is found, possibly under Jewish influence, in *PG*, I, 12, 196, and there may be a slight connection between this and 1 Clem. 59.3. See E. Peterson, 'La Libération d'Adam de l' Ἀνάγκη', *RB* 55 (1948), 204.

10 See Kittel and von Rad, *TDNT*, II, 233ff, especially p. 245.

11 See F. Hauck, *TDNT*, IV, 644ff.

12 G. Dix, *Jew and Greek* (London, 1953), p. 65.

13 The name 'Thomas' is also a genuine Greek name. See BDF 53.2d. In addition to the Gospel of Thomas, the tradition is preserved in the Acts of Thomas; see especially 31. In the Fourth Gospel the term λεγόμενος means 'translated by'. The author, therefore, in 11: 16 and 21: 12 is pointing out, for those who would not know it, that 'Thomas' means 'twin'. The Syrian texts, however, omit this, presumably since the readers would know the meaning. The tradition recurs in 14: 22, where in the reference to 'Judas not Iscariot' sy^S inserts the word 'Thomas' and sy^C adds 'Judas Thomas'. In addition, Eusebius, *HE* 1.13.11 refers to Judas Thomas in the account of Agbar of Edessa, although as Koester notes (*Trajectories*, p. 128, n. 30), only in those parts where he is quoting the legend word for word. See also on this G. Bornkamm, Hennecke–Schneemelcher, I, 426f, and A. J. F.

Klijn, *The Acts of Thomas* (Leiden, 1962), p. 158.

14 'Ιουδας 'Ιακωβου, who is mentioned in Luke 6: 16 and Acts 1: 13 reappears in *Act. Thom.* 1, but this may be only a conventional list. It is the remarkable superscription in Jude that draws attention to the name. Kelly, *I Peter*, p. 234, stresses the value of the name 'James' against the mention of Jude, but reckons that Judas Thomas as the twin brother of Jesus was honoured only in some gnostic circles. Yet this belief may be also distinctive of Christianity in eastern Syria in the early years. Indeed, James himself may have carried some authority among the Syrian Christians: see Daniélou, *Theology of Jewish Christianity*, p. 58. This may, however, merely reflect their membership of the Jewish–Christian world and may not be over-stressed: see Koester, *Trajectories*, p. 136.

15 See H. C. Puech, Hennecke–Schneemelcher, I, 282; W. C. van Unnik, *Newly Discovered Gnostic Writings* (ET London, 1960), pp. 49f. A valuable caution is expressed by B. Ehlers, 'Kann das Thomasevangelium aus Edessa stammen?', *NovT* 12 (1970), 284ff, but it is answered by A. J. F. Klijn, 'Christianity in Edessa and the Gospel of Thomas', *NovT* 14 (1972), 70ff.

16 See G. Strecker, Hennecke–Schneemelcher, II, 102ff, and P. Vielhauer, *ibid.* I, 123ff. W. Bauer, *Orthodoxy and Heresy in Earliest Christianity* (ET Philadelphia, 1971), pp. 32 and 39ff, notes that the canon at Edessa included additional Pauline correspondence, and Koester, *Trajectories*, p. 137, n. 61, notes that the sectarian heirs of the Thomas tradition in Syria, the Manichaeans, also positively valued Paul.

17 For the general background see L. W. Barnard, 'The Church in Edessa during the First Two Centuries A.D.', *VC* 22 (1968), 161ff.

18 Bigg, *I Peter*, pp. 311ff, has attempted to find some links, but without success. His connections are solely due to a common Christian confession.

19 Those who argue the reverse generally do so in order to preserve genuine Petrine authorship. See especially E. M. B. Green, *2 Peter Reconsidered* (London, 1961).

20 Prior to 2 Peter it is only noted in the fifth century B.C. historian Acusilaus.

21 Noah as herald to the righteous is found in Josephus, *AJ* 1.74 and Jub. 7.20ff, and the Christian use is as early as *1 Clem.* 7.6 and 9.4. The fall of Sodom, so that only ashes remained, is not part of the Judaean legends but is found in Philo, *Vit. Mos.* 2.56.

22 Rabbinical texts mainly treat Lot as sinful (see S–B, III, 669ff), but Christians (e.g. *1 Clem.* 11.1) used another tradition that he was the paradigm of faithfulness. See e.g. Wis. 10: 16.

23 The Christological basis of the word seems to be eroded. The suggestion of Bigg, *Peter and Jude*, p. 279, which is followed by E. M. B. Green, *A Commentary on II Peter and Jude* (London, 1968), p. 105, that this refers to ecclesiastical authority, cannot be assumed without some evidence.

24 So, excellently, Kelly, *I Peter*, p. 336.

25 On this use of ὅπου see BDF, 456.3.

26 Against Kelly, *I Peter*, p. 338. This is not 'the most banal of truisms'.

27 Noted also by Spicq, *S. Pierre*, p. 234, but his comparison of 2 Macc. 4: 15 is irrelevant. The δόξαι there are 'Greek opinions' or 'habits of life'.

28   On the Greek versions of this myth see Glasson, *Greek Influence*, p. 62.
29   The style of the epistle is a recognised Asiatic florid type (see E. Norden, *Die Antike Kunstprosa* (Leipzig, 1898), I, 131ff), coupled with many semitisms. J. Chaine, *Les épîtres catholiques* (Paris, 1939), p. 18, gives a complete page of examples.
30   See Green, *2 Peter and Jude*, p. 22, n. 1; also A. L. Moore, *The Parousia in the New Testament* (Leiden, 1966), pp. 151ff.
31   Its absence from the Syrian canon is not a major objection to this view, since that list is selective. See A. Souter (rev. C. S. C. Williams), *The Text and Canon of the New Testament*, 2nd ed. (London, 1954), pp. 50ff and 209. On the Petrine traditions of western Syria see Strecker, Hennecke-Schneemelcher, II, 102ff and Koester, *Trajectories*, pp. 124ff.

7 Ignatius of Antioch

1   S. E. Johnson, 'Unsolved Questions about Early Christianity in Anatolia', in D. E. Aune (ed.), *Studies in the NT and Early Christian Literature* (Leiden, 1972), pp. 181ff.
2   R. Bultmann, 'Ignatius and Paul', ET in S. M. Ogden (ed.), *Existence and Faith* (London, 1961), pp. 267ff.
3   On the text see Lightfoot, *The Apostolic Fathers*, II.1, 70ff, and M. P. Brown, *The Authentic Writings of Ignatius* (Durham N.C., 1963).
4   See especially H. Schlier, *Religionsgeschichtliche Untersuchungen zu den Ignatiusbriefen* (Geissen, 1929); C. C. Richardson, *The Christianity of Ignatius of Antioch* (New York, 1935); H. W. Bartsch, *Gnostisches Gut und Gemeindetradition bei Ignatius von Antiochen* (Gütersloh, 1940); and V. Corwin, *Saint Ignatius and Christianity at Antioch* (New Haven, 1960).
5   *Smyrn.* 6.1; *Phil.* 2.1; *Eph.* 13.2; *Trall.* 5.1f; 9.1.
6   Clearly in *Eph.* 20.2. See Richardson, *Christianity of Ignatius*, pp. 55ff.
7   Against Lightfoot, *Apostolic Fathers*, II.2, 67, but also strongly suggested by BAG *s.v.* ὄλεθρος.
8   The genitives are genitives of place. See BDF 186.1.
9   *Apostolic Fathers*, II.2, 67.
10   Lightfoot, *Apostolic Fathers*, II.2, 165.
11   The 'Song of the Star' has been the focus of many studies. See especially Bartsch, *Gnostisches Gut*, pp. 133ff. A. Cabaniss, 'Wis 18.14ff. An Early Christian Christmas Text', *VC* 10 (1956), 97ff, suggests that there may be a primitive Christmas liturgy behind this passage. The fact, however, that Ignatius himself proposes further elucidation suggests that the 'hymn' and its implications were less well known than some later commentators have assumed.
12   Schlier, *Religionsgeschichtliche Untersuchungen*, ch. 1.
13   Corwin, *St. Ignatius*, pp. 177f.
14   *Ibid.* pp. 118ff.
15   *Ibid.* p. 123; and see *Mag.* 8.2.
16   See Lightfoot, *Apostolic Fathers*, II.2, 80, and contrast the view of the author of Hebrews (1: 1f).
17   See Daniélou, *Theology of Jewish Christianity*, pp. 214ff.
18   See J. M. Allegro, 'Further Messianic References in the Qumran Literature',

JBL 75 (1956), 174ff.

19 See K. Stendhal, *The School of St. Matthew* (Uppsala, 1954), pp. 155f. Test. Naph. 5: 1–4 is cited as a parallel development by Daniélou (*Theology of Jewish Christianity*, p. 221).

20 χόρος, which is also found of worship in *Rom.* 2: 2, perhaps shows the influence of pagan patterns of worship. See K. Lake, *The Apostolic Fathers* (London, 1912), I, 193, n. 2. The word is used of companies of stars in *1 Clem.* 20.3 with reference to their orderly arrangement.

21 E.g. Tertullian, *de idol.* 9; Origen, *contra Cels.* 1.60; and compare Justin, *1 Apol.* 1.14 and Tertullian, *Apol.* 23. The fact that Ignatius was writing to the Ephesians may be significant in view of the fame of Ephesus as a centre for magic.

22 The Magi are ambivalent in early Christian thought: they are associated with magic and are therefore evil. This view may be connected with the increasing stature of Simon Magus: see Bidez and Cumont, *Les mages hellénisés*, I, 155. Alternatively, they are earnest seekers after truth: see below on Theodotus. Justin, *Dial.* 78.9, seems to hold both views at once.

23 There is much to be said for Lightfoot's suggestion, which omits διεφθείρετο and puts a comma after δέσμος and after ἀγνοία and after βασιλεία, thus associating spells and magic. See *Apostolic Fathers*, II.2, 83f.

24 Origen, e.g., associated magic with demons (*contra Cels.* 1.60), but this is not the case for Ignatius, for whom the word is still neutral in the Greek manner. See *Smyrn.* 3.2.

25 See A. D. Nock in a review in *JTS* 31 (1929/30), 311, who illustrates this from the growing use of the title 'Saviour' for Christ in Ignatius. This too came to fruition in some gnostic thinking. He also aptly cites Sallustius, περὶ θεῶν καὶ κόσμος, 4.

8 The angelomorphic Christology of early Jewish Christianity

1 Definition of the term 'Jewish Christianity' is a notorious difficulty. In this context it is applied to a social phenomenon and the phrase 'Judaeo-Christian' is reserved for styles of thinking and theological positions. In general see Daniélou, *Theology of Jewish Christianity*, pp. 77ff, and the note by the translator, J. A. Baker, to the second volume, *Gospel Message and Hellenistic Culture* (ET London, 1973). Also R. N. Longenecker, *The Christology of Early Jewish Christianity* (London, 1970), pp. 1ff.

2 The word is defended by Longenecker, *ibid.* pp. 26ff.

3 M. Werner, *Die Entstehung des christlichen Dogmas* (Leipzig, 1941), and the detailed criticism by W. Michaelis, *Zur Engelchristologie im Urchristentum* (Basel, 1942).

4 This example should not be taken to imply a close connection between Justin and early Jewish Christianity. This is discussed below.

5 Tertullian, *de carn. Christi.* 14; Epiphanius, *Pan.* 30.16.4.

6 See P. Vielhauer, Hennecke–Schneemelcher, II, 629ff. The work has a fundamentally paraenetic intention, which means that doctrinal points are assumed rather than expounded. In the *Mandates* and *Similitudes* especially there is an emphasis upon faith and experience, which assumes a certain understanding of the role of an angel: see e.g. *Sim.* 6.3 and *Mand.* 7.2.

7 Daniélou, *Theology of Jewish Christianity*, pp. 121ff.

8 Hippolytus, *Comm. Dan.* 4.57, also divides the men in Ezek. 9: 2 into the six plus one, who is the Word. See also an amulet reported by E. Peterson, 'Das Amulet von Akra', *Aegyptus* 33 (1953), 172ff.

9 See the table in A. R. C. Leaney, *The Rule of Qumran and its Meaning* (London, 1966), pp. 50ff. Once the Testaments of the Twelve Patriarchs and 2 Enoch are regarded as primarily Christian, there is little evidence for the doctrine of two spirits outside Qumran and Jewish Christianity. See Seitz, 'Two Spirits', pp. 82ff.

10 See Daniélou, *Theology of Jewish Christianity*, pp. 127ff. I, however, consider he overemphasises trinitarian doctrine.

11 E.g. the stars (Asc. Is. 4: 8 and 2 En. 4) and nature (Test. Lev. 3: 2 and 2 En. 6). See generally Bietenhard, *Die himmlische Welt*, pp. 123ff.

12 See R. McL. Wilson, 'The Early History of the Exegesis of Gen. i.26', *Studia Patristica* (Berlin, 1957), II, 420ff. The Valentinians preferred Gen. 2: 7.

13 Flemming and Duensing, Hennecke–Schneemelcher, II, 642; Charles *APOT*, II, 158. The interesting, but speculative, suggestion that it is an account of the history of the Dead Sea Sect in its early stages is worth note. See D. Flusser, 'The Apocryphal Book of the *Ascensio Isaiae* and the Dead Sea Sect', *IEJ* 3 (1953), 30ff.

14 Daniélou, *Theology of Jewish Christianity*, pp. 189f.

15 *Ibid.* p. 191, overestimates the difference between the firmament and the lower air in Ascension. The last major stage in the Redeemer's descent is into the firmament, where he again gives the password. But no password is needed in the lower air, ostensibly because its denizens are too busy fighting. But the mark of each heaven and the firmament has been the requirement of a password, and the absence of this feature in the lower air suggests that it is not a separate entity from the firmament.

16 Porphyry, *de abst.* 2.37ff. The idea of hostile demons developed in paganism also from the end of the first century, perhaps through the influence of Zoroastrianism. See Cumont, *Religions orientales*, pp. 180f and 281, n. 55. On earlier hints in the same direction see F. Andres, 'Daemon', *RE Supp.* III (1918), 267ff, and Delling, *TDNT*, II, 3ff.

17 Plato, *Symp.* 202E, and note how peculiarly Greek this is. See H. J. Rose, 'Numen inest: "Animism" in Greek and Roman Religion', *HTR* 28 (1935), 237ff, especially pp. 243f.

18 See Foerster, *TDNT*, I, 165. Rabbinic Judaism is devoid of deep teaching on demons, just as it is shy of the doctrine of fallen angels. See R. A. Stewart, *Rabbinic Theology*, pp. 54ff, especially p. 86, and Foerster, *TDNT*, II, 12f.

19 See also Minucius Felix, 26.11: 'Hostanes daemonas prodidit terrenos, vagos, humanitatis inimicos.'

20 A complex and obscure question. See H.-J. Schoeps, 'Ebionite Christianity', *JTS* n.s. 4 (1953), 219ff, and, on the anti-Paulinism of the Kerygmata Petrou, G. Strecker, *Das Judenchristentum in den Pseudo-Clementinen* (Berlin, 1958). After Ignatius there is no detectable Pauline Christianity in western Syria.

21 See A. Aleith, *Paulusverständnis in der alten Kirche*, BZNW 18 (Berlin, 1937).

9 The Greek apologists

1   In general see F. Andres, *Die Engellehre der griechischen Apologeten des zweiten Jahrhunderts und ihr Verhältnis zur griechischen-römischen Dämonologie* (Paderborn, 1914).

2   See Daniélou, *Gospel Message*, pp. 7ff.

3   1 Cor. 10: 20f. For Justin's use of the Gospels see A. J. Bellinzoni, *The Sayings of Jesus in the Writings of Justin Martyr* (Leiden, 1967).

4   *1 Apol.* 45.1 (cf. *Dial.* 110) may indicate knowledge of 2 Thess. 2: 6f, but there is insufficient detail for certainty. In *Dial.* 35 there appears to be a quotation of 1 Cor. 11: 19, but it more probably comes directly from a tradition of Jesus: see J. Jeremias, *The Unknown Sayings of Jesus* (ET London, 1957), pp. 59ff.

5   See Andres, *Die Engellehre*, pp. 36ff. In general Athenagoras is more urbane and sympathetic to pagan life than the other apologists.

6   The same confusion is found in Athenagoras, *Leg.* 25, and may be due to an attempted harmonisation of Gen. 3: 1ff and Gen. 6: 1ff. See Daniélou, *Gospel Message*, p. 433, n. 19.

7   See H. A. Kelly, *Towards the Death of Satan* (London, 1968), pp. 85ff. In *Dial.* 79 Justin argues for the fall of the angels without recourse to Gen. 6. Trypho the Jew considers belief in rebellious angels to be blasphemous, thus reminding us of the strongly Christian character of this belief.

8   See L. W. Barnard, *Justin Martyr: His Life and Thought* (Cambridge, 1967), pp. 124f.

9   See Daniélou, *Gospel Message*, pp. 346ff, and especially *1 Apol.* 60.1ff and *2 Apol.* 6.3.

10   Even Tatian seems not to allow for the experience of Fate after baptism. Hence the need for gnosis and the strength of the gnostic approach, which is most clearly expounded on this point in Clement of Alexandria, *Exc. ex Theod.* 69ff and 84f.

11   *Orat.* 17. See Bidez and Cumont, *Les mages hellénisés*, I, 167ff; Cumont, *Religions orientales*, pp. 168ff and 292ff. The historical Hostanes dates to the reign of Xerxes, but the ideas attributed to him came into prominence during the second century A.D. See Nilsson, *Geschichte*, II, 650.

12   See M. Elze, *Tatian und seine Theologie* (Göttingen, 1960), especially pp. 100ff.

10 Clement of Alexandria

1   On this aspect of Plato see R. Schaerer, *Dieu, l'homme et la vie d'après Platon* (Neuchâtel, 1944), pp. 123ff. On Clement see E. F. Osborn, *The Philosophy of Clement of Alexandria* (Cambridge, 1957), pp. 65ff.

2   See Philo, *de op. mund.* 4f, and Osborn, *Philosophy*, pp. 41ff. On Clement's debt to Philo see S. R. C. Lilla, *Clement of Alexandria: A Study in Christian Platonism and Gnosticism* (Oxford, 1971), pp. 19ff.

3   ἐξουσίαι is added before ἀρχαί in D, and after it in C, some lesser texts, and notably in Tertullian and Origen.

4   See Osborn, *Philosophy*, pp. 127ff.

5   *Ibid.* pp. 82ff.

6   Daniélou, *Gospel Message*, pp. 183ff, argues that the defeat of the powers

is fundamental to Clement, as to other early Christian writers. As evidence he cites *Protr.* 1.7.4 and 11.111.1, but neither of these passages expounds the defeat of the powers. In the latter the defeat of Satan (here associated with death – cf. Origen, *Comm. in Matt.* 13.9 and Heb. 2: 14), is mentioned in passing as Clement discusses the freedom of the Christian from the bonds of pleasure. Note again the psychological interpretation.

7 On Clement's angelology see R. P. Casey, *The Excerpta ex Theodoto of Clement of Alexandria* (London, 1934), pp. 105ff.

8 For a survey of this distinctively Christian connection of the angels and the days see M.-Th. d'Alverny, 'Les anges et les jours', *CA* 9 (1957), 271ff.

9 This theme is derived from Gen. 2: 4. See *Strom.* 6.16 and Daniélou, *Theology of Jewish Christianity*, pp. 168ff.

11 The influence of gnosticism

1 See U. Bianchi (ed.), *Le Origini dello Gnosticismo* (Leiden, 1967), pp. xxviff.

2 On Simon Magus see *adv. haer.* 1.16.2, also Justin, *1 Apol.* 26. Simon's particular contribution does not matter for our purpose, but see W. Foerster, *Gnosis* (ET Oxford, 1972), I, 28. There is a problem between the Latin and Greek texts of this passage of Irenaeus, but the Latin may have been affected by what is later said of Basilides. See W. W. Harvey, *Sancti Irenaei Episcopi Lugdunensis Libros quinque adversus Haereses* (Cambridge, 1857), I, 194.

3 See Wilson, 'Early Exegesis', pp. 427ff. This may suggest that Saturnilus had close links with the Judaeo-Christian tradition, by contrast with Valentinus, who tends to follow Gen. 2: 7.

4 The accounts of Basilides in Hippolytus, *Ref.* 7.20, and other fragments (see Foerster, *Gnosis*, I, 74ff) give a different interpretation but include reference to astrology.

5 On this and the term 'mathematici', which is used of the Ophites in *adv. haer.* 1.19.4, see Harvey, *Sancti Irenaei*, I, 203, n. 6.

6 On this persistent problem in gnosticism see R. A. Bullard, *The Hypostasis of the Archons* (Berlin, 1970), n. 375.

7 On the sense of 'dualism' see Proposal B, V from Messina in Bianchi, *Le Origini*, pp. xxviii.

8 The Fathers in general frequently use such lists with many variations. It is always difficult to know whether there is a direct quotation of Col. 1: 16 or not. See for example H. J. Frede (ed.), *Vetus Latina* (Freiburg, 1966–71), XXIV.2, 350.

9 The most important passage on the demons (*adv. haer.* 5.28) shows a clear dependence on the Revelation of St John the Divine.

10 See T. W. Manson, *On Paul and John* (London, 1963), p. 27. G. Aulén rightly remarks that Irenaeus does not separate incarnation from atonement, but he overestimates the concept of victory over cosmic powers in the thought of Irenaeus. See *Christus Victor* (ET London, 1931), p. 34. Irenaeus was less an innovator and more an expositor of Paul. See E. Brunner, *The Mediator* (ET London, 1934), pp. 229f.

11 This is clearly expounded by Wilson, 'Early History', pp. 421ff. The danger was combated by Jewish polemic against any plurality in the Godhead. The

Gnostic proliferation of powers is integral to their conception of God as two – Father Unknown and Demiurge. See P. Boyancé, 'Dieu cosmique et dualisme', *Le Origini*, pp. 354ff.

12   *Adv. haer.* 5.17.3 (Col. 2: 14); *Frag.* xxxvii (Greek) (Col. 2: 16).

13   *Adv. haer.* 1.18 cites a Valentinian use of the text that includes the word θεότητες, which Theodoret (Harvey, *Sancti Irenaei*, I, 38, n. 6) describes as a Valentinian interpolation. See M. L. Peel, *The Epistle to Rheginos* (London, 1969), p. 63, who rightly questions a direct dependence on Col. 1: 16 and suggests that the list in *Rheginos* 44.37f with θεότητες may be 'a random allusion to two orders of beings known in the Valentinian system or remembered vaguely from Paul's writings'.

14   A convenient edition is that of R. A. Bullard, *Patristische Texte und Studien*, X (Berlin, 1970). A recent, extensive critical edition and translation is that by B. Layton in *HTR* 67 (1974), 351ff and 69 (1976), 31ff.

15   *HA* 134.21ff reads: 'the great apostle said to us concerning the Powers (ἐξουσίαι) of darkness: Our fight is not against flesh and blood, but it is against the powers of the world (ἐξουσίαι) and the spirituals of evil.'

16   The text is Coptic, but there is no reference to ἀρχαί.

17   Bullard, *Patristische Texte*, X, 45.

18   This characteristic is well expounded for the concept of time by H.–C. Puech, 'La Gnose et le temps', *Eranos Jahrbuch* 20 (1951), 57ff, especially p. 110.

19   See S. Giversen, *Apocryphon Johannis* (Copenhagen, 1963), pp. 203 and 216ff.

20   On Jewish varieties of this legend see Ginzberg, *Legends*, V, 69ff. For a good example of Christian development at this point see the tract edited by R. Reitzenstein, 'Eine frühchristliche Schrift von der dreierlei Früchten', *ZNW* 15 (1914), 60ff, especially p. 82.

21   See d'Alverny, 'Les anges et les jours'. Also S. Pétrement, 'Le mythe des sept archontes créateurs, peut-il s'expliquer à partir du Christianisme?', *Le Origini*, pp. 477ff.

22   See Colson, *The Week*, pp. 39ff and 60f, on the growth of the two seven-day systems and their gradual mutual assimilation.

23   E.g. Hippolytus, *Phil.* 8.14.1, where, as often, the angels number only six.

24   For the possible effects of such general pressure of anti-materialism on the Jews and Christians see G. Quispel, 'The Origins of the Gnostic Demiurge', *Kyriakon. Festschrift Johannes Quasten* (Münster, 1970), I, 271ff.

25   On the Jewish background of these beings see R. M. Grant, 'Les êtres intermédiaires dans le Judaisme tardif', *Le Origini*, pp. 141ff, which expands his general stance in *Gnosticism and Early Christianity* (New York, 1966). Boyancé's attempt ('Dieu cosmique') to demonstrate Platonic origins for the archons is not convincing. The importance of Plato, *Leg.* 5.906Bff in neo-Platonism is not in dispute, but it is difficult to see in it, coupled with *Pol.* 270D and the *Timaeus*, a source for gnostic archons. Boyancé proposes Philo, especially through *de opificio mundi*, as the means. In Plato's treatment of the gods in the *Timaeus* they are related to the stars, which, according to Philo, rule on analogy with the archons of a city (*de spec. leg.* 1.13). Philo uses archons here in their political sense, but Plato uses it of the lower gods and thus the planetary archons of gnosticism

are derived from Plato. However, this cannot stand. In view of the Jewish connections with gnosticism, it is more probable that the term derives from the mixture of Jewish and Christian ideas that has been mentioned above. Plato, possibly via Philo, may have later made a contribution, for 'Judaism in its broadest sense' must include Philo. See R. McL. Wilson (*Le Origini*, p. 691), 'it is Judaism in its broadest sense which provides the immediate background and at least one of the focal points for the development of Gnosticism'.

26 See W. H. C. Frend, 'A Note on Jews and Christians in Third Century North Africa', *JTS* n.s. 21 (1970), 93: 'nearly always at the heart of Tertullian's controversial writing is the contemporary situation'.

27 See T. D. Barnes, *Tertullian: An Historical and Literary Study* (Oxford, 1971), pp. 60ff, and compare W. H. C. Frend, *The Donatist Church* (Oxford, 1952), pp. 87ff.

28 See Barnes, *Tertullian*, pp. 68f and 273ff. He generally allows the Jews insufficient significance: see Frend, 'A Note on Jews and Christians', pp. 92ff, and W. Horbury, 'Tertullian and the Jews in the Light of *de spectaculis* xxx. 5–6', *JTS* n.s. 23 (1972), 455ff.

29 *Apol.* 35. Astrology is fundamentally opposed to God, but its status has been changed by the coming of the Magi to Christ (*de idol.* 9). It is a fact of life for which the Christian has no use, but not a threat. Exorcisms are daily affairs: *ad Scap.* 2; *Apol.* 27; *Apol.* 23.

30 *Adv. Prax.* 12. For details and parallels see the edition by E. Evans (London, 1948), pp. 258ff.

31 *de cult. fem.* 1.2; *de idol.* 9; *de or.* 22; *de virg. vel.* 7.

32 'Elementorum' = τὰ στοιχεῖα, which in Tertullian are always physical. See *de praesc. haer.* 33 and *Apol.* 17. 'Spiritus' is a vague term in Tertullian, but, when used of men, seems to mean 'the soul'.

33 In *de orat.* 4 he spiritualises 'thy will be done on earth as in heaven' into a distinction between flesh and spirit.

34 The usual translation in Vetus Latina is 'mundi tenentes' or 'mundi rectores'. See Frede, *Vetus Latina*, XXIV.1, 290ff. On Tertullian's text of the NT, an acute problem, see Barnes, *Tertullian*, pp. 276ff.

35 This is also the mark of the martyrologies, which hold to the sovereignty of God through cosmology and to the actuality of evil through demonologies. See H. Musurillo, *The Acts of the Christian Martyrs* (Oxford, 1972), references by page and line: Apollonius, 2; Fructuosus, 2.4; Pionius, 8.3; Carpus, 22.14; Justus, 58.17.

36 See e.g. the oft quoted remarks of S. J. Chase, *The Origins of Christian Supernaturalism* (Chicago, 1946), p. 1.

37 E.g. the Ophite system as reported by Origen, *contra Cels.* 6.31ff. On the ascent of the soul see H. Chadwick, *Origen: Contra Celsum* (Cambridge, 1953), p. 334, n. 2.

38 There is always the hope that the stars may be understood and thus manipulated to one's own end. For details generally see E. Pfeiffer, *Studien zum antiken Sternglauben* (Leipzig and Berlin, 1916). See also E. R. Dodds, *Pagan and Christian in an Age of Anxiety* (Cambridge, 1965), p. 15.

39 See Pétrement, 'Les sept archontes', pp. 484f.

40 See A. D. Nock, 'Gnosticism', *HTR* 57 (1964), 256f.

41 E.g. *CIL*, V, 3466, of a gladiator from Verona. The Lambiridi inscription is published in J. Carcopino, *Aspects mystiques de la Rome païenne* (Paris, 1942), pp. 208ff.

42 Frend, *Donatist Church*, pp. 94ff.

43 Cyprian, *ad Donatum*, pp. 3f.

12 Origen

1 See generally J. Daniélou, *Origène* (Paris, 1948), and for the angelology, pp. 220ff. See also the assessment by J. Quasten, *Patrology* (Utrecht, 1950–60), II, 40ff.

2 *De princ. praef.* 10, which should be compared with *de princ.* 1.7.2f, in which Job 25: 5, a favourite text, is cited. See too *contra Cels.* 5.10 where worship of the stars is allowed, but not because of the light that amazes the masses, but because the stars are rational and good beings. Origen seems not to have fatalistic notions about the stars. See Chadwick, *contra Celsum*, p. 271, n. 8.

3 *Comm. in Cant.* 3f. For Origen's close associations with the rabbis and Jewish influence on his thought, see Moore, *Judaism*, I, 165.

4 Note too the curious use of the story of the wrestling of Jacob, which was with the help of the angel and not against him: *de princ.* 3.2.5.

5 In the same context he takes the ἄρχοντες of 1 Cor. 2: 6ff as hostile powers. Cf. *de princ.* 3.3.2.

6 In *Exhort. ad mart.* 48 he links Luke 6: 48ff with Eph. 6: 12 to make this point more vividly.

7 On the ἐπινοῖαι see Chadwick, *contra Celsum*, p. 390, n. 1, and C. Bigg, *The Christian Platonists of Alexandria* (Oxford, 1886), pp. 168ff and 210ff.

8 *Exhort. ad mart.* 41; *Comm. in Joh.* 6.54. While Col. 2: 15 forms a theme for Origen's doctrine of the atonement, he offers other views too. See Bigg, *Christian Platonists*, pp. 208ff and notes.

Conclusion to part 3

1 In general the change that occurred in the understanding of the angels may be attributed to Origen. The biblical concern with 'officium angelicum' gave place to a patristic concern with 'angelica natura'. The peak of this development was reached in the writings of Pseudo-Dionysius – *de hierarchia ecclesiastica* and *de divinis nominibus*. Written *c.* 500 A.D. these texts exercised considerable influence and represent the climax of those angelological concerns that begin with Origen.

2 Although this period coincides with a decline in popularity and interest in the Pauline letters, which might in part explain the absence of reference to Col. 2: 15, the fact remains that there is no general evidence for a belief in mighty cosmic forces. The revival of interest in Paul coincided with a new approach to this fundamental question, and this allowed Origen to produce his innovative exegesis.

Final remarks

1 See J. N. D. Kelly, *Early Christian Creeds*, 3rd ed. (London, 1972), pp. 378ff.

2 Bousset, *Kyrios Christos*, pp. 60ff, has attempted to show that this belief is of much earlier date, but his arguments presuppose a centrality for the notion of Christ's battle, which we have shown to be unjustified. Another attempt has been made by A. Cabaniss to link the harrowing of hell with the first century. See 'The Harrowing of Hell, Psalm 24, and Pliny the Younger', *VC* 7 (1953), 5ff. The argument is speculative, and the evidence for a widespread belief is not found prior to the fourth century. An early and detailed account is in *Gospel of Nicodemus* (Greek Version) 6 (22). For an account of this development, see F. Loofs, 'The Descent to Hades (Christ's)', *ERE*, IV, 659ff.

SELECT BIBLIOGRAPHY

In the interests of brevity only a select bibliography is offered. There is no mention of the numerous commentaries and works of wider reference that are alluded to in the text and footnotes.

Abrahams, I., *Studies in Pharisaism and the Gospels* (Cambridge, 1917–24).

Affeldt, W., *Die weltliche Gewalt in der Paulus-exegese: Römer 13, 1–7 in den Römerbriefkommentaren der lateinischen Kirche bis zum Ende des 13. Jahrhunderts* (Göttingen, 1969).

Aleith, A., *Paulusverständnis in der alten Kirche*, BZNW 18 (Berlin, 1937).

Allan, J. A., 'The "in Christ" Formula in Ephesians', *NTS* 5 (1958), 54ff.

Allegro, J. M., 'Further Messianic References in the Qumran Literature', *JBL* 75 (1956), 174ff.

Altmann, A., 'The Gnostic Background of the Rabbinic Adam Legends', *JQR* 35 (1944), 371ff.

d'Alverny, M.-Th., 'Les anges et les jours', *CA* 9 (1957), 271ff.

Andres, F., 'Daemon', *RE Supp.* iii (1918), pp. 267ff.

Die Engellehre der griechischen Apologeten der zweiten Jahrhunderts und ihr Verhältnis zur griechischen–römischen Dämonologie (Paderborn, 1914).

Angus, S., *The Religious Quests of the Graeco-Roman World* (London, 1929).

Anwander, A., 'Zu Kol 2, 9', *BZ* 9 (1965), 278ff.

Arai, S., 'Die Gegner des Paulus im I. Korintherbrief und das Problem der Gnosis', *NTS* 19 (1973), 430ff.

Aulén, G., *Christus Victor* (ET London, 1931).

Babelon, E., 'Bacchius Judaeus', *RBN* 47 (1891), 5ff.

Balsdon, J. P. V. D., *The Emperor Gaius* (Oxford, 1934).

Bammel, E., 'Ein Beitrag zur paulinischen Staatsanschauung', *TLZ* 11 (1960), 837ff.

'The Commands in I Peter ii.17', *NTS* 11 (1964), 279ff.

'Versuch zu Kol 1, 15–20', *ZNW* 52 (1961), 88ff.

Bandstra, A. J., *The Law and the Elements of this World* (Kampen, 1964).

Barbel, J., *Christos Angelos. Die Anschauung von Christus als Bote und Engel in der gelehrten und volkstümlichen Literatur des christlichen Altertums* (Bonn, 1941), with supplement (1964).

Barnard, L. W., 'The Church in Edessa during the First Two Centuries A.D.', *VC* 22 (1968), 161ff.

Justin Martyr: His Life and Thought (Cambridge, 1967).

Barnes, T. D., 'An Apostle on Trial', *JTS* n.s. 20 (1969), 405ff.
Tertullian: A Historical and Literary Study (Oxford, 1971).

Barnett, A. E., *Paul becomes a Literary Influence* (Chicago, 1941).

Barnikol, E., 'Römer 13. Der nichtpaulinische Ursprung der absoluten Obrigkeitsbejahung von Römer 13, 1–7', in *Studien zum NT Patristik. E. Klostermann zum 90. Geburtstag dargebracht* (Berlin, 1961), pp. 65ff.

Baron, S. W., *A Social and Religious History of the Jews in Palestine*, 2nd ed. (New York, 1957).

Barrett, C. K., 'The Acts and the Origin of Christianity', in *New Testament Essays* (London, 1972), pp. 105ff.
'Christianity at Corinth', *BJRL* 46 (1963), 269ff.

Barton, G. A., 'Demons and Spirits (Hebrew)', *ERE*, IV, 594ff.
'The Origin of the Names of Angels and Demons in the Extra-canonical Apocryphal Literature to 100 A.D.', *JBL* 31 (1912), 156ff.

Bartsch, H. W., *Gnostisches Gut und Gemeindetradition bei Ignatius von Antiochien* (Gütersloh, 1940).

Bauer, W., *Orthodoxy and Heresy in Earliest Christianity* (ET Philadelphia, 1971).

Baumann, R., *Mitte und Norm des Christlichens. Eine Auslegung von I Korinther 1. 1–3. 4* (Münster, 1968).

Baynes, N. H., *The Hellenistic Civilisation and East Rome* (London, 1946).

Beasley-Murray, G. R., *Baptism in the New Testament* (London, 1962).

Beaujeu, J., *La religion romaine à l'apogée de l'empire* (Paris, 1955).

Bedale, S., 'κεφαλή in the Pauline Letters', *JTS* n.s. 5 (1954), 211ff.

Bellinzoni, A. J., *The Sayings of Jesus in the Writings of Justin Martyr* (Leiden, 1967).

Benoit, P., 'Qumran et le Nouveau Testament', *NTS* 7 (1960), 276ff.

Bertram, G., ὕψωμα, *TDNT*, VIII, 614.

Betz, H. D., 'The Mithras Inscriptions of Santa Prisca and the New Testament', *NovT* 10 (1968), 62ff.

Beulier, E., *Le culte imperiale, son histoire et son organisation depuis Auguste jusqu'à Justinien* (Paris, 1891).

Bianchi, U., (ed.), *Le Origini dello Gnosticismo. Colloquio di Messina, 13–18 Aprile, 1966* (Leiden, 1967).

Bidez, J., and Cumont, F., *Les mages hellénisés* (Paris, 1938).

Bietenhard, H., *Die himmlische Welt im Urchristentum und Spätjudentum* (Tübingen, 1951).

Bigg, C., *The Christian Platonists of Alexandria* (Oxford, 1886).

Blaiklock, E. M., 'The Acts of the Apostles as a Document of First Century History', in W. W. Gasque and R. P. Martin (eds.), *Apostolic History and the Gospel* (Exeter, 1970), pp. 41ff.

Blanchette, O. A., 'Does the Cheirographon of Col. 2. 14 represent Christ Himself?', *CBQ* 23 (1961), 306ff.

Blinzler, J., 'Lexikalisches zu dem Terminus τὰ στοιχεῖα τοῦ κόσμου bei Paulus', *Studiorum Paulinorum Congressus Internationalis Catholicus 1961* (Rome, 1963), II, 429ff.

Boismard, E., *Quatre hymnes baptismales dans la première épître de Pierre*

(Paris, 1961).

Bonner, C., 'An Obscure Inscription on a Gold Tablet', *Hesperia* 13 (1944), 134.

Bonsirven, J., *Le judaisme palestinien au temps de Jésus Christ* (Paris, (1950).

Bornkamm, G., 'Die Häresie des Kolosserbriefes', *Das Ende des Gesetzes – Paulusstudien, Gesammelte Aufsätze* (Munich, 1966), pp. 139ff.

'Die Hoffnung im Kolosserbrief', *Geschichte und Glaube* (Munich, (1971), II, 206ff.

Bouché-Leclerq, A., *L'astrologie grec* (Paris, 1899).

Histoire de la divination dans l'antiquité (Paris, 1880).

Bousset, W., *Kyrios Christos* (ET New York, 1970).

Bowen, C. R., 'The Original Form of Paul's Letter to the Colossians', *JBL* 43 (1924), 177ff.

Bowersock, G. W., *Augustus and the Greek World* (Oxford, 1965).

Bowker, J. W., '"Merkabah" Visions and Paul's Visions', *JSS* 16 (1971), 157ff.

Boyancé, P., 'Dieu cosmique et dualisme. Les archontes de Platon', in U. Bianchi (ed.), *Le Origini dello Gnosticismo*, pp. 340ff.

Brehier, E., *Les idées philosophiques et religieuses de Philon d'Alexandrie*, 3rd ed. (Paris, 1950).

Brown, M. P., *The Authentic Writings of Ignatius* (Durham N.C., 1963).

Brown, R. E., 'The Semitic Background of the New Testament *mysterion*', *Biblica* 39 (1958), 426ff and 40 (1959), 70ff.

Bruce, F. F., 'St. Paul in Rome. 4. The Epistle to the Ephesians', *BJRL* 49 (1966), 318ff.

Buckler, W. H., 'An Epigraphic Contribution to Letters', *CR* 41 (1927), 119ff.

'Some Lydian Propitiatory Inscriptions', *BSA* 21 (1941), 169ff.

Bullard, R. A., *The Hypostasis of the Archons.* Patristische Texte und Studien X (Berlin, 1970).

Bultmann, R., 'Ignatius and Paul', in S. M. Ogden (ed.), *Existence and Faith* (London, 1961), pp. 267ff. ET of 'Ignatius und Paulus', in J. N. Sevenster and W.C. van Unnik (eds.), *Studia Paulina in honorem Johannes de Zwaan septuagenerii* (Haarlem, 1953), pp. 37ff.

Cabaniss, A., 'Wis. 18.14ff. An Early Christian Christmas Text', *VC* 10 (1956), 97ff.

Calder, W. M., 'The Cult of the Homonades', *CR* 24 (1910), 76ff.

'The Epigraphy of Anatolian Heresies', in W. H. Buckler and W. M. Calder (eds.), *Anatolian Studies presented to Sir W. M. Ramsay* (Manchester, 1923), pp. 59ff.

Carcopino, J., *Aspects mystiques de la Rome païenne* (Paris, 1942).

Carr, A. W., 'The Rulers of this Age – I Corinthians II. 6–8', *NTS* 23 (1976), 20ff.

'Two Notes on Colossians', *JTS* n.s. 24 (1973), 492ff.

Carrington, P., *The Primitive Christian Catechism* (Cambridge, 1940).

Case, S. J., *The Origins of Christian Supernaturalism* (Chicago, 1946).

Casey, R. P., *The Excerpta ex Theodoto of Clement of Alexandria* (London, 1934).

Cerfaux, L., *Le Christ dans la théologie de Saint Paul*, 2nd ed. (Paris, 1954).
  'L'Influence des "mystères" sur les épîtres de Saint Paul aux Colossiens et Ephésiens', in J. Coppens, A. Descamps and É. Massaux (eds.), *Sacra Pagina. Miscellanea Biblica Congressus Internationalis Catholici de Re Biblica* (Brussels, 1959), II, 373ff.
  'Vestiges d'un florilège dans I Cor. i. 18 – iii. 24?', *RHE* 27 (1931), 521ff.
Chadwick, H., 'Die Absicht des Epheserbriefes', *ZNW* 51 (1960), 145ff.
  'All Things to All Men – I Cor. ix. 22', *NTS* 1 (1954), 259ff.
  The Circle and the Ellipse (Oxford, 1959).
Chapot, V., *La province romaine proconsulaire d'Asie* (Paris, 1904).
Colson, F. H., *The Week: An Essay on the Origin and Development of the Seven Day Cycle* (Cambridge, 1926).
Conzelmann, H., *An Outline Theology of the New Testament* (London, 1969).
Cooke, G., 'The Sons of (the) God(s)', *ZAW* 76 (1964), 22ff.
Corwin, V., *Saint Ignatius and Christianity at Antioch* (New Haven, 1960).
Coutts, J., 'The Relationship of Ephesians and Colossians', *NTS* 4 (1957), 201ff.
Craddock, F. B., '"All things in Him" – A Critical Note on Col. I. 15–20', *NTS* 12 (1965), 78ff.
Cramer, F. H., *Astrology in Roman Law and Politics* (Philadelphia, 1954).
Cranfield, C. E. B., *A Commentary on Romans 12 and 13* (Edinburgh, 1965).
Cross, F. M. Jnr., 'The Council of Yahweh in Second Isaiah', *JNES* 12 (1953), 274ff.
Crouch, J. E., *The Origin and Intention of the Colossian Haustafel* (Göttingen, 1972).
Cullmann, O., *Christ and Time* (ET London, 1962).
  The Christology of the New Testament (ET London, 1963).
  'The Kingship of Christ and the Church in the New Testament', ET in *The Early Church* (London, 1956), pp. 101ff.
  'On the most recent discussion of ἐξουσίαι in Rom. 13.1', Excursus to *The State in the New Testament*, pp. 94ff.
  The State in the New Testament (ET London, 1957).
  'The Tradition: The Exegetical, Historical and Theological Problem', ET in *The Early Church* (London, 1956), pp. 55ff.
Cumont, F., 'Les anges du paganisme', *RHR* 72 (1951), 159ff.
  Astrology and Religion among the Greeks and Romans (London, 1912).
  L'Egypte des astrologues (Brussels, 1937).
  Lux Perpetua (Paris, 1949).
  'Les mystères de Sabazius et le Judaisme', *CRAI* (1906), 63ff.
  The Mysteries of Mithra (ET London, 1903).
  'Le mysticisme astral dans l'antiquité', *BCLARB* (1909), 256ff.
  Les religions orientales dans le paganisme romain, 4th ed. (Paris, 1929).
  Textes et monuments figurés relatifs aux mystères de Mithra (Brussels, 1894–9).
Cumont, F., and Canet, L., 'Mithra ou Sarapis ΚΟΣΜΟΚΡΑΤΩΡ?', *CRAI* (1919), 313ff.

Dahl, N. A., 'Paul and the Church at Corinth according to I Corinthians 1–4', in W. R. Farmer, C. F. D. Moule and R. R. Niebuhr (eds.), *Christian History and Interpretation. Studies presented to John Knox* (Cambridge, 1967), pp. 313ff.

Dalton, W. J., *Christ's Proclamation to the Spirits. A Study of I Peter 3.18–4.6.* (Rome, 1965).

Daniélou, J., *Les anges et leur mission d'après les pères de l'église* (Paris, 1953).

Gospel Message and Hellenistic Culture (ET London, 1973).

'Le mauvais gouvernement du monde d'après le gnosticisme', in U. Bianchi (ed.), *Le Origini dello Gnosticismo*, pp. 448ff.

Origène (Paris, 1948).

Philon d'Alexandrie (Paris, 1958).

'Les sources juives de la doctrine des anges des nations chez Origène', *RechSR* 38 (1951), 132ff.

The Theology of Jewish Christianity (ET London, 1964).

Daube, D., 'Participle and Imperative in I Peter', in E. G. Selwyn, *The First Epistle of St. Peter*, 2nd ed. (London, 1947), pp. 467ff.

Davies, W. D., 'Paul and the Dead Sea Scrolls: Flesh and Spirit', in K. Stendahl (ed.), *The Scrolls and the New Testament* (London, 1958), pp. 157ff.

Paul and Rabbinic Judaism (London, 1948).

Day, J., *An Economic History of Athens under Roman Domination* (New York, 1942).

Dehn, G., 'Engel und Obrigkeit: ein Beitrag zum Verständnis von Röm. 13.1–7', in E. Wolf (ed.), *Theologische Aufsätze für Karl Barth* (Munich, 1936), pp. 90ff.

Deissmann, A., *Light from the Ancient East* (ET London, 1910).

Delcor, M., *Le livre de Daniel* (Paris, 1971).

Delling, G., ἀρχή, *TDNT*, I, 481ff.

θριαμβεύω, *TDNT*, III, 159ff.

πλήρωμα, *TDNT*, VI, 298ff.

στοιχεῖον, *TDNT*, VII, 670ff.

τάσσω, *TDNT*, VIII, 27ff.

Römer 13, 1–7 innerhalb der Briefe des NT (Berlin, n.d.).

Deniel, R., 'Omnis potestas a Deo. L'origine du pouvoir civil et sa relation à l'église', *RechSR* 56 (1968), 43ff.

Dexinger, F., *Sturz der Gottessöhne oder Engel vor der Sintflut* (Vienna, 1966).

Dibelius, M., *Die Geisterwelt im Glauben des Paulus* (Göttingen, 1909).

'Die Isisweihe bei Apuleius und verwandte Initiations-riten', *Botschaft und Geschichte. Gesammelte Aufsätze II* (Tübingen, 1956), pp. 30ff.

'Rom und die Christen im ersten Jahrhundert', *Botschaft und Geschichte*, pp. 177ff.

Studies in the Acts of the Apostles (ET London, 1956).

Dibelius, M., and Kümmel, W. G., *Paul* (ET London, 1953).

Dieterich, A., *Nekyia: Beiträge zur Erklärung der neuentdeckten Petrus-apocalypse*, 2nd ed. (Leipzig, 1913).

Dix, G., *Jew and Greek* (London, 1953).

'The Seven Archangels and the Seven Spirits', *JTS* 28 (1927), 233ff.
Dodd, C. H., *According to the Scriptures* (London, 1952).
    The Bible and the Greeks (London, 1935).
Dodds, E. R., *The Greeks and the Irrational* (Berkeley, 1951).
    Pagan and Christian in an Age of Anxiety (Cambridge, 1965).
    'Supernormal Phenomena in Classical Antiquity', *The Ancient Concept of Progress and Other Essays in Greek Literature and Belief* (Oxford, 1973), pp. 156ff.
Doeve, J. W., *Jewish Hermeneutics in the Synoptic Gospels and Acts* (Assen, 1954).
Doresse, J., *The Secret Books of the Egyptian Gnostics* (ET London, 1960).
Downey, G., *A History of Antioch in Syria* (Princeton, 1961).
Dunn, J. D. G., *Baptism in the Holy Spirit* (London, 1970).
Dupont-Sommer, A., *The Jewish Sect of Qumran and the Essenes* (New York, 1955).
Dussaud, R., 'Jupiter Heliopolitanus', *Syria* 1 (1920), 1ff.
Duthoy, R., *The Taurobolium* (Leiden, 1969).
Easton, B. S., 'The New Testament Ethical Lists', *JBL* 51 (1932), 1ff.
Edelstein, E. J. and L., *Asclepius* (Baltimore, 1945).
Egan, R. B., 'Lexical Evidence on Two Pauline Passages', *NovT* 19 (1977), 34ff.
Ehlers, B., 'Kann das Thomasevangelium aus Edessa stammen?', *NovT* 12 (1970), 284ff.
Ehlers, W., 'Triumphus', *RE* vii.2, 493ff.
Eitrem, S., ''EMBATEYΩ – Note sur Col. 2, 18', *ST* 2 (1948), 90ff.
Ellingsworth, P., 'Colossians 1.15–20 and its Context', *ExT* 73 (1961), 252ff.
Elze, M., *Tatian und seine Theologie* (Göttingen, 1960).
Ernst, J., *Pleroma und Pleroma Christi. Geschichte und Deutung eines Begriffs der paulinischen Antilegomena* (Regensburg, 1970).
Everling, O., *Die paulinische Angelologie und Dämonologie* (Göttingen, 1888).
Festugière, A.-J., *Personal Religion among the Greeks* (Berkeley, 1954).
Feuillet, A., 'Les "chefs de ce siècle" et la sagesse divine d'après I Cor. 2.6–8', *Studiorum Paulinorum Congressus Internationalis Catholicus 1961* (Rome, 1963), I, 383ff.
    Le Christ, Sagesse de Dieu d'après les épîtres pauliniennes (Paris, 1966).
Field, F., *Notes on the Translation of the New Testament* (Cambridge, 1899).
Findlay, G. C., 'St. Paul's Use of ΘPIAMBEYΩ', *The Expositor* 10 (1879), 403ff.
Fitzmyer, J. A., 'A Feature of Qumran Angelology and the Angels of I Corinthians xi.10', *NTS* 4 (1958), 48ff.
Flusser, D., 'The Apocryphal Book of *Ascensio Isaiae* and the Dead Sea Scrolls', *IEJ* 3 (1953), 30ff.
    'The Dead Sea Sect and Pauline Christianity', in C. Rabin and Y. Yadin (eds.), *Aspects of the Dead Sea Scrolls*, Scripta Hierosolymitana 4 (Jerusalem, 1958), pp. 215ff.

Foerster, W., ἀήρ, *TDNT*, I, 165.
  δαίμων, *TDNT*, II, 1ff.
  ἐξουσία, *TDNT*, II, 562ff.
  ἐχθρός, *TDNT*, II, 811ff.
  πύθων, *TDNT*, VI, 917ff.
Foucart, P. F., 'Les empereurs romains initiés aux mystères d'Eleusis', *RP* 23 (1893), 197ff.
Francis, F. O., 'Humility and Angelic Worship in Col. 2, 18', *ST* 16 (1962), 109ff.
  'Visionary Discipline and Scriptural Tradition at Colossae', *LexTQ* 2 (1967), 77ff.
Francis, F. O., and Meeks, W. A. (eds.), *Conflict at Colossae* (Montana, 1973).
Frend, W. H. C., *The Donatist Church* (Oxford, 1952).
  'A Note on Jews and Christians in Third Century North Africa', *JTS* n.s. 21 (1970), 92ff.
Fridrischen, A., 'THELON. Col 2, 18', *ZNW* 21 (1922), 135ff.
Friedrich, G., εὐαγγέλιον, *TDNT*, II, 707ff.
Frye, R. N., 'Reitzenstein and Qumran revisited by an Iranian', *HTR* 55 (1962), 261ff.
Gärtner, B., 'Paulus und Barnabas in Lystra. Zu Apg. 14. 8–15', *SEÅ* 27 (1962), 63ff.
  The Temple and the Community in Qumran and the New Testament (Cambridge, 1965).
Galloway, A. D., *The Cosmic Christ* (London, 1951).
Gaselee, S., 'Petronius Arbiter', *OCD*, p. 672.
Gasque, W. W., *Sir Wm. Ramsay, Archaeologist and New Testament Scholar* (Grand Rapids, 1966).
Gerber, U., 'Rom. viii. 18ff als exegetisches Problem der Dogmatik', *NovT* 8 (1966), 69ff.
Gibbs, J. G., 'The Cosmic Scope of Redemption according to Paul', *Biblica* 56 (1975), 13ff.
  Creation and Redemption. A Study in Pauline Theology (Leiden, 1971).
Ginzberg, L., *The Legends of the Jews* (Philadelphia, 1938–47).
Giversen, S., *Apocryphon Johannis* (Copenhagen, 1963).
Glasson, T. F., *Greek Influence in Jewish Eschatology, with Special Reference to the Apocalypses and Pseudepigrapha* (London, 1961).
Goodenough, E. R., *Jewish Symbols in the Greco-Roman Period* (New York, 1953–68).
Goodspeed, E. J., *The Key to Ephesians* (Chicago, 1956).
Grant, F. C., *Roman Hellenism and the New Testament* (London, 1962).
Grant, M., *The Jews in the Roman World* (London, 1973).
Grant, R. M.,'Les êtres intermédiaires dans le judaisme tardif', in U. Bianchi (ed.), *Le Origini dello Gnosticismo*, pp. 141ff.
  Gnosticism and Early Christianity, 2nd ed. (New York, 1966).
  'Like Children', *HTR* 39 (1946), 71ff.
Grässer, E., 'Kol. 3. 1–4 als Beispiel einer Interpretation *secundum homines recipientes*', *ZThK* 64 (1967), 139ff.

Green, E. M. B., *2 Peter Reconsidered* (London, 1961).
Groton, W. M., *The Christian Eucharist and the Pagan Cults* (New York, 1914).
Grundmann, W., ἄγγελος, *TDNT*, I, 74ff.
　δύναμις, *TDNT*, II, 284ff.
Gundel, W., 'Astralreligion', *RAC*, I, 810ff.
　'Astrologie', *RAC*, I, 817ff.
Hadas, M., *Hellenistic Culture* (Oxford, 1959).
Hammerton-Kelly, R. G., *Pre-Existence, Wisdom, and the Son of Man* (Cambridge, 1973).
Harrison, P. M., 'Onesimus and Philemon', *ATR* 32 (1950), 268ff.
Hatch, W. H. P., 'τὰ στοιχεῖα in Paul and Bardaisan', *JTS* 28 (1927), 181ff.
Hatzfeld, J., *Les trafiquants italiens dans l'orient hellénique* (Paris, 1910).
Hauck, F., μιαίνω, *TDNT*, IV, 644ff.
Hauck, F., and Schulz, S., πορεύομαι, *TDNT*, VI, 566ff.
Haufe, G., 'Hellenistische Volksfrommigkeit', in J. Leipoldt and W. Grundmann (eds.), *Umwelt des Urchristentums*, I (Berlin, 1967).
Hauvette-Besnault, A., and Dubois, M., 'Inscriptions de Carie', *BCH* 5 (1881), 179ff.
Hay, D. M., *Glory at the Right Hand. Psalm 110 in Early Christianity* (Nashville, 1973).
Hegermann, H., *Die Vorstellung vom Schöpfungsmittler im hellenistischen Judentum und Urchristentum* (Berlin, 1961).
Henderson, B. W., *Five Roman Emperors* (Cambridge, 1927).
Hogarth, D. G., and Ramsay, W. M., 'Apollo Lermenus', *JHS* 8 (1887), 376ff.
Hooker, M. D., 'Were there false teachers in Colossae?', in B. Lindars and S. S. Smalley (eds.), *Christ and the Spirit in the New Testament. Studies in honour of C. F. D. Moule* (Cambridge, 1973), pp. 315ff.
Jeremias, J., *Jerusalem at the Time of Christ* (ET London, 1969).
　Μιχαήλ, *TDNT*, IV, 854ff.
Johnson, S. E., 'The Dead Sea Manual and the Jerusalem Church', in *The Scrolls and the New Testament*, ed. K. Stendahl (London, 1958), pp. 129ff.
　'Laodicea and its Neighbours', *BA* 13 (1950), 1ff.
　'A Sabazius Inscription from Sardis', in *Religion in Antiquity*, ed. J. Neusner (Leiden, 1968), pp. 542ff.
　'Unsolved Questions about Early Christianity in Anatolia', in *Studies in the New Testament and Early Christian Literature*, ed. D. E. Aune (Leiden, 1972), pp. 181ff.
Jones, A. H. M., *Cities of the Eastern Roman Provinces* (Oxford, 1937).
de Jonge, M., *The Testaments of the Twelve Patriarchs* (Assen, 1953).
　'The Testaments of the Twelve Patriarchs', *NovT* 2 (1960), 18ff.
Judge, E. A., 'St. Paul and Classical Society', *JAC* 15 (1972), 31ff.
　The Social Pattern of Christian Groups in the First Century (London, 1960).
Jung, L., *Fallen Angels in Jewish, Christian and Mohammedan Thought* (Philadelphia, 1926).
Juster, J., *Les juifs dans l'empire romain* (Paris, 1914).

Kallas, J., 'Romans xiii. 1-7: An Interpolation', *NTS* 11 (1965), 365ff.
Kamlah, E., 'ΥΠΟΤΑΣΣΕΣΘΑΙ in den neutestamentlichen "Haustafeln"', in *Verborum Veritas*, ed. O. Böcher and J. Haacker (Wuppertal, 1970), pp. 237ff.
Kaplan, C., 'Angels in the Book of Enoch', *ATR* 12 (1930), 423ff.
Käsemann, E., 'Ephesians and Acts', in *Studies in Luke-Acts*, ed. L. E. Keck and J. L. Martyn (New York, 1966), pp. 288ff.
  'On the Subject of Primitive Christian Apocalyptic', ET in *New Testament Questions of Today* (London, 1966), pp. 108ff.
  'A Primitive Christian Baptismal Liturgy', ET in *Essays on New Testament Themes* (London, 1964), pp. 149ff.
  'Principles of Interpretation of Romans 13', ET in *New Testament Questions*, pp. 196ff.
  'Römer 13, 1-7 in unserer Generation', *ZThK* 56 (1959), 316ff.
Kehl, N., *Der Christushymnus im Kolosserbrief: eine motivgeschichtliche Untersuchung zu Kol. 1, 12-20* (Stuttgart, 1967).
Kelly, H. A., *Towards the Death of Satan* (London, 1968).
Kelly, J. N. D., *Early Christian Creeds*, 3rd ed. (London, 1972).
Kennedy, H. A. A., *Paul and the Mystery Religions* (London, 1913).
Kerényi, K., *Die Mysterien von Eleusis* (Zurich, 1962).
Kirby, J. C., *Ephesians, Baptism and Pentecost. An Inquiry into the Structure and Purpose of the Epistle to the Ephesians* (London, 1968).
Kittel, G., ἄγγελος, *TDNT*, I, 80ff.
  δόγμα, *TDNT*, II, 230ff.
Kittel, G., and von Rad, G., δόξα, *TDNT*, II, 233ff.
Klijn, A. J. F., 'Christianity in Edessa and the Gospel of Thomas', *NovT* 14 (1972), 70ff.
Knox, W. L., *Paul and the Church of the Gentiles* (Cambridge, 1939).
  Paul and the Church of Jerusalem (Cambridge, 1925).
Koester, H., and Robinson, J. M., *Trajectories through Early Christianity* (Philadelphia, 1971).
Koets, P. J., *Deisidaemonia: A Contribution to the Knowledge of Religious Terminology in Greek* (Purmerend, 1929).
Kraabel, A. T., 'Hypsistos and the Synagogue at Sardis', *Greek, Roman and Byzantine Studies* 10 (1969), 81ff.
Kramer, W., *Christ, Lord, and Son of God* (ET London, 1966).
Kümmel, W. G., *Introduction to the New Testament* (ET London, 1966).
Kuhn, H. B., 'The Angelology of the Non-Canonical Jewish Apocalypses', *JBL* 67 (1948), 217ff.
Kuhn, K. G., 'The Epistle to the Ephesians in the Light of the Qumran Texts', in J. Murphy-O'Connor (ed.), *Paul and Qumran* (London, 1968), pp. 115ff.
Lähnemann, J., *Der Kolosserbrief, Komposition, Situation, und Argumentation* (Gütersloh, 1971).
Lampe, G. W. H., 'The New Testament Doctrine of *ktisis*', *SJT* 17 (1964), 449ff.
Langkammer, H., 'Die Einwohnung der "absoluten Seinsfülle" in Christus. Bemerkungen zu Kol. 1, 19', *BZ* 12 (1968), 258ff.

Langton, E., *The Essentials of Demonology* (London, 1949).
Latte, K., 'Schuld und Sühne in der griechischen Religion', *ARW* 20 (1921), 292ff.
Laumonier, A., *Les cultes indigènes en Carie* (Paris, 1958).
'Inscriptions de Carie', *BCH* 58 (1934), 291ff.
Layton, B., 'Critical Prolegomena to an Edition of the Coptic *Hypostasis of the Archons*', in M. Krause (ed.), *Essays on the Nag Hammadi Texts, in Honour of Pahor Labib* (Leiden, 1975), pp. 90ff.
'The Hypostasis of the Archons', *HTR* 67 (1974), 351ff and 69 (1976), 31ff.
Leaney, A. R. C., *The Rule of Qumran and its Meaning* (London, 1966).
Le-Bas, P., and Waddington, W. H. *Voyage archéologique en Grèce et en Asie Mineure II: Inscriptions grecques et latines* (Paris, 1847–73).
Lee, J. Y., 'Interpreting the Demonic Powers in Pauline Thought', *NovT* 12 (1970), 54ff.
Leivestad, R., *Christ the Conqueror: Ideas of Conflict and Victory in the New Testament* (London, 1954).
Leon, H. J., *The Jews of Ancient Rome* (Philadelphia, 1960).
Lerle, E., 'Die Predigt in Lystra', *NTS* 7 (1960), 46ff.
Levi, D., 'Aion', *Hesperia* 13 (1944), 269ff.
Levick, B., *Roman Colonies in Southern Asia Minor* (Oxford, 1967).
Lévy, I., *La légende de Pythagore de Grèce en Palestine* (Paris, 1927).
'Notes d'histoire et d'épigraphie', *REJ* 41 (1900), 174ff.
Liebermann, S., *Hellenism in Jewish Palestine*, 2nd ed. (New York, 1962).
Lilla, S. R. C., *Clement of Alexandria: A Study in Christian Platonism and Gnosticism* (Oxford, 1971).
Lincoln, A. T., 'A Re-examination of "The Heavenlies" in Ephesians', *NTS* 19 (1973), 468ff.
Lindars, B., *New Testament Apologetic* (London, 1961).
Loewe, H., 'Demons and Spirits (Jewish)', *ERE*, IV, 612ff.
Lohse, E., 'Ein hymnisches Bekenntnis in Kol. 2. 13c–15', in A. Descamps and A. de Halleux (eds.), *Mélanges bibliques en hommage au R. P. Béda Rigaux* (Gembloux, 1970), pp. 427ff.
'Paränese und Kerygma im I Petrusbrief', *ZNW* 45 (1954), 68ff.
Longenecker, R. N., *The Christology of Early Jewish Christianity* (London, 1970).
Loofs, F., 'The Descent to Hades (Christ's)', *ERE*, IV, 659ff.
Lyonnet, S., 'L'épître aux Colossiens (Col. 2.18) et les mystères d'Apollon Clarien', *Biblica* 43 (1962), 93ff.
'S. Paul et le gnosticisme', in U. Bianchi (ed.), *Le Origini dello Gnosticismo*, pp. 211ff.
Macgregor, G. H. C., 'Principalities and Powers: The Cosmic Background of Saint Paul's Thought', *NTS* 1 (1954), 17ff.
McKelvey, R. J., 'Christ the Cornerstone', *NTS* 8 (1961), 352ff.
The New Temple. The Church in the New Testament (Oxford, 1969).
Magie, D., *Roman Rule in Asia Minor* (Princeton, 1950).
Maly, K., *Mündige Gemeinde. Untersuchung zur pastoralen Führung des Apostels Paulus im I Korintherbrief* (Stuttgart, 1967).
Manson, T. W., *On Paul and John* (London, 1963).

Manson, W., 'Principalities and Powers', *SNTSBull* 3 (1952), 7ff.

Marshall, I. H., 'Palestinian and Hellenistic Christianity: Some Critical Comments', *NTS* 19 (1973), 271ff.

Martin, R. P., *Carmen Christi. Philippians ii. 5–11 in Recent Interpretation and in the Setting of Early Christian Worship* (Cambridge, 1967).

'An Epistle in search of a Life Setting', *ExT* 79 (1968), 296ff.

Mary, Sister Sylvia, '2 Cor. 12.1–4 and the Recent Discussion on "height" and "depth"', in F. L. Cross (ed.), *Studia Evangelica*, IV = *Texte und Untersuchungen*, 102 (Berlin, 1968), 462ff.

Mattingly, H., and Sydenham, E. H., *The Roman Imperial Coinage* (London, 1926).

Mees, M., *Die Zitate aus dem Neuen Testament bei Klemens von Alexandrien* (Rome, 1970).

Megas, G., 'Das χειρόγραφον Adams. Ein Beitrag zu Kol. 2, 13–15', *ZNW* 27 (1928), 305ff.

Metzger, B. M., 'Methodology in the Study of the Mystery Religions and Early Christianity', *HTR* 48 (1955), 1ff.

Michaelis, W., κοσμοκράτωρ and παντοκράτωρ, *TDNT*, III, 913ff.

Zur Engelchristologie im Urchristentum (Basel, 1942).

Michel, O., 'Zur Exegese von Phil. 2, 5–11', *Theologie als Glaubenswagnis. Festschrift Karl Heim* (Hamburg, 1954), pp. 79ff.

οἰκέω, *TDNT*, V, 119ff.

ὁμολογέω, *TDNT*, V, 199ff.

Milik, J. T., with the collaboration of M. Black, *The Book of Enoch: Aramaic Fragments of Qumran Cave 4* (Oxford, 1976).

Miller, G., ''ΟΙ ΑΡΧΟΝΤΕΣ ΤΟΥ ΑΙΩΝΟΣ ΤΟΥΤΟΥ – A New Look', *JBL* 91 (1972), 522ff.

Minear, P. S., 'The Cosmology of the Apocalypse', in W. Klassen and G. F. Snyder (eds.), *Current Issues in New Testament Interpretation* (London, 1962), pp. 23ff.

Mitton, C. L., 'The Authorship of the Epistle to the Ephesians', *ExT* 67 (1955), 195ff.

The Epistle to the Ephesians (Oxford, 1951).

Moore, G. F., *Judaism in the First Centuries of the Christian Era: The Age of the Tannaim* (Cambridge, Mass., 1946–8).

Morgenstern, J., 'The Mythological Background of Ps. 82', *HUCA* 14 (1939), 29ff.

Morrison, C. D., *The Powers that Be. Earthly Rulers and Demonic Powers in Romans 13. 1–7* (London, 1960).

Moule, C. F. D., 'A Reconsideration of the Context of Maranatha', *NTS* 6 (1960), 307ff.

Moulton, J. H., 'The Iranian Background of Tobit', *ExT* 11 (1899), 257ff.

Munck, J., 'Jewish Christianity in post-Apostolic Times', *NTS* 6 (1960), 103ff.

'The New Testament and Gnosticism', *ST* 15 (1961), 181ff.

Paul and the Salvation of Mankind (ET London, 1959).

Murphy-O'Connor, J., 'Truth: Paul and Qumran', *Paul and Qumran* (London, 1968), pp. 179ff.

Mussner, F., *Christus das All und die Kirche. Studien zur Theologie des*

Epheserbriefes (Trier, 1955).
'Contributions made by Qumran to the Understanding of the Epistle to the Ephesians', in J. Murphy-O'Connor (ed.), *Paul and Qumran*, pp. 159ff.
Musurillo, H., *The Acts of the Christian Martyrs* (Oxford, 1972).
Neugebauer, F., 'Zur Auslegung von Röm. 13.1–7', *KuD* 8 (1962), 151ff.
Nilsson, M. P., *The Dionysiac Religion of the Hellenistic and Roman Age* (Lund, 1957).
Geschichte der griechischen Religion (Munich, 1955).
Greek Piety (Oxford, 1948).
Greek Popular Religion (New York, 1940).
'Roman and Greek Domestic Cult', in *Opuscula Selecta* (Lund, 1960), pp. 271ff.
Nineham, D. E., 'The Case against Pauline Authorship', in F. L. Cross (ed.), *Studies in Ephesians* (London, 1956), pp. 29ff.
Nock, A. D., 'The Augustan Restoration', *CR* 39 (1925), 60ff, reprinted in *Essays on Religion and the Ancient World*, ed. Zeph Stewart (Oxford, 1972), I, 16ff.
'Early Gentile Christianity and its Hellenistic Background', in A. E. J. Rawlinson (ed.), *Essays on the Trinity and on the Incarnation* (London, 1928), pp. 51ff, reprinted in *Essays*, I, 49ff.
'The Emperor's Divine *comes*', *JRS* 37 (1947), 102ff, reprinted in *Essays*, II, 653ff.
'Gnosticism', *HTR* 57 (1964), 255ff, reprinted in *Essays*, II, 940ff.
'A Vision of Mandulis Aion', *HTR* 27 (1934), 83ff, reprinted in *Essays*, I, 357ff.
'The Vocabulary of the New Testament', *JBL* 52 (1933), 132ff, reprinted in *Essays*, I, 341ff.
Nock, A. D., and Festugière, A.-J. (eds.), *Hermès Trismégiste* (Paris, 1960).
Norden, E., *Agnostos Theos. Untersuchungen zur Formengeschichte religiöser Rede* (Leipzig, 1913).
Die antike Kunstprosa (Leipzig, 1898).
Noth, M., 'Die Heiligen des Höchsten', *Gesammelte Studien zum AT*, 2nd ed. (Munich, 1960), pp. 247ff.
Odeberg, H., *The View of the Universe in the Epistle to the Ephesians* (Lund, 1934).
Oepke, A., and Kuhn, K. G., πανοπλία, *TDNT*, V, 295ff.
Osborn, E. F., *The Philosophy of Clement of Alexandria* (Cambridge, 1957).
Osten-Sacken, P. von der, *Gott und Belial. Traditionsgeschichtliche Untersuchungen zum Dualismus in der Texten aus Qumran* (Göttingen, 1969).
Römer 8 als Beispiel paulinischer Soteriologie (Göttingen, 1975).
Pagels, E. H., 'Conflicting Versions of Valentinian Eschatology: Irenaeus' Treatise vs. The Excerpts from Theodotus', *HTR* 66 (1974), 35ff.
Parsons, W., 'The Influence of Rom. 13 on pre-Augustinian Political Thought', *TS* 1 (1940), 337ff.
Peel, M. L., *The Epistle to Rheginos* (London, 1969).
'Gnostic Eschatology and the New Testament', *NovT* 12 (1970), 141ff.

Percy, E., *Die Probleme der Kolosser- und Epheserbriefe* (Lund, 1946).
Perdrizet, M., 'Reliefs mysiens', *BCH* 23 (1899), 592ff.
Peterson, E., 'Das Amulet von Akra', *Aegyptus* 33 (1953), 172ff.
    'I Korinther 1.18ff und die Thematik des jüdischen Busstages', *Biblica* 32 (1951), 97ff.
    'La libération d'Adam de l' Άναγκή', *RB* 55 (1948), 199ff.
    'La problème du nationalisme', in J. Daniélou, *Les anges et leur mission*, appendix.
Pétrement, S., 'Le mythe des sept archontes créateurs, peut-il s'expliquer à partir du Christianisme?', in U. Bianchi (ed.), *Le Origini dello Gnosticismo*, pp. 460ff.
    'La notion de gnosticisme', *RMM* 65 (1960), 385ff.
Pettazzoni, R., 'Confessions of Sin and the Classics', *HTR* 30 (1937), 1ff.
Pfeiffer, E., *Studien zum antiken Sternglauben* (Leipzig and Berlin, 1916).
Pfitzner, V. C., *Paul and the Agon Motif. Traditional Athletic Imagery in the Pauline Literature* (Leiden, 1967).
Picard, C., 'Un oracle d'Apollon Clarios à Pergame', *BCH* 46 (1922), 190ff.
Pleket, H. W., 'An Aspect of the Emperor Cult: Imperial Mysteries', *HTR* 58 (1965), 231ff.
Pope, R. M., 'Studies in Pauline Vocabulary: Of the Heavenly Places', *ExT* 23 (1912), 365ff.
Prat, F., 'Le triomphe du Christ sur les principautés et les puissances', *RechSR* 3 (1912), 210ff.
Preisker, O., ἐμβατεύω, *TDNT*, II, 535ff.
Proksch, O., ἅγιος, *TDNT*, I, 88ff.
Puech, H.-C., 'La Gnose et le temps', *Eranos Jahrbuch* 20 (1951), 57ff.
Quispel, G., 'The Origin of the Gnostic Demiurge', *Kyriakon. Festschrift Johannes Quasten* (Münster, 1970), I, 271ff.
Ramsay, W. M., 'Artemis-Leto and Apollo Lairbenus', *JHS* 10 (1889), 216ff.
    The Cities and Bishoprics of Phrygia (Oxford, 1897).
    The Cities of St. Paul (London, 1907).
    'Religious Antiquities in Asia Minor', *BSA* 18 (1911), 44ff.
    The Social Basis of Roman Power in Asia Minor, ed. J. G. C. Anderson (Aberdeen, 1941).
Reicke, B., *The Disobedient Spirits and Christian Baptism. A Study of I Peter 3.19 and its Context* (Uppsala, 1946).
    'The Law and this World according to Paul. Some Thoughts concerning Gal. 4.1–11', *JBL* 70 (1951), 261ff.
Reitzenstein, R., 'Ein frühchristliche Schrift von der dreierlei Früchten', *ZNW* 15 (1914), 74ff.
    Die hellenistischen Mysterienreligionen (Leipzig, 1910).
Richardson, C. C., *The Christianity of Ignatius of Antioch* (New York, 1935).
Ringgren, H., *The Faith of Qumran. The Theology of the Dead Sea Scrolls* (ET Philadelphia, 1963).
    'The Problem of Fatalism', in *Fatalistic Belief in Religion, Folklore, and Literature* (Stockholm, 1967), pp. 7ff.
Robert, L., *Les gladiateurs dans l'orient grec* (Paris, 1940).

'Rapport sommaire sur un second voyage en Carie', *RevArch* 6 (1935), 152ff.
'Reliefs votifs et cultes d'Anatolie', *Anatolia* 3 (1958), 103ff.
Robinson, J. A. T., *The Body. A Study in Pauline Theology* (London, 1952).
'The Most Primitive Christology of All?', *JTS* n.s. 7 (1956), 177ff.
Robinson, J. M., 'A Formal Analysis of Col. 1.15–20', *JBL* 76 (1957), 270ff.
Roller, O., 'Das Buch mit sieben Siegeln', *ZNW* 36 (1937), 98ff.
Rose, H. J., 'Numen inest: "Animism" in Greek and Roman Religion', *HTR* 28 (1935), 237ff.
Rowley, H. H., *Jewish Apocalyptic and the Dead Sea Scrolls* (London, 1957).
The Relevance of Apocalyptic, 3rd ed. (London, 1963).
Russell, D. S., *The Method and Message of Jewish Apocalyptic* (London, 1964).
Sanders, E. P., 'Literary Dependence in Colossians', *JBL* 85 (1966), 28ff.
Sanders, J. A., 'Dissenting Deities and Philippians 2, 1–11', *JBL* 88 (1969), 279ff.
Sanders, J. N., 'The Case for Pauline Authorship', in F. L. Cross (ed.), *Studies in Ephesians* (London, 1956), pp. 9ff.
Sanders, J. T., *The New Testament Christological Hymns: Their Historico-Religious Background* (Cambridge, 1971).
Schaerer, R., *Dieu, l'homme et la vie d'après Platon* (Neuchâtel, 1944).
Schaferdiek, K. L., and Foerster, W., Σατανᾶς, *TDNT*, VII, 163ff.
Schlier, H., βάθος, *TDNT*, I, 517ff.
κεφαλή, *TDNT*, III, 673ff.
Principalities and Powers in the New Testament (ET Edinburgh and London, 1961).
Religionsgeschichtliche Untersuchungen zu den Ignatiusbriefen, BZNW 8 (Giessen, 1929).
Schmidt, K. L., ἐκκλησία (καλέω), *TDNT*, III, 506ff.
θρησκεία, *TDNT*, III, 155ff.
'Die Natur- und Geistkräfte im paulinischen Erkennen und Glauben', *Eranos Jahrbuch* 14 (1947), 87ff.
Schmithals, W., *Die Gnosis in Korinth: eine Untersuchung zu den Korintherbriefen*, 2nd ed. (Göttingen, 1965).
Schmitz, O., θρόνος, *TDNT*, VI, 160ff.
Schniewind, J., 'Die Archonten dieses Äons: I Kor. 2, 6–8', *Nachgelassene Reden und Aufsätze* (Berlin, 1951), pp. 104ff.
Schoeps, H.-J. 'Ebionite Christianity', *JTS* n.s. 4 (1953), 219ff.
Paul: The Theology of the Apostle in the Light of Jewish Religious History (ET London, 1961).
Scholem, G. G., *Jewish Gnosticism, Merkabah Mysticism, and Talmudic Tradition* (New York, 1960).
Schrenck, G., ἐκδίκησις, *TDNT*, II, 442f.
εὐδοκέω, *TDNT*, II, 738ff.
Schweizer, E., 'Die "Elemente der Welt", Gal. 4, 3, 9: Kol. 2, 8, 20', in O. Bocher and K. Haacker (eds.), *Verborum Veritas. Festschrift für*

Gustav Stählin zum 70. Geburtstag (Wuppertal, 1970), pp. 245ff.
πνεῦμα, *TDNT*, VI, 396ff.

Seitz, O. J. F., 'Two Spirits in Man: An Essay in Biblical Exegesis', *NTS* 6 (1959), 82ff.

Sevenster, J., *Do You Know Greek?* (Leiden, 1968).
Paul and Seneca (Leiden, 1961).

Sherwin-White, A. N., *The Roman Citizenship* (Oxford, 1939).
Roman Society and Roman Law in the New Testament (Oxford, 1963).

Skehan, P., 'A Fragment of "The Song of Moses" (Deut. 32) from Qumran', *BASOR* 136 (1954), 12ff.

Smith, D. M., 'Goodenough's *Jewish Symbols* in Retrospect', *JBL* 86 (1967), 53ff.

Smith, J. Z., 'The Prayer of Joseph', in J. Neusner (ed.), *Religion in Antiquity* (Leiden, 1968), pp. 253ff.

Sokolowski, F., 'A New Testimony on the Cult of Artemis of Ephesus', *HTR* 58 (1965), 427ff.
'Sur le culte d'Angelos dans le paganisme grec et romain', *HTR* 53 (1960), 225ff.

Souter, A., *The Text and Canon of the New Testament*, 2nd ed. (London, 1954).

Sperber, D., 'The Seventy Nations', *Encyclopaedia Judaica*, XII, 882ff.

Starr, C. G., *Civilisation and the Caesars. The Intellectual Revolution in the Roman Empire* (New York, 1954).

Steinleitner, F., *Die Beicht im Zusammenhange mit der sakralen Rechtspflege in der Antike* (Leipzig, 1913).

Stern, A., 'Wo trügen die Korinthischen Christen ihre Rechthändel aus?', *ZNW* 59 (1968), 86ff.

Stewart, J. S., 'On a Neglected Emphasis in New Testament Theology', *SJT* 4 (1951), 292ff.

Stewart, R. A., *Rabbinic Theology – An Introductory Study* (Edinburgh, 1961).

Stock, S. G., 'Fortune (Greek)', *ERE*, VI, 93ff.

Strathmann, H., and Meyer, R., λαός, *TDNT*, IV, 29ff.

Strecker, G., *Das Judenchristentum in den Pseudo-Klementinen* (Berlin, 1958).

Strobel, A., 'Furcht, wem Furcht gebuhrt: zum profangriechischen Hintergrund von Röm. 13.7', *ZNW* 55 (1964), 58ff.
'Zum Verständnis von Römer 13', *ZNW* 47 (1956), 67ff.

Strugnell, J., *The Angelic Liturgy at Qumran* (Leiden, 1960).

Takahashi, M., 'An Oriental's Approach to the Problem of Angelology', *ZAW* 78 (1966), 343ff.

Tarn, W. W., and Griffith, G. T., *Hellenistic Civilisation*, 3rd ed. (London, 1952).

Taylor, L. R., *The Divinity of the Roman Emperor* (Middletown, 1931).

Tcherikover, V. A., *Hellenistic Civilisation and the Jews* (Philadelphia, 1961).

Testuz, M., *Les idées religieuses du livre des Jubilés* (Paris and Geneva, 1960).;

Thackeray, H. St J., *Josephus, the Man and the Historian* (New York, 1929).

The Septuagint and Jewish Worship (London, 1923).

Tinh, T. T., *Le culte d'Isis à Pompeii* (Paris, 1964).

Toutain, J., *Les cultes païens dans l'empire romain* (Paris, 1907).

Traub, H., ἐπουράνιος, *TDNT*, V, 540ff.

Treves, M., 'The Two Spirits and the Rule of the Community', *RQ* 3 (1961), 449ff.

Van der Horst, P. W., 'Observations on a Pauline Expression', *NTS* 19 (1973), 181ff.

Van Roon, A., *The Authenticity of Ephesians* (Leiden, 1974).

Van Unnik, W. C., 'The Gospel of Truth and the New Testament', in F. L. Cross (ed.), *The Jung Codex* (London, 1955), 79ff.

Newly Discovered Gnostic Writings (ET London, 1960).

Vermeule, C. C., *Roman Imperial Art in Greece and Asia Minor* (Cambridge, Mass., 1968).

Versnel, H. S., *Triumphus: An Inquiry into the Origin, Development, and Meaning of the Roman Triumph* (Leiden, 1970).

Vischer, L., *Die Auslegungsgeschichte von I Kor. 6, 1-11* (Tübingen, 1955).

Von Campenhausen, H., 'Zur Auslegung von Röm. 13. Die dämonistische Deutung des *exousia*-Begriffes', in W. Baumgartner, O. Eissfeldt, K. Elliger and L. Rost (eds.), *Festschrift A. Bertholet zum 80. Geburtstag* (Tübingen, 1950), pp. 97ff.

Wagner, G., *Pauline Baptism and the Pagan Mysteries* (ET Edinburgh, 1967).

Wambacq, B. N., 'Per eum reconciliare . . . quae in caelo sunt. Col. 1.20', *RB* 55 (1948), 35ff.

Weiss, H., 'The Law in the Epistle to the Colossians', *CBQ* 34 (1972), 294ff.

Wernberg-Moeller, P., 'A Reconsideration of the Two Spirits in the Rule of the Community – IQS III.13 – IV.26', *RQ* 3 (1961), 413ff.

Werner, M., *Die Entstehung des christlichen Dogmas* (Leipzig, 1941); ET *The Formation of Christian Dogma* (London, 1957).

Whiteley, D. E. H., 'The Christology of Ephesians', in F. L. Cross (ed.), *Studies in Ephesians* (London, 1956), pp. 51ff.

Wilckens, U., σοφία, *TDNT*, VII, 465ff.

Weisheit und Torheit: eine exegetisch-religionsgeschichtliche Untersuchung zur I Kor. 1 und 2 (Tübingen, 1959).

Williams, A. L., 'The Cult of Angels at Colossae', *JTS* 10 (1909), 413ff.

Williamson, L., 'Led in Triumph: Paul's Use of THRIAMBEUO', *Interp* 22 (1968), 316ff.

Wilson, R. McL., 'The Early Exegesis of Gen. 1.26', in *Studia Patristica* (Berlin, 1957), II, 429ff.

Gnosis and the New Testament (Oxford, 1968).

The Gnostic Problem (London, 1958).

'How Gnostic were the Corinthians?', *NTS* 19 (1972), 65ff.

'Some Recent Studies in Gnosticism', *NTS* 6 (1959), 32ff.

Witt, R. E., *Isis in the Graeco-Roman World* (London, 1971).

Wolfson, H., 'The Pre-existent Angel of the Magharians and Al-Nahawāndī', *JQR* 51 (1960), 89ff.

Wright, G. E., 'The Lawsuit of God: A Form-Critical Study of

Deuteronomy 32', in B. W. Anderson and W. Harrelson (eds.), *Israel's Prophetic Heritage* (London, 1962), pp. 26ff.

Wuellner, W., 'Haggadic Homily Genre in I Corinthians 1–3', *JBL* 89 (1970), 199ff.

Wuilleumier, P., 'Cirque et astrologie', *Mélanges d'archéologie et d'histoire de l'École française de Rome* 44 (1927), 184ff.

Wunsch, R., *Antike Flüchtafeln* (Bonn, 1907).
 'Neue Flüchtafeln', *RhMP* n.f. 55 (1900), 62ff.

Wycherley, R. E., 'Saint Paul at Athens', *JTS* n.s. 19 (1968), 619ff.

Yadin, Y., *The Scroll of the War of the Sons of Light against the Sons of Darkness* (ET London, 1962).

Yamauchi, E., *Pre-Christian Gnosticism* (London, 1973).
 'Qumran and Colossians', *BibSac* 121 (1964), 141ff.

Zsifkovits, V., *Der Staatsgedanke nach Paulus in Röm. 13.1–7 mit besonderer Berücksichtigung der Umwelt und der patristischen Auslegung* (Vienna, 1964).

INDEX OF PASSAGES CITED

Suetonius
Augustus
47	179
52	179

Vitellius
14	181

Tacitus
Dial. 38.7   182

Hist. 2.8   178f

Ann.
2.54	181
4.37	179
10.44	179

Thucydides
5.47	183
6.54	183

Varro
De ling. lat.
6.68	190

De re rust.
1.31.2	181

Vettius Valens
42.12	94
141.26	198

Zeno
2.3	186

J. INSCRIPTIONS

CIG
3082	179

CIL
III. 6070	179, 182
III. 6983	180
III. 7118	179, 182
V. 3466	210
VI. 504	180
VI. 510	180

IGRR
III. 328	180

ILS
8393	181
8781	179

InscBM
894	179

OGIS
458	179
530	191

SEG
II. 549	179

INDEX OF MODERN AUTHORS